Ambrose Beatty Rathborne

**Camping and Tramping in Malaya,**

fifteen years' pioneering in the native states of the Malay peninsula

Ambrose Beatty Rathborne

**Camping and Tramping in Malaya,**
*fifteen years' pioneering in the native states of the Malay peninsula*

ISBN/EAN: 9783337289416

Printed in Europe, USA, Canada, Australia, Japan

Cover: Foto ©Andreas Hilbeck / pixelio.de

More available books at **www.hansebooks.com**

# CAMPING AND TRAMPING
IN
# MALAYA

FIFTEEN YEARS' PIONEERING IN THE NATIVE
STATES OF THE MALAY PENINSULA

BY

AMBROSE B. RATHBORNE, F.R.G.S.

*LONDON*
SWAN SONNENSCHEIN & CO., LIM.
1898

TO
MY WIFE

# PREFACE

COMPARATIVELY little has hitherto been written about the Malay Peninsula, and possibly it may be of interest to describe the early days of a country which has just emerged from a state of barbarism, slave-dealing, and disorder, into a prosperity under British protection that has been seldom equalled in so short a space of time.

I have endeavoured to convey to the reader a fair and accurate idea of the country, its people, and the events that have assisted this awakening and enlightenment, by conducting him through the Western Native States of the Malay Peninsula, which I traversed many times as a humble worker in the spread of civilization and pioneer of progress. I will only add that any absence of literary skill is to be excused by the fact of my hand being more accustomed to wield the parang, for cutting my way through the jungle, than the pen, and that my study was chiefly confined to the forest, and the life found therein, where the points of the compass were my only guide.

I have gratefully to acknowledge the assistance I have obtained in the corroboration of various facts and the verification of events from the papers and reports in the Colonial Office Library, and in that of the Royal Asiatic Society.

I am specially indebted to my friend Mr. D. H. Wise, Secretary to the High Commissioner of the Protected Malay States, for the numerous photographs, taken by himself, which he has kindly placed at my disposal for the illustration of this book, and which add very materially to its interest.

AMBROSE B. RATHBORNE.

27, EVELYN GARDENS, LONDON, S.W.
*March 9th*, 1898.

# CONTENTS

### CHAPTER I.

The Malay Peninsula—Arrival at Singapore—General Description—Chinese Population—Suburban Residences of Merchants—Straits of Johore—Spirit and Opium farmers—Chandu Farm—Sailing and Rowing in Malay boat—Helmsman with an evil repute—Pepper Garden—Gambler Plantation—Coolies' house and Opium smoker—Return to Singapore—The late Sultan of Johore . . . 1–16

### CHAPTER II.

The late Sir Frederick Weld, G.C.M.G.—Departure from Singapore—Squall at sea—Arrival at Malacca—Malacca and its Malays—The Malacca Baba—Interior of Malacca—Paddy fields, houses, and inhabitants—Villages, trades, marriages, and divorces—Tapioca planting—Tenure of Agricultural Lands . . . . . . 17–38

### CHAPTER III.

Departure for Sungie Ujong—Striking upon sunken rocks—Journey up river—Crocodiles—Captain Murray, R.N., Her Majesty's Resident—Honourable Martin Lister—Black panthers—Rantau—Seremban—Gunong Brembong—Coffee planting—Native Labour—Characteristics of Malays—Pay days . . . . . . . 39–62

### CHAPTER IV.

Monkeys—Flying squirrels and lizards—Wild dogs—Jakuns—Benighted—The jungle—Birds—Wild beasts—Leeches—Ticks—Snakes—Fish—Scenery—Coffee planting—Cholera—Fall over rocks—Waris families—The Chief of Sungie Ujong—Sword dance—Berok monkey—Malay attacked by tigress—Death of tigress and cub—Growth of coffee—Difficulties of labour—Government dilatory—Abandonment of estates . . . . . 63–87

## CONTENTS

### CHAPTER V.

PAGE

Exploring and Surveying—Rassa—Events which caused British Intervention—Man-eating tiger—Camping in the jungle—Sleeping man seized and carried off by tiger—My syce killed and partially eaten by tiger—Placing spring guns—Alone with a tiger—A shot at a tiger—Village of Lukut—Port Dickson—Cape Ricardo . . . . 88–104

### CHAPTER VI.

S'tul—Brennang—Samunieh—Pudu—Kwala Lumpor—Frequent fires—The Capitan China—Secret Societies—Events which caused British Intervention—Kwala Selangor—Lombong tin mining—Winning, sluicing, and smelting of tin ore—Division of profits—Miners' houses—Sheds for dying coolies . 105–124

### CHAPTER VII.

Gambling houses—Hua-Hoey lotteries—Lampan working—Superstitions regarding tin ore—Malay Pawang—Dwellers around mines—Malay wood-cutters, felling, sawing, and squaring of timber—Buffaloes at work—Charcoal burners—Buffalo carts—Reverberatory furnaces—Alluvial deposits, and the lode formation of tin and gold . . 125–140

### CHAPTER VIII.

Communications in Selangor—Forest—Rattan—Journey to Klang—Timber—Night in the jungle—Wood-cutters—Kwala Lumpor, its central position—Resident-General—Leaving Kwala Lumpor—Travelling northward—Limestone hill and caves—Soil—Wild animals—Rogue elephant—Former denizens of the jungle—Camp—Insects—Scorpions—Horse leeches—Crossing Pass—Ulu Yam—Benighted on horseback—Bathing—Sunset—Remains of Siamese tin workings 141–166

CONTENTS                                    ix

## CHAPTER IX.
                                              PAGE
Ulu Selangor—Destroyed by dam bursting—Trade—Kalompong
—Ulu Bernam—River—Mountains—Herd of elephants—
Kwala Slim—Crossing swamps—Kwala Galeting—Death of
the only Europeans in this district—Fish-hook ants—
Trollah—Crute—Small-pox—Sungkai River—Kwala Lepis
—Catching wild elephants—Jungkau—Tapah and country
round—Hanging over precipice—Sakais        . 167-191

## CHAPTER X.
Chanderiang—Night at Malay miners' camp—A Sikh policeman
and his prisoner—Kwala Dipang—Sungie Rya—Ipoh—
Gunong Meerut—The Sensitive Plant—Coolies' loads—
Kwala Kangsar—The Regent—Sir Hugh Low, G C.M.G.—The
Perak War—A journey down—Birds—Fish—The Sultan—
Road to Thaiping—Charged by a rhinoceros—Seladang—
Herd of wild pig—Pass in the hills—Bukit Gantong—
Events which caused British intervention and the Perak
War—Slavery     .        .        .        .        . 192-217

## CHAPTER XI.
Thaiping — Introduction of Pumping Machinery — Orderly
behaviour of Chinese miners—Outbreak of Secret Societies,
punishment and stampede—Hospitals—Rhinoceros visiting
a ward—Sanatorium—View from the hills above Thaiping—
Return to Thaiping—Tamil Festival—Churches—Town Life
—Government Offices—Theatres and plays—Storms and
lightning—Malay running amuck        .        .        . 218-234

## CHAPTER XII.
Leaving Thaiping—Journeying on elephants, their obedience
and sagacity—The Kurow River—Nearly drowned—Ijuk—
Wild elephants—Salamah—Attacked by wasps—Red ants—
Elephants wander, and start delayed—Ascent of Gunong
Inas—A disagreeable night—Descent—Janing—Shooting
Rapids on the Perak River—Bruar—Kwala Plus—A thunder-
storm—Ipoh—A Coffee Plantation, death of manager,
typical of many others—British sense of duty        235-253

# CONTENTS

## CHAPTER XIII.

Pigeon shooting—Krian—Snipe shooting—A Tamil ruse—Buffaloes—Nipa palms, and making attaps—Province Wellesley sugar planting, and Indian immigrants—Penang—Its Botanical Gardens and hills—The dwellers in the Island on the Esplanade—Drying and salting fish—Fishing stakes . . . . . . 254-271

## CHAPTER XIV.

Island of Pangkor—Dutch Fort—Pirates—District Officer murdered—Station moved to Lumut—S'tiawan—Pandah Karim—Start upon a Survey—Tamil boy murdered—Three weeks in a swamp—Thorns and mosquitoes—A tiger—Kota Stia—Rowing up the Perak River to Teluk Anson—The bridle path to Tapah—Poling up the Kinta and Tapah Rivers, and descending them . . 272-294

## CHAPTER XV.

Mr. Noel Denison—An arduous exploration through floods—Destruction of gutta trees—Method of collecting gutta by Dyaks—Through the floods of the Bernam River—Fever-stricken followers—Rembau, its stockades, politics, and inhabitants—Tampin—Johol—Jempol—Ulu-Moar—S'trimenanti—Exploring—A message from the Datoh—Small-pox—A cock-fight—Coffee trees—Fruit trees—Irrigation—Graves—Eam Tuan of S'trimenanti—Bukit Putus, its defence and capture—Meeting between Sir Frederick Weld and Chiefs—Appointment of Resident . . 295-317

## CHAPTER XVI.

Jellebu—Crossing the Mountains—Tigers—Kanaboi—Tin—Kwala Klawang—Eam Tuan—Terrified elephants—Bukit Tanah—Exploring hills—Road-making—Malays—Chinese—Tamils—The Malay Peninsula—Geology—Climate and rainfall—Some of its products, flora, fauna, and minerals—Its inhabitants, education, and administration—Comparisons of Revenue and Trade . . . 318-339

# LIST OF ILLUSTRATIONS

|  | PAGE |
|---|---|
| A Malay Hill Mine | *Frontispiece* |
| Malay Woman Husking Paddy | 29 |
| Liberian Coffee | 47 |
| A Group of Malays | 51 |
| Tamils | 85 |
| The Sultan of Selangor and Followers | 113 |
| Lombong Mining | 119 |
| Bullock Cart | 145 |
| Bathing a Captive Elephant | 181 |
| Sakais with Blow-Pipes | 187 |
| Sakais Playing Flute | 190 |
| A Bag of Wild Pig | 211 |
| Elephant and Riders | 237 |
| A Street in Penang | 261 |
| Chinese Fishing Village | 269 |
| River at Tapah | 291 |
| Malay House | 297 |
| Eam Tuan of S'trimenanti and Followers | 313 |
| A Road through the Jungle | 329 |

# CAMPING AND TRAMPING IN MALAYA.

## CHAPTER I.

The Malay Peninsula—Arrival at Singapore—General Description—Chinese Population—Suburban Residences of Merchants—Straits of Johore—Spirit and Opium Farmers—Chandu Farm—Sailing and Rowing in Malay Boat—Helmsman with an Evil Repute—Pepper Garden—Gambier Plantation—Coolies' House and Opium Smoker—Return to Singapore—The late Sultan of Johore.

My first experiences of the East were gained in the island of Ceylon, where I spent some years before proceeding, in January, 1880, to the Native States of the Malay Peninsula, and acquired knowledge that was to be most useful to me in my after life of pioneering in that new and hitherto undeveloped country, amongst a people unaccustomed to intercourse with Europeans and unused to the trammels of civilization.

The Malay Peninsula is a long strip of land, a continuation of British Burmah and Siam, extending southward almost to the equator, and separated from the island of Sumatra by the Straits of Malacca, which is used by steamers proceeding to China and Japan, as well as by numbers of small trading craft. The strongly-fortified coaling depôt of Singapore, situated at the southern extremity of the peninsula, is one of the principal British strongholds between Aden and the Far East, and together with Malacca, the Dindings, and the island of Penang, form the Colony of the Straits Settlements; the rest of the peninsula is divided into numerous native states, each ruled by a chief, who is now either under British or Siamese control, these two nations having each their agreed-upon sphere of influence in Malaya. Formerly the greatest anarchy prevailed in these native states, inhabited by Malays; and it was for the security and the preservation of the small trading schooners, the suppression of piracies and internal disturbances, which were becoming of frequent occurrence, that active steps were taken to put a stop to the prevalent lawlessness, and to exercise more direct control over their affairs by an administration of British officials, as owing to their geographical position (bordering on the Straits of Malacca), and their propinquity to the colony, a continuance of this chronic unrest and pillage was intolerable.

The first circumstances that strike the traveller on reaching Singapore are the bustle and stir going on around, the busy Chinese hurrying hither and thither, the air of prosperity pervading all, and the rich greenness of the vegetation caused by the moist heat and the constant showers, for throughout the year there is but seldom any prolonged period of drought.

The houses are substantially built, and the godowns of the European merchants are fine;

there are here not only many black races, but numerous white nationalities as well, each and all happy and flourishing under the British flag, which makes no difference between them, permitting all to trade and compete without distinction of race, to pay the same taxes, and to be in every way equal.

The Government buildings are palatial, an excellent club-house overlooks the outer harbour, which is a fine natural anchorage sheltered from the prevailing winds, and facing the China Sea, and full of ceaseless activity, cargo boats going backwards and forwards, a perfect fleet of steamers trading with every part of the world, embarking and discharging goods, and a constant succession of small boats, carrying passengers, plying to and fro. Chinese junks with their great brown sails, and sailing craft of every description, which trade between the numerous small and thriving villages dotted round the shores of the many surrounding islands, are busy going and coming, or anchored in the distance off the beach, where the native quarter of the town reaches down to the sea. Singapore is a city of considerable size; one portion of it is taken up by the European and business community, another by the Chinese traders and retail dealers; Tamils, Javanese, and Malays occupy other portions, and the rest of the town is composed of a polyglot collection of inhabitants with more than a proportionate number of Chinese, as the shopkeeping and local trade of the country is principally carried on by them. At night they are still to be seen hard at work when others' shops are closed, for they are strenuous and indefatigable when toiling for their own gain.

  The lower classes of Chinese live closely crowded together, earning a livelihood by many forms of manual labour, and the celerity with which ships coal in the harbour is due to their work, for they follow one another in quick succession, a seemingly endless chain of men carrying baskets full of coal on their backs from the sheds to the ships, and returning with them empty in their hands for fresh loads. As a community they are hardworking and generally law-abiding, but should any rule or regulation be issued by the Government which is not to their liking, they become riotous and violent, making the occasion an excuse to satisfy their innate love of a row, to insult Europeans, and do a little looting on their own account. Those who take part in these tumults possess no houses or wives, have deposited their earnings in safe keeping, and have nothing to deter them from joining in the fun and fray, knowing that at most a broken head, which they do not mind, or a term of imprisonment in jail, where they have better food and are more comfortable than they are outside, is all that usually falls to their lot if they get within reach of the police, as directly severe measures for repression are taken these disturbances quickly cease. The better class of Chinese usually have nothing to do with these outbreaks, for there is an excellent and salutary law that provides for the deportation of any person not a natural-born subject of Her Majesty, who at any time may be proved to be associated with secret societies dangerous to the peace, or to be an instigator or participator in any riots or disturbances; so that those who have anything to lose think twice before intriguing and running the risk of being sent out of the country. They are hospitable and friendly, pressing their visitors to drink brandy and champagne instead of the ubiquitous tea. They are fond of reiterating emphatic expressions of their own opinions, and this appears to be their most popular form of argument. Many of them speak English, but Malay is the universal language of this part of the world, and forms the medium of conversation between the different races. The only master they recognize is superior force, and our system of administering justice is so different to what they have been accustomed to, that they are filled with delight to think that so long as they keep within the law, no one else can interfere with them, and this subject forms an oft-recurring source of conversation. They are fond of their children, and liberal in subscribing to local sports and amusements.

The suburban residences of the merchants are situate at some little distance from the town, and are good substantial houses, each one built on a portion of the many small hills which are so numerous on the island of Singapore. They stand sequestered in their own grounds amongst beautiful and shady trees and well-kept lawns, forming a pleasing and home-like prospect; and it is to these comfortable and attractive dwelling-places, with their cool, lofty rooms, that the merchant returns in the evening after his day's work is done, driving thereto along a smooth and well-watered road, passing beneath an avenue of trees which makes the way agreeable and shady even on the hottest days.

Singapore is now the principal town of the Malay Peninsula; its early history is somewhat obscure, but the island is supposed to have been devastated by the Javanese about 1252, and to have remained almost uninhabited after that time, until it was taken possession of by Sir Stamford Raffles in 1819, by virtue of a treaty with the Johore princes, when the present city was founded.

Desirous of visiting the neighbouring state of Johore, I drove across the island till I reached the straits of that name, at a place situated opposite to the present palace of the Sultan, which can be distinctly seen across the water. On the way I passed many dead nutmeg trees, all that now remained to indicate that a flourishing plantation had previously covered the hillside, for disease and blight had completely killed the trees, and destroyed the industry.

In former times the passage through the Straits of Johore was both tedious and dangerous for sailing ships. The narrow fairway allows but little room for tacking; the breezes are most fitful; and the ships, either drifting helplessly with the current, or anchored, waiting for a change of tide or wind, afforded a tempting prey to the piratical inhabitants who lived along the coast and lay in hiding amongst the numerous creeks, from which they would suddenly row out in their long, swift *prahus*, and appear at the side of the ill-fated ship almost as soon as an alarm could be given. Then ensued a fierce struggle, ending in certain death to those attacked if overcome.

As the boat which I had arranged should meet me had not as yet arrived, I awaited it at the police station, which, like many others, consisted merely of a couple of rooms—one on each side, an open space in the middle, at the far end of which was the lock-up, somewhat resembling a cage with wooden bars in front placed close together, so that the prisoner could not squeeze through whilst waiting to be taken in to headquarters; a verandah with a table and a couple of chairs, a stand of arms and cutlasses, and a sentry walking up and down, completed the picture. When not on duty, the sergeant, or corporal in charge, and his few men occupy quarters close by, where each married man is apportioned a good-sized room. Their duties are not severe; smuggling troubles them but little, as the port and island of Singapore is free to all goods excepting spirits and opium, for each of which there is what is locally termed a farm. This means that they are let during a term of years to a Chinaman, or syndicate of Chinese, who for a stipulated monthly payment are allowed under certain conditions to have the entire control of the collection of the duty on these articles, and receive every assistance on the part of the Government to enable them to carry on the business.

The spirit farmer collects the duty on all imported spirits, no shopkeeper being able to dispose of a bottle without giving to the purchaser a pass to show that the duty has been paid. He also manufactures a native spirit called samshu, made from rice, not only intoxicating, but, like absinthe, peculiarly mischievous in its permanent effects.

The opium farmer has the sole right of cooking opium, that is, preparing it for smoking—a rather peculiar process. The opium is moistened, boiled, and stirred, then mixed with water, the solution being evaporated until of the consistency of a thin treacly extract, known locally as chandu, which the farmer retails at a certain fixed rate, much higher than its intrinsic value. Half the revenue of the colony comes from these two farms, and the profits of the farmer would be seriously interfered with were there much smuggling or illicit manufacture, so he employs a large number of detectives who are constantly on the look-out.

When the time approaches for these farms to be renewed the excitement is intense, and the competition between the different sects of Chinese most keen; and deservedly so, for the possession of them gives to the successful competitors an all-pervading influence for a term of years. Upon their good faith in great measure depend the strength and quality of the spirit, and the purity of the prepared opium. Their detectives search and examine their countrymen on arrival, thrusting their hands into the pockets of their clothes, and ransacking their baggage.

This system of chandu farming is not confined to the island of Singapore, but extends to the coast districts of the native states, where an attempt to introduce it into the mining districts of the interior provoked such serious riots and discontent that the endeavour had to be abandoned, and the duty is now collected upon the unprepared opium as it arrives, leaving its preparation to the smokers themselves.

The whole principle of farming revenues is pernicious in the extreme, and unbefitting a strong and stable government; for in times of prosperity the opium farmer makes large profits, but when the reverse occurs the loss ultimately falls upon the Government, as the farmer fails to pay the instalments when due, necessitating the cancelling of his contract and realization of his pledges.

Eastern races have but small appreciation of punctuality; but at last all was ready, and I embarked on a long, shallow boat, crank and narrow, with only about six inches of freeboard. The crew consisted of five Malays, the helmsman, a fine, strongly-built, powerful-looking man, pleasant-mannered, decided and energetic, a worthy descendant of the pirates of former times; he was an amusing companion, an excellent sailor, and we made many expeditions together. Some years afterwards he was tried and acquitted of the charge of murdering a Chinese trader; not the only victim by any means, if report can be credited. His method in each case was supposed to be very similar. He ingratiated himself into the confidences of some unsuspecting Chinese trader, and having persuaded him of the profits to be obtained, they would start together in a boat for some of the numerous islets and creeks along the coasts. The Chinaman who brought the money to pay for his purchases was never heard of again, and the Malay returned to his home with the story that his Chinese companion had travelled on to some neighbouring village.

The fact of each side of these waters being under different jurisdiction made the suppression of such crimes difficult, especially so in the case of a Chinese life, which was not regarded of much value by the Malays, who naturally did their best to screen their countrymen and co-religionists.

As there was a favourable breeze we hoisted sail, and in order to keep the boat upright and in trim as she scudded along, ropes were fastened to the mast, having loops on the lower end in which some members of the crew sat, with their feet on the gunwale, and at every stronger puff of wind they would push themselves out from the boat with their toes, craning their bodies over the water, and with their weight counteracting each gust and preventing the boat from turning turtle. The number of men hanging out depended on the strength of the wind, a one, or two, or more man breeze, as it is termed.

Crossing the straits and coasting along the opposite shore, we enjoyed a most exhilarating sail, when, suddenly turning into a narrow creek, invisible from a distance, we found ourselves in a perfect calm, so thick were the mangrove trees on either side. The sail was hauled down, and the boatmen made ready to row. A round piece of twisted rattan, which in this country serves for rope and string, placed over a wooden peg stuck into the side of the boat, was the primitive arrangement that took the place of rowlocks. The oar blades, which were not so large as those of a small scull, were nailed, and tied with rattan, on to straight poles not much thicker than broomsticks, and the handles being passed through the rattan rings the rowers dip these rude oars into the water, and at the end of each stroke they give a mild sort of jerk, which is sufficient to cause the light craft to glide over the water, although so little power is applied. After a short row up the creek, which gradually became narrower and narrower, until the bushes on either side touched the oars, we reached a roughly constructed landing-stage, to which was fastened a primitive ladder, and climbing up it we found ourselves in a pepper garden, with its gambier plantation adjoining, both cultivations being at the time very profitable occupations, and much pursued in the state of Johore, being owned and worked by Chinese. These pepper gardens, although small in size, are expensive to open and keep in a proper state of cultivation, and it is necessary to have adjacent a considerable reserve of jungle, where burnt earth can be made, for it is the principal manure used, and has a great effect on the health and productiveness of the vines.

When a Chinaman is desirous of making a pepper garden, the first thing he does is to engage Malays to fell and burn the jungle and build a house, the sides and roof of which are covered with attap leaves, cut from that most useful palm, *nipa fruticans*. He then procures Sinkehs; these are Chinese who, wishing to leave their country and seek work elsewhere, are collected and brought to Singapore by some broker, who keeps them in his house until a purchaser arrives, and buys them of him for a certain sum per head. These coolies are then taken to the Chinese protectorate, where they sign articles to work at fixed rates of pay during the period of their indenture, at the expiration of which they are free to go where they choose.

Pepper cuttings are next purchased, but are often difficult to procure, as the best kinds are obtainable only when the young vines have to be cut back. After being struck, they are planted against posts, to which they are tied, and up which they climb, and ultimately cover. The vines are perennial, with leaves of a somewhat hard, dark green colour; and a person walking through the garden seems to be in the midst of a forest of posts encircled with vines of a uniform cylindrical shape, with short lateral branches growing outwards, from which clusters of green peppercorns hang down in small bunches, speckled and brightened here and there by a few reddening ones riper than the rest, showing that the time for harvesting has arrived, as the vines are injured by allowing the berries to ripen on them, which therefore are gathered when full grown, but before being thoroughly mature, so that they may not lose their pungency, or shed and fall to the ground.

If black pepper is made, the berries are detached from the stem and sun-dried on mats. Should white pepper be required, the bunches are allowed to ripen by keeping them some days in the house after gathering; the stalks and pulp are then removed, and the white seeds dried.

The Chinese overseer conducted me over the plantation, and passing through a belt of forest we suddenly emerged into an adjacent gambier plantation, which appeared to be in the last stage of productiveness, for the bushes were bare and straggling, with only a few leaves remaining at the end of their branches. This cultivation rapidly exhausts the soil, and as but little care is taken of the trees, whose younger shoots are being continually cut, no wonder that in a few years' time the bush itself becomes choked and dies. Coolies were carrying bundles of gambier sticks to the shed, where the leaves and the young shoots are put into a large shallow pan with water, a fire being lighted underneath; and, after sufficient boiling, the leaves are taken out and drained, so that none of the liquor shall be lost. When sufficiently evaporated, the liquid is stirred up and down with a piece of soft wood until it thickens, the whole becoming a mass resembling soft, yellowish clay, which is then placed in shallow trays, and when somewhat hardened cut into cubes, dried in the shade, and sold under the name of gambier, being used for tanning and dyeing. The boiled leaves are not wasted, but serve as a top dressing for the roots of the pepper vines.

On returning to the house, some tea was at once poured out into small, round, handless cups; for on the table of every Chinese dwelling a tea-pot invariably stands ready for use, containing a weak fluid with just a flavour of tea, which passers-by are constantly pouring out and taking a sip of. Along two sides of the house was a wide bench raised some two feet from the ground, and made with sticks, covered with pieces of bark stripped from large trees. This was divided into cubicle partitions by large blue mosquito nets hanging down, suspended from cords overhead. Each coolie occupied one of these, in which he rested after work, and slept. A long-drawn, gulping, rasping, snorting sound proceeding from inside a net, together with the peculiar sickly odour, made it evident that some opium smoker was within.

The opium smoker lies at full length with his head resting on a log, hollowed out to fit the back of his neck, and square underneath, so as to remain firmly fixed and not roll about. A little tray holds the necessary paraphernalia, which consists of a curiously shaped pipe with a large, hollow, closed-in bowl, having only a small aperture, a needle, a little pot of prepared opium, and an oil lamp over which there is a glass globe, or shade, with an opening at the top, so as to protect the flame from draughts and enable it to burn steadily.

The smoker turns towards the tray, takes up his pipe, sees that the tiny hole is clear, places a little pill of the treacly drug upon a needle, and rests it exactly over the central hole of the pipe bowl; he then warms the charge, and works at it with his needle until a small orifice remains; then holding it over the flame he ignites the opium, and sticking his needle into the burning mass two or three times to keep the passage into the pipe clear, he draws the vapour into his chest with the gurgling sound that attracted my attention; then slowly exhaling the smoke he closes his eyes, and appears to be in the calm, placid enjoyment of some phantasm of the brain, which leaves his body in a listless, inanimate trance. The opium smoker who inhales to excess is always easily distinguishable; his body loses its sleek, well-fed appearance, becoming thin, skinny, and dried, and he has a peculiarly sickly tinge, and a hard, wizened, drawn appearance about the face.

The smell of cooking in the verandah, and the sound of splashing water as the coolies bathed, told us that they would shortly be coming in to have a meal, and as the afternoon was drawing in we left on our homeward journey. The wind had died away, a perfect calm prevailed as we paddled along in the cool of the evening with the stars shining brightly overhead. The splash of the dipping oars, the recurring click as they rose from the water, and now and again some desultory conversation between the boatmen, was all that disturbed the tranquil stillness of the night, till the grating of the boat against the steps of the landing-place aroused me from a pleasant drowsiness.

The state of Johore, although formerly more accessible than the native states to the northward, has not kept its place in the progressive development and material advancement that has ensued elsewhere from British protection and better administration, owing to its lack of mineral wealth. At the time of my visit several Ceylon planters, attracted by its accessibility from Singapore, had commenced opening lands in several districts in the interior for coffee arabica, but owing to the poorness and unsuitability of the soil, the low elevation of the hills (only a few hundred feet in height), the difficulties of the labour supply, and the unhealthiness of the climate, this industry, as far as coffee arabica is concerned, has entirely ceased, although estates of Liberian coffee and tea, more conveniently situated, are still in existence.

It is the only one of the native states in the British sphere of influence that has preserved its semi-independence, and whose affairs are not directly administered by a British resident, aided by an organized staff of officials. The ruler of this state was the late genial Sultan Abu Baakar, so well known in England, where he died whilst on a visit. Many visitors to Singapore must have taken away with them agreeable reminiscences of the hospitality, and the sumptuous entertainments he gave in his palace overlooking the straits. In Singapore society he was a popular figure, a patron and staunch supporter of all sports, and especially so of the local race meetings, in which several of his horses always competed; and when residing in the island on these occasions, his fine house was the centre of much amusement and gaiety.

## CHAPTER II.

*The late Sir Frederick Weld, G.C.M.G.—Departure from Singapore—Squall at sea—Arrival at Malacca—Malacca and its Malays—The Malacca Baba—Interior of Malacca—Paddy fields, houses and inhabitants, villages, trades, marriages, and divorces—Tapioca planting—Tenure of agricultural lands.*

In the late Sir Frederick Weld, G.C.M.G., the Straits Settlements were fortunate in having a Governor whose experience amongst the Maoris of New Zealand well befitted him for the task of supervising the consolidation of the states already brought under British protection, and of increasing the area of our rule to other states as yet free and independent.

He was much respected by the chiefs throughout the Malay Peninsula, whom he visited, and whose confidence he entirely won by a never-varying straightforwardness and candour. His reputation for trustworthiness and uprightness materially helped the peaceful absorption of many fresh states, prevented outbreaks, and quieted numerous feuds; thus carrying to a successful issue the system inaugurated by Sir Andrew Clark of placing a British official as adviser to the native chiefs.

As the steamer which was to take me part of the way towards Sungei Ujong—at that time a state but little known—started from the outer harbour, I stepped into a sampan from the jetty close by the club-house, and was soon alongside of the steamer, where the noise of the donkey-engine, the rattling of chains, the loud quacking of the ducks as they were slung on board, betrayed the activity that was going on in order to get the ship off to time.

The decks were piled with crates of fowls and ducks; jars of spirits, tubs of fish, cases of kerosene oil, lined the sides; and on the hatchways being closed they were immediately taken possession of by the many deck passengers, who opened and spread their mats upon which they reclined, making themselves as comfortable as they could. An awning was stretched across overhead as a protection against sun and rain. Every vacant nook was occupied by some being or some thing, a most varied and miscellaneous assortment as we looked down upon it all from the poop.

The steamer seems to have no buoyancy, for she is below her Plimsoll mark and overloaded, the passengers are greatly in excess of her licensed number; but what matter? Europeans seldom travel in her, she is under the control of a Chinese supercargo who thinks only of profit, and the port rules were not at this time stringently enforced; so as much as could be crammed on board was taken, until the lapping of the water high up along the steamer's sides warns even the most heedless that it were folly to load her more.

The whistle sounds, the rattle of the chain is heard as the anchor rises, the steamer slowly threads her way through the shipping, and turns to go a short way into the Straits of Malacca, by passing through the inner harbour where there is a narrow channel between two islands. On the one side wharves stretch from end to end, alongside of which big ocean-going steamers are moored. The number of warehouses behind the quay testify to the large trade being carried on, for we are just leaving the great emporium of Malaya, where steamers coal on their outward and homeward voyages, and where goods are transhipped and distributed to all parts of the world. The docks are situated here; ships are being repaired, and the constant clang of hammers is heard as we along.

On the other side a silent dulness pervades the reddish-coloured hills, the summits of which have since been planted with trees, giving cover to strong fortifications and big guns, which it is hoped make Singapore impregnable to attack from the seaward, whilst boards at the water's edge mark the position of some submarine mines placed across the narrow entrance of the harbour. Passing between two red bluffs, we emerge into a well-buoyed channel that guides us into the straits beyond.

The sun has set, the outline of the coast fades from view, the night is fine and clear, a cool breeze makes a ripple on the water, and tempts me to have my bed made up on deck; but sleep has hardly come when the noise of hurrying feet is heard, then the flapping of the side awnings as the sailors lower and make them fast: none too soon, for a black bank of clouds has formed ahead, the breeze has freshened, and we are soon struck by the squall, accompanied by torrents of rain and blinding darkness. The steamer slacks her speed, begins to pitch, and the waves splash over her dipping bows; her human freight seeks shelter as best it may. An hour, and all is over; dripping decks, dead and dying ducks and fowls that have been smothered or trampled upon by their fellows, and small crested waves alone remain to tell of the squall we have just gone through, an experience very frequent in these waters at certain seasons of the year.

Early the next morning we approach Malacca, and on nearing the coast perceive that the whole shore is lined with a deep fringe of cocoanut-trees, whilst in the distance can be discerned the hills and mountains which form the dividing range of the Peninsula. We pass a number of small canoe-shaped fishing boats, in each of which a man is seated, having a wide conical hat upon his head, which looks like an inverted mushroom, as a protection from the sun. These tiny boats rock to every ripple, causing anyone affected with seasickness to shudder as he watches their occupants quietly fishing, entirely undisturbed by the pitching and tossing of their little craft. As we draw near the anchorage speed is slackened, but before the engines are stopped the ship is waylaid by a number of boats, which the rowers fasten on to her sides and up which they clamber, and rush amongst the passengers to seek for fares. They vociferate excitedly, for competition is keen, and pick up and secure the goods of their bespoken fares to prevent their changing their minds and engaging their passage to the shore with someone else. These boats are rowed by four or six men; they are capacious and strong, carrying a large sail, and able to withstand rough weather, a necessary attribute, as owing to the shallow foreshore steamers are obliged to anchor more than a mile out, and the journey to and fro is sometimes unpleasantly lively.

Malacca formerly was the principal trading port of this part of the world, and a place of considerable importance. In 1511 the Portuguese under Albuquerque attacked the town, commencing their assault by attacking the bridge spanning the river that intersects it. They then stormed the stockades on each side, which they took, and after setting fire to both parts of the city, which had been defended by 20,000 fighting men, they withdrew to their ships.

The king of Malacca, and his son-in-law the king of Pahang, were present at the battle, and, escaping capture, returned and commenced repairing the damage done, and refortified the town.

The Portuguese shortly made a second attack, and, having effected a landing, kept up a constant bombardment for ten days, in which their ships assisted. At last the city was taken and sacked, and its inhabitants—men, women, and children—massacred, for orders were given that all Malays and Moors should be put to death. On their side a number of Portuguese soldiers died of wounds inflicted by poisoned darts expelled from blow tubes.

In 1641 the Dutch under Caartekoe took Malacca

by assault, after besieging it for five months, and Portuguese ascendency came to an end.

It was taken by the English in 1795, but restored to the Dutch in 1818, to be transferred once more to the English in 1824 in pursuance of the treaty of Holland.

The ruins of the church built by the Portuguese still stand on the top of a steep conical hill, whence a fine view of the surrounding country is obtained. On one side you look down on the red-tiled roofs of houses half hidden amongst the cocoanut-trees, against whose green leaves they make a pleasing contrast of colour as the sun shines upon them; on the other side white gravestones on the adjacent hills mark the burial place of the Chinese merchants who have made this land their home, whilst at our feet is the sea glittering in the sunshine, and in the distance a steamer passes by, leaving a trail of smoke behind.

The fortifications have all been levelled, and a postern gate at the base of the hill is all that is left to show where the ramparts once stood, and nothing now remains to mark the spot by the river where assailants and besieged fought hand to hand, giving no quarter and expecting none.

The entrance to the river itself has become so silted up that it is only at high tide that a sailing craft of not more than a few tons can now enter, and at low water even small boats are unable to pass the bar.

The town was formerly the principal trading station and the great mart of this part of the world, where goods coming from China and the many islands of Malaysia and the Pacific Ocean, as well as from India, were bartered and sold, but its former glories have entirely departed, and its commerce has been transferred to the more recent settlements of Penang and Singapore, both of which places are more favourably situated as ports of call and for the transhipment of cargoes.

The Malays of Malacca are a prosperous and contented community, having everything at hand that is necessary to make life easy and happy. They have mosques wherein to worship, fish can be had for the taking, in their paddy fields close at hand they grow their rice, they dwell under the shade of fruit and cocoanut trees, the produce of which, being easily marketable, is sold for sufficient to supply them with the little extra luxuries they require for the year.

The women are clever at embroidery, especially with silver and gold thread, as well as in the art of preserving fruits in a manner somewhat similar to our crystallized ones, and in the making of many kinds of sweetmeats and pickles; in fact, the Malacca Malay, when compared with those in the interior of the native states, is far advanced in civilization.

The costume of the men consists of a kind of short smock, reaching only down to the hips, made of some imported cotton stuff of flowery pattern or gaudy colour, and called a baju, or coat. There is not much shape about this garment, which has a pocket on each side, a circular hole at the top fits the neck, an opening in front makes it easy to put on or take off over the head, and it is fastened either with small gold or common mother-of-pearl buttons, according to the means of the wearer. A sarong, or cloth fastened round the waist, hangs down to near the feet; the head is covered sometimes by a round cap, but more generally by a coloured cloth not much larger than a handkerchief, which twisted round forms a skimpy kind of turban. Should any one of them wish to appear very civilized and smart, he affects trousers, in which case he ties his sarong so that it does not fall below the knee, and dons white canvas shoes.

The women's costume is equally light and airy, and consists of a gay-coloured jacket, which, opening all the way down in front, reaches to the knees; the upper portion is fastened by three brooches, and their sarongs are similar to those worn by the men. Their hair is tied in a rolled knot behind, and kept tidy by long pins stuck through it, and when they wish to be very smart they thrust their feet into gold-embroidered, heelless slippers, which strike the ground with a flapping noise as they walk along; and they envelop the upper portion of their bodies and their heads in a sarong, the corners of which being extended are held outstretched by the hands at the level of their eyes, so that only an opening just sufficient to look out of is left, and usually the uglier the wearers are the more closed do they keep this aperture.

Amongst themselves, the discussing of their neighbours and the latest scandal seems to form the chief subject of their conversation, in the same way as Tamil women will talk of food for hours, and seem never tired of this—to them—fascinating subject.

The outskirts of Malacca are thickly populated by Malays, whose gardens, bordering on fine stretches of paddy fields, contain both fruit and cocoanut trees, in whose produce there is quite a brisk trade at certain seasons of the year; and the decks of the steamers trading to Singapore are crowded with a miscellaneous assortment, amongst which are the far-famed and prickly durian, so obnoxious to new comers, but delicious to those who have succeeded in overcoming its peculiar smell and taste; dukas, a fruit for which Malacca is famous, and equal in flavour to a nectarine; mangosteens, encased in a peculiar covering that hardens as the fruit ripens, and has a little crown on the top with a leaf for every division of the fruit inside, which is delicate in flavour, but does not keep good for many days; wholesome langsats that have a pleasant acid taste, but whose stone is bitter; red rambutans, with their prickly skins, beneath which a large seed is thinly coated with a luscious covering; and the rambai, a fruit that hangs down in bunches like yellow grapes, full of seeds inside, and somewhat bitter in flavour. Besides these there are the tampuni, pulasan, papaya and guava, all edible and pleasant to the taste.

The red colour of the roads is an agreeable change from the white granite thoroughfares of Singapore. Good laterite is easily procurable, and the streets are paved with this material, which is softer than granite, and pleasanter to drive along in fine weather.

The sea-wall is faced with blocks of hard laterite, having a honeycombed appearance on the outside. These stones are quarried and cut in a soft state, and after exposure to the air and weather for a year they become hard, making excellent building material, and are much used. The esplanade is lined with flamboyant trees, or "flame of the forest" as it is sometimes called, and when in blossom the flowers form a mass of gorgeous colour.

No description of Malacca would be complete without mention being made of the Malacca Babas, who are Malacca-born Chinamen, and form a considerable community, many of them being ignorant of the language of their forefathers, and only speaking Malay. They are of a gregarious disposition, and even the wealthy live in their business houses in the town, although they have fine residences and gardens some little distance away in the country, to which they only resort for recreation and change.

The interior of Malacca is less thickly populated, the country is undulating, and the principal settlements are within easy distance of the roads, which are numerous. Wherever there are valleys and gulleys the opportunity has been taken to convert them into paddy fields, which once a year are prepared for planting by having the weeds and grasses growing in them cut down and burnt. Then they are inundated with water, the ground is dug with a long-handled hoe, buffaloes are driven to and fro to churn up the earth, or a small wooden plough is used, depending upon the nature of the soil; the water is then let off, the surface smoothed and made ready to receive the plants.

On some suitable spot adjacent to the rice field the paddy seed has already been sown in a nursery, where it germinates and grows, forming little tufts of plants. These are pulled up, and after the top portion of their growth is cut to within a few inches of their roots, they are carried and planted out in the fields by women; the water is once more admitted, and there is nothing left to do but to regulate it and to wait until the grain is ripe, when all hands turn out with baskets and small knives or sickles, and cut the golden ears from off their stalks and carry them to the drying grounds, where, after being exposed to the sun, the grain falls from the stalks, and is stored in round cylinders made of bark—through which rats cannot penetrate—to be taken out as required. The grain, as long as it is in the ear, is called paddy, but when husked it is called rice. In order to prepare the paddy for household use it is re-dried on mats, then placed in a rude wooden mortar, which is formed merely out of a hollowed log, and pounded with a long-handled pestle; but more usually this pestle is a short piece of wood let into a wooden beam, the centre of which is fastened to a frame, and made so as to allow the person working it to easily depress one end by placing her foot and weight upon it, thus raising the pestle from the mortar. Directly the foot and weight is removed from the end of the beam the pestle falls upon the paddy, breaking the outside husk a little at each blow. The process continues until the paddy placed in the mortar is sufficiently husked to allow of its being winnowed. Should there be the slightest breath of air, this is done by letting the husked paddy fall gradually from a height, and the lighter and smaller particles get blown away, but the heavier fall on to the mat below, from which they are taken up, and winnowed anew by placing them by small quantities at a time in a flat triangular tray, made of plaited reeds fastened to a wooden frame. The broad side of this frame is laid hold of and held in both hands, and by shaking and tossing it in a peculiar manner the husks are made to go to the top of the triangle, out of which they are tossed by a deft movement and jerk of the tray, and this is continued until nothing but the rice is left behind, and after any black specks or foreign matter have been picked out by hand, it is ready for cooking.

On the hill slopes by the side of these fields there are fringes of cocoanut and fruit trees, and amongst them the Malay builds his house, which of itself is rather a peculiar structure. The builder takes six or eight stones, depending on the size of the house he intends to erect; these are placed on the surface of the ground, a little bed having been made for them to rest upon; then he fells and squares the required number of hard wood posts, cutting a hole in them at the height he requires his flooring to be from the ground, generally about five feet, and shaping the tops so as to leave a small square projection in the centre. These posts are then rested upon the stones, the joists and beams are let into the holes already cut, and secured by wooden pegs; light pieces of wood are stretched across the top, and fit over the small square projections, making the framework of the house complete. The sides of the dwelling are either formed of attaps, or of long strips of bark; the roof is steep-pitched and made with thin long saplings, just sufficiently strong to bear the weight of the men who cover them with attaps, or palm leaves. Sticks placed across the joists, and covered with a lattice of split rattan, or narrow laths cut

from the nibong palm, form the floor, which shakes and quivers as you walk across it.

Fortunately tornadoes and violent gales are unknown in these parts, or these houses would soon be blown away, and deposited in some neighbouring swamp.

Mats woven from rushes are unrolled and laid flat, and upon these the inmates sit and sleep. Formerly a common practice of seeking a cowardly revenge was to creep underneath the house and thrust a spear up through the interstices of the flooring into the sleeper above; the only difficulties were to be sure of sticking the right person and not someone else, and to prevent alarm being given by poisoning or killing the half-starved, miserable-looking dog that fed around the house upon the refuse thrown out, but which was usually never admitted inside. Nowadays wooden planks are used by the better class of natives for the sides and floors of their houses.

A fireplace or hob is made by filling a shallow box with earth, and on this a few stones are placed upon which rest the saucepans and cooking pots, whilst a few sticks ignited underneath make all the fire required to cook the rice and food. Overhead a sort of rough shelf made of sticks is the receptacle for the cooking utensils when not in use. The boiling rice is skimmed with a spoon made of a portion of a cocoanut shell, through which a piece of wood is stuck to form a handle. The larder of the household hangs down from the roof, suspended by strings of rattan threaded through the centre of the half of a cocoanut shell, the rounded side of which is uppermost, and hanging a little above the article to be protected against the ravages of rats. This clever and simple device never fails, for although the rat is able to climb down the string, directly it reaches the smooth rounded outside of the cocoanut shell it meets with an obstacle it cannot get round; and whilst endeavouring to do so, it causes the shell to tip a bit, and as its smooth surface affords no foothold, the rat falls to the floor below.

A curious dislike prevails amongst the inmates to having trousers hung up inside the house; they think it unbecoming to sit or sleep beneath anyone's pantaloons, although any other garment does not cause the same offence.

Water for cooking and drinking is brought from an adjoining open well or stream, in gourds made from a large species of pumpkin, the inside of which has been taken out, leaving the hard outside shell, and when new they give to the water kept in them a somewhat muddy taste.

Cooking operations are simple, for the meal usually consists of boiled rice, small pieces of dried fish heated over the embers of the fire, and a concoction of hot red chillies that have been ground with salt into a paste. The smoking rice is put in the centre of the floor; pieces of dried fish and fiery chillies ground up with salt are the usual relishes, and around this simple fare the family sit with their legs crossed; and should there be a stranger within the house he is always invited to join in the meal, to which each one helps himself, and places as much as he cares to take upon a leaf spread in front of him, which serves the purpose of a plate. No one speaks, all being too busily engaged taking handfuls of rice, which, with a dexterous movement of the fingers, they place within their mouths. Upon completion of the meal many of them have a disgusting habit of showing their satisfaction by belching, after which they wash their hands and rinse out their mouths.

The materials used in chewing are then passed

round to each person in succession, commencing with the principal guest, who selects a betel leaf, which he spreads out flat, and places upon it a little moist and finely ground lime; then he folds the leaf in four, and putting it into his mouth helps himself to a small piece of gambier, and a little areca nut to flavour what he is chewing; next he takes a quid of tobacco, with which he first of all rubs his teeth, then places it in his mouth, so that his cheek bulges out, and for a few minutes solely occupies himself with chewing; then he commences to expectorate a nasty red fluid down through the openings of the floor. The chewing mixture without the tobacco is not unpleasant, for it has a pungent, aromatic taste, but it was not sufficiently agreeable for me to try it more than once. What it was like mixed with the quid of tobacco I cannot say, for although I smoked continuously, I could never bring myself to chew the leaf. This habit of constant chewing is very bad for the teeth, which become black and decayed until they are quite unfit for use, and even then the old people do not discontinue the custom, but putting the harder ingredients into a mortar, they chop them up with a chisel-headed pestle before putting them into their mouths. Around each dwelling several vines may be seen trained up posts, and it is from these that the betel leaves are plucked. The aromatic nut is supplied by the tall, slender areca-nut palms which grow so freely, and look so picturesque crowned with a few dark green leaves beneath which hang clusters of nuts in their tough outer covering, the colour of which, as the fruit ripens, changes from green to yellow. The lime induces expectoration, and the gambier is somewhat insipid, having a peculiar gummy kind of taste.

After the meal washing up takes place. The refuse water is thrown through the interstices in the floor, a dirty habit, as underneath the house an offensive-smelling pool forms, from which the fowls and ducks gather the eatable leavings, scrambling for them with the mangy-looking dog that lurks around the house. Although everything is brought into the house by the door, Malays have this unpleasant habit of throwing rice skimmings, fish bones, and all refuse through a hole in the floor by the side of the cooking place.

The size of a Malay village in the interior varies in proportion to the extent of land in the immediate vicinity suitable for rice growing and under irrigation. The houses are built a little distance apart, and stand in their own grounds close to the paddy fields, and surrounded by fruit trees. There is often a little shed in the compound that shelters a fireplace, scooped out of the hillside, and having two openings, one a horizontal shaft in which the firewood is placed, joined at the end to a perpendicular outlet, on the top of which rests the large cauldron used by Malay women to make the delicious sugar cakes of jaggery they are all so fond of, and which is manufactured by evaporation from the sap of the palm trees that grow around. Ducks and fowls wander about, and broody hens sit on nests beneath the houses.

The ground is covered with close-cropped sward, eaten short by buffaloes and goats. The former, when wanted for work, are tethered at night to a stake driven into the ground; a fire is lighted near to keep the mosquitoes from annoying them, but at other times they are allowed to roam at will, and congregate in herds, making innumerable tracks in the low scrub in the vicinity of the villages. The latter are shut up at night in small houses, elevated some eight or ten feet off the ground on posts, and made accessible by steps scooped out of a log that leans against the doorway, in order to prevent the goats from being carried off by the tigers and panthers prowling around, which otherwise would speedily be their fate.

Malay silversmiths, blacksmiths, and carpenters are fast being superseded by Chinese, and as the villagers have no trades to give them occupation during the time there is nothing doing in the fields, many of the men leave their homes in search of employment, returning at frequent intervals, for they are able by working three months in the year to supply themselves with all the necessaries they require for the remaining nine. The women stay at home, and beyond their household duties have little else to occupy themselves with, for they do not weave, and sew but little, as they usually purchase their apparel ready made. Their only excitement is connected with religious festivals and marriages. The cost of the latter ranges from twenty dollars to two thousand dollars, according to the wealth of the parents and whether the bride has been married before, because it is only on first marriages that so much money is spent, and the wedding of a divorcee takes place more quietly.

The bride is prepared for the nuptials by having her hair cut so as to leave a fringe in front, and her teeth filed, and on the appointed day she powders her face, dyes her eyelids, borrows the finest garments she can and as much jewellery as she is able from all her friends, and is seated on a daïs to be admired by her kind. The bridegroom is dressed in his best, as are all his friends, who stroll about in the neighbourhood of the house and make him the object of their congratulations as the time approaches for him to seat himself beside the bride, when the assembled company chant some verses of the Koran, and the recognized priest or Haji proceeds to perform the ceremony. The bride and bridegroom grasp each other's right hand, and a cloth or handkerchief is placed over them by the Haji, who, holding their hands, prefaces the words of the marriage contract with an exhortation and prayer. After the ceremony the bride and bridegroom sit together for a short while for the edification of the guests, and then the feast takes place.

The Mohammedan religion has caused the marriage-tie to be very loose and easily broken, for it is only necessary that the husband should repudiate his wife to render them both free; the woman, however, has to wait three months before she can marry again. There are three degrees of divorce; should the husband repudiate his wife only once or twice the divorce is revocable, but if he does so three times, then it is irrevocable; and to become revocable the woman must be married to, and divorced from, some other man before remarrying with her former husband. Connected with this, the Malays have a custom of presenting one, two, or three pebbes to the divorcee by way of intimating which degree of separation they wish it to be, but the simple holding-up of three fingers has been held to be a sufficiently implied and legal dissolution of the bond of matrimony.

Notwithstanding this apparently simple method of divorce, family relations and questions of money often prevent it from being so easily effected; besides, the freedom the Malay women enjoy cause them to be quite capable of looking after their own interests in this respect. Perhaps the jealous disposition of the men helps to make the marriage-tie more binding, for Malay women seldom appear to have any difficulty in marrying again after they are once divorced; and, although the husband may be ready enough to get rid of his wife, he does not like seeing her comfortably settled with another, or to be himself the object of her covert jibes and sneers.

Both sexes are fond of their children, and these often become the strongest tie of all; and when they are young the father may frequently be seen carrying one about perched on his hip with its legs akimbo or teaching it to walk, amusing and playing with it; and when he returns it to its mother she tosses it in the air, catching and letting it go and talking to it the while, then she kisses it by placing her nose against its face and sniffing once or twice loudly—a peculiar manner of caress according to our notions; and swinging the child round she places it on her hip, and holds it there with her arm round its body.

Chinese tapioca planters owned much of the land in the interior portions of Malacca that was unoccupied by Malays; and during the years of their prosperity, before the price of tapioca fell, gave abundance of employment to the inhabitants of the neighbouring villages. Large numbers of carts were required to carry the manioc roots to the central factories, and the manufactured product down to the coast, and, being principally owned by Malays, became the means of earning for their owners an easy and comfortable livelihood.

The method of tapioca cultivation as pursued in the Straits is wasteful and devastating. Fine forest trees are cut down and burned, manioc cuttings are planted short distances apart, and soon grow up several feet from the ground with long spindly stems, on the tops of which are a few leafy branches, whilst yam-like tubers form underneath the ground and usually reach maturity in a little more than a year, when they are uprooted, detached from the stalks, and carried in carts to the central factory, which is erected in some place where there is a plentiful supply of good water procurable, a most important requisite in the preparation of tapioca, and much depends upon its being pure and clean. The roots are first peeled, then grated and carried with the water into vats, where they are kept some days, and the water is constantly changed. The juice of the root is extracted by pressure, and the residue, after drying and sifting, is baked in pans over slow fires in order to free the flake from the small quantity of hydrocyanic or prussic acid that it contains. Manioc roots roasted whole in the embers of a wood fire make an excellent substitute for potatoes, and have not the sweet taste peculiar to yams. As soon as the crop has been gathered the ground is dug over and a fresh lot of cuttings are planted, but by the time this crop is harvested, or at most one more, the soil is exhausted, and the land, already very dirty, is abandoned, and becomes choked with weeds, scrub, and lalang grass; the latter soon predominates, and turns the country where it flourishes into a wilderness of long grass with white fluffy seeds that are wafted about in every direction. In dry weather this grass burns easily, afterwards growing up stronger than ever, for it has a network of roots that go down some distance below the surface of the ground, and are always ready to push forth fresh shoots, consequently it is most difficult to eradicate by digging, but if the young blades are eaten back by buffaloes or cattle the lalang ceases to make further growth, and other grasses take its place.

The tenure by which all agricultural lands are held is by payment of an annual quit rent, which sum covers all rates and taxes. Should the tenant fail to pay, the Government can distrain for the amount, and in cases where the occupiers desert their holdings, which often happens, and especially in new districts, the Government after a while re-enter into possession of the land.

# CHAPTER III.

Departure for Sungie Ujong—Striking upon sunken rocks—Journey up river—Crocodiles—Captain J. P. Murray, R.N., Resident—Honourable Martin Lister—Black panthers—Rantau—Seremban—Gunong Brembong—Coffee planting—Native labour—Characteristics of Malays—Pay days.

In order to reach Sungie Ujong from Malacca it was necessary to embark on board another small steamer, which combined the maximum of discomfort with the minimum of speed. We steamed along parallel with the coast, and not far out from the shore, passing on our way some small conical rocks that were straight in our course, and which the ebbing tide had left uncovered and exposed to view. At this point rather a curious incident occurred some years later, during one of the many times in which I took this journey. It was on a somewhat larger steamer, in command of which there was a new captain, who, either not being thoroughly acquainted with the proper course to be steered, or unmindful of these rocks, was lolling on a seat, not troubling himself about the ship, which was left to the control of the helmsman.

I happened also to be sitting on the bridge at the time, and suddenly was surprised to see the bows of the steamer rise in the air, and she came almost to a standstill; then her bows dipped, and we continued on our way. We had struck and slid over one of these rocks. Fortunately they were covered with just sufficient water to allow of this being done, for had the tide been lower and the rocks nearer the surface there would no doubt have been a bad smash; as it was, it was quite enough to make one satisfied with the usual humdrum monotony of steaming through the water, and not to wish for the more lively sensation of jumping obstacles on the way. Meanwhile the captain's face had been a study—blank astonishment and dismay at first, followed by intense relief.

Crossing the bar at the entrance of the Linggi river, we steamed up it. As the tide was low, the mud-coloured banks of the mangrove swamp on each side were exposed to view, and a crocodile was now and then to be seen lying basking on the shelving slope, until, disturbed by the approaching steamer, it would suddenly turn round with a nimbleness quite amazing and disappear beneath the water. Another again would be floating with its head just visible, when all at once it would sink out of sight, and vanish so quietly as to leave no perceptible sign or movement in the water behind to mark the spot where its uncanny head had so lately appeared.

These pests make the rivers dangerous; generally women are taken and carried off when bathing or fetching water, but they have been known to attack the occupants of a small boat. Once their jaws close firmly on the victim, unless help is very close at hand, there is no reopening of their mouths, and if their hold is relaxed it is simply because the teeth have torn along through the flesh to the end of the part laid hold of.

I have never seen anyone taken by a crocodile myself, but an eye-witness has described how in one instance he saw a man holding on to the side of a boat to prevent himself from being dragged down, shrieking for help, which could not reach him, until overcome he let go, to disappear and rise no more. These reptiles are reputed to bury their prey in the mud at the bottom of the river, and to feed upon them when they have become decomposed. From a distance a crocodile looks more like a log lying on the bank than anything else, and it is only on nearer approach that the outline of this repulsive-looking monster is distinctly defined.

The river gets narrower as we proceed, the bends become sharper, and the branches of the mangrove trees brush against the sides of the steamer, which is sometimes obliged to stop to permit of her bows being pushed round to enable her to turn some corner; but there is nothing to recall to mind that, but a few years previously, this highway had been stopped by the inhabitants of the neighbouring state of Rembau, and a blockade maintained—causing distress, and threatening famine to the Chinese miners in the interior—which the people of Sungie Ujong were unable to raise until two men-of-war sent a force of bluejackets and marines in boats to their assistance.

Occasionally a tribe of monkeys were descried sitting on the branches of trees, peering out through the foliage and seeming to take quite an intelligent interest in what was passing, or the sudden rustling of leaves would attract my attention in time to see branches alive with motion as the monkeys ran along them and jumped or swung from tree to tree. The swamp on each side of the river is a perfect network of mangrove roots, amongst which colonies of crabs have their home, and immediately on being disturbed they scuttle away, and, popping into their holes, disappear, or sometimes, if not too frightened, they will linger at the entrance, only half hidden from view, wondering at the unwonted disturbance.

I had almost forgotten to mention that ubiquitous species of little animal, *Poriophthalmus Koelrenteri*, which seems to thrive amidst the pestilential mud of the mangrove swamps. It skids along the banks at a tremendous pace, disporting itself on the still wet, slimy mud which the receding tide has but recently uncovered, and when alarmed darts into the water so quickly as to puzzle the observer who sees it for the first time, because, apparently, it has no means of propulsion, as from a distance nothing can be seen except the little creature gliding over the soft mud on its belly. On closer examination a mark on the surface is visible where its stomach has scraped, and on each side little cuts where its pectoral fins have struck the mud as it nimbly slid on its way.

At night the channel is plainly defined by a sparkling mass of tiny lights, as myriads of fireflies flit and scintillate amongst the leaves of the bordering mangrove trees; and I have often watched with fascination these twinkling sparks, until my eyes have become tired with gazing upon the glittering lines between which the boat slowly wended its way to the highest point of the river practicable for a small steamer to reach, where was situated a landing stage and a few houses clustered together, the only port, at this time, of the state, and named Linggi. Some years later this port was given up for another further down the river, which in its turn was abandoned for one on the sea coast called Port Dickson, after a Colonial Secretary of the Straits Settlements, the late Sir Frederick Dickson, who was also for some while Acting Governor.

The river at Linggi was so narrow that in order to turn the steamer about her stern had to be shoved in amongst the branches of the trees on one bank, whilst her bow was pushed and dragged round through the branches on the other. A few small boats took what cargo there was for Seremban, a long and difficult four days of poling up stream, and often longer when there was either too much or too little water in the river.

There was a police station near the landing place, and I was fortunate in meeting Capt. Murray, R.N., the genial and kindly Resident, who was on his way to Malacca; but before leaving the next day he ordered a policeman to escort me to Seremban, and bid me make myself at home in his house. Not long afterwards he met with a fall, which, followed by a long day's journey and exposure to the sun, brought on an illness to which he succumbed a few days after reaching Malacca, whither he had gone for medical advice.

Travelling with Captain Murray was the Hon.

Martin Lister, who was at that time engaged in opening a Liberian coffee plantation at Linsum; afterwards joining the Civil Service, he was appointed the first Resident of the Negri Sembilan, a group of neighbouring states; and it was in large measure owing to his tact and influence with the inhabitants that this change in administration was accepted peacefully and quietly by the people concerned. Later on he became Resident of Sungie Ujong, in addition to his duties in the Negri Sembilan; but his health having completely broken down he was ordered home, but never arrived there, succumbing to his malady at Suez. It is a touching coincidence that the last portion of the career of each of these two friends should have been so similar; they were both stricken with a mortal illness whilst Residents of Sungie Ujong, and departed from the state never to return; but they left behind them with the people amongst whom they lived, memories of many a kindly action and reputations for unvarying justice and uprightness, qualities amongst those in authority that have made our Empire what it is.

At certain seasons of the year in the neighbourhood of Linggi, towards evening, great numbers of flying foxes—which are a kind of large bat, having reddish-coloured backs and brown heads—were to be seen sailing along high up in the air, following one another in quick succession, and journeying from the land across the straits towards the hills of the interior.

Some of the villagers were very expert at setting traps for tigers and panthers, which were numerous and frequently captured, and after being allowed to remain for some days to quieten down and become tamed, they were carried to the villages in cages, only just large enough to hold the wretched, half-starved animal, which was generally so weak and stiff from want of food and long confinement as to be incapable of moving. The tigers would lie in quiet calmness, taking but little notice when poked with a stick, whereas the black panthers were always ready with a spiteful snarl, game and vicious to the last. The latter are not dangerous when unmolested, but are most ferocious if attacked. I have constantly observed them cross the road scarce fifty yards away when I have been walking or driving, and there was one special locality where sometimes two or three were to be seen at dusk; but I never troubled about them, nor did they ever interfere with me in any way. I remember seeing a magnificent female of this variety which had only been some months in captivity. She was intensely savage, and the sight of anyone sent her into paroxysms of rage and fury, so that no one dared to go too near the bars of the spacious cage in which she was confined. She was given a male companion, but at the end of a week they had a tremendous fight, in which she came off the victor and he was killed. Although they are called black panthers, on a nearer view their bodies are seen to be prettily dappled with brown.

It was a twenty-two mile walk to Seremban; the road was undulating, ever going up or down some hill, villainously bad, scarcely passable for carts, and utterly unfit for any description of buggy. The first portion of the journey skirted straggling Malay villages; then, with the exception of a tapioca clearing, there was nothing but jungle, until the pioneer Liberian coffee estate at Linsum was reached, and adjacent to it the village of Rantau.

The cultivation of Liberian coffee was as yet in an experimental stage in the Straits, and it was still uncertain whether it would take kindly to the soil and climate, or become the failure it afterwards was in Ceylon. Wherever planted in these regions it proved itself to be hardier and more robust than the Arabian variety, growing at a lower elevation, and thriving where well cared for and liberally cultivated. The trees grow to a considerable size, and have to be planted at longer intervals apart than Arabian coffee—nine feet by nine feet being quite close enough; the leaf is large, and of a dark green colour; the bean, which is enclosed in a thick, tough berry, is bigger than the latter, and unless picked and prepared with care the infusion has a bitter taste, and is not so pleasant to drink as the other variety, consequently it fetches a lower price in the market. The berries hang for a considerable while and ripen slowly, so that there is a great temptation to gather them before they are thoroughly ripe and mature. The trees are topped at about five feet from the ground to make them spread laterally. The yield per acre is largely in excess of the Arabian variety, and should this coffee recover its price, the planting of it cannot fail to become a most lucrative industry. Arabian coffee was also planted at Linsum, but in a few years it overbore itself, the climate at this elevation proving too hot and forcing for it unless planted under shade, when its bearing capabilities are checked, and instead of producing fruit it runs to wood and leaves. Cocoa was also planted on this estate, but proved only a qualified success, some trees growing and bearing magnificently,

whilst their neighbours were stricken and stunted, under, to all appearances, exactly similar conditions. The pepper vines did well, and the sago palms grew luxuriantly in any swampy localities.

The road for the remaining twelve miles lay mostly through jungle, but for some distance before reaching Seremban it traversed a country which had once been planted but since abandoned, and which had become covered with a kind of short scrub and lalang, across which there was no shade; and as it was intensely hot, the last portion of the tramp was very exhausting and wearisome, especially as I was not as yet accustomed to the damp, moist heat of the Straits, which to a new comer is at first very enervating and trying, and from being so lately cooped up on board ship I was somewhat out of condition.

On reaching Seremban I found that Captain Murray's residence consisted of two houses, each of two stories. The dining-room, Government offices, and store-rooms were on the ground floor; whilst above were the sitting-room, study, and bedrooms. The houses were joined together by a bridge, which connected the two broad verandahs that ran round the outside of both houses, and one of them being somewhat higher than the other was called the quarter-deck. A little tame honey-bear cub wandered about the house, and was most wilful in its ways. It much disliked being chained up, and when annoyed would throw itself down on the floor and cry and shake with rage just like some naughty, badly-brought-up child. Its end was sad, for in one of its fits of temper it upset an oil lamp that was standing on the ground, and got so badly burnt that it had to be destroyed. The estate for which I was bound was fifteen miles further up country, and situated in the main range of hills at an elevation of about fifteen hundred feet. A gang of men were employed in cutting a road over this intervening distance, but it was some years before it was completed. The track to the hills traversed undulating country till it reached the foot of the main range of mountains, where there were extensive paddy fields, and a large Malay village called Pantai.

From this point there was an uphill climb the whole way through dense forest, along a narrow path that followed the course of the main stream, the waters of which could be heard dashing and tumbling below with a perpetual roaring sound, the noise of which increased or decreased as the road either approached closer to the river or receded, winding round one of the numerous valleys, where tiny rivulets divide the ridges that intersect the spurs of Gunong Brembong.

A small house had been built, a little clearing, of Arabian coffee, planted by way of commencement, and some extent of forest felled by a European, who shortly after was invalided home, and has since died. In these parts nature always revenges herself for being interfered with. Fever-laden vapours rise from the land despoiled of its trees, and the soil disturbed by digging emits noxious gases, and these reign paramount until a new growth has taken the place of the one destroyed, or time and exposure have weakened the banefulness of the fumes. The fever in these hills was of a very malignant type—for weeks at a time attack would succeed attack. The best means of cure was change; but as work had to be looked after and directed, it was impossible to leave the place, so there was nothing to be done but to endure it. Alternate days were generally worse than the intervening ones, although sometimes the fever would be continuous for days and weeks with slight intermissions, and its course was much as follows. Each morning the fever-stricken subject, with emaciated body and weak, tottering footsteps, would seek a couch in the verandah in which to enjoy the deliciously fresh and cool air of the hills, until after a short while of languid but refreshing rest a cold shivering fit would compel him to return to his bed, and to cover himself, head and all, with blankets, seeking warmth. Then followed an awful continuous sickness, a great rise in temperature, and a burning head that felt as though it were striving to split asunder, making the temples throb and ache, until the consciousness that the limit of endurance was nearly reached came as a consolation, and providential light-headedness supervened, giving relief from suffering. The climate otherwise was pleasant, and as cool as it would have been at a much higher elevation in Ceylon.

The labourers were Malays from the adjacent independent states, many of whom had never seen a white man, nor had they ever been accustomed to any systematic work. It was my custom to give out money to be taken to the villages where labour was procurable, and many a man was persuaded to come and work by the temptation of being able to supply his home with a few dollars before he started. Some would come and work until their advances were repaid, and then without a word would return home again; others stayed for a longer period, trying to put some money by; whilst many would arrive on the estate out of curiosity, being told by some

A GROUP OF MALAYS.

comrade about what was going on, and they would pay me a visit just because they were inquisitive to see a white man.

I always entertained them to tea, and their wonder was at the clock, whose pendulum swung backwards and forwards with constant regularity; and the ticking of my watch would surprise and amuse them as they placed it to their ears. Photographs they did not seem to understand at all, nor could they make anything of them, looking at them turned upside down as often as not; and even when objects were pointed out and the subject explained, it seemed to be entirely beyond their comprehension; and although they would, out of politeness, continue to look at the photograph in an absent-minded way, they were always intensely relieved when the subject was changed. Notwithstanding the strangeness of their surroundings they never appeared *gauche* or awkward except when sitting on a chair for the first time, and then they would sit gingerly on the very edge of the seat, and were apparently half afraid lest it should give way beneath their weight. I used to suggest to them that they should try and see what the routine of work on the estate was like, and help me by joining what, in Malay, I called my force of "labourer children,"—a usual and well-understood expression to signify not only the good feeling and pleasant terms that existed between employer and employed, but that the one in authority entertained a considerate care for those under him—and I always received the invariable answer, "I have not as yet made up my mind." However, the next day they were generally to be seen out in the fields amongst the men, and after working hours came for an advance of money, for they were most suspicious at first that they might not get paid, and considered prepayment as the only means for protecting themselves from imposition.

The peculiar distinctive qualities of Malays are so diverse that any generalization of their character is extremely difficult; but the constant association and friendly acquaintance I had with so many of them, coming from different states, and yet unaffected by the influences of civilization, gave me an opportunity of observing their idiosyncrasies, and the many traits recounted will enable the reader to form a fair opinion.

The children play about from quite an early age entirely uncontrolled; a sharp slap, casually administered, is about all the correction given. The women cook, carry water, see to the house, and work in the fields, where a great proportion of the manual labour is done by them. The men, when at home, build and keep their houses in repair, collect rattan from the neighbouring jungle, do all the fencing requisite, make traps for catching fish and game, and seek for forest fruits and edible roots. They attend to the buffaloes and drive them when ploughing, for these animals are somewhat dangerous to handle, and when being led along the narrow paths through the jungle by a rope of rattan passed through their nose their attendant has to be on the alert, for should any sudden noise or movement frighten the one he is leading it will rush blindly forward, and then it is difficult to keep clear of its horns and to check its onward course and calm its fears. In the towns every buffalo is obliged to have a stick fixed across its horns and made fast to its head, so that should it become terrified or savage it cannot do much harm.

The inhabitants of each little independent state have some peculiarities and characteristic traits, by means of which the locality from whence they come can be determined, and when they speak a difference of dialect is easily detected.

The Malays, as a race, are very slow to acquire confidence in a stranger; they are polite with an innate courtesy, and should they suddenly be confronted by a novel or difficult situation, their self-control and grace of movement is so inborn that they go through the most trying ordeal without the slightest awkwardness. They can be led or shamed by words into doing almost anything; but once let them imagine that they are being driven or forced against their will, they turn mulish and stubborn, and it is difficult to overcome their obstinacy. They are reserved, never taking liberties, and equally disliking any to be taken, quick to judge character or to take offence, disliking coarseness, flattered by small attentions and agreeable glibness of speech. Notwithstanding an apparent frank openness of manner, and seeming candid light-heartedness attractive in the extreme, they possess a self-restraint and control that enables them to narrate only just as much as they think it expedient for the listener to know. They parry an awkward question with commendable dexterity, and their face assumes a blank mask impossible to pierce. If caught in a flagrant lie, with imperturbable good humour they own that their "tongue has made a slip," and that you are better informed than they. An indolent love of ease and pleasure makes them dislike the monotony of any continuous work. They seldom trouble to enter into an argument, preferring outwardly to agree, but inwardly they still retain their own opinions of unshaken and undisturbed superiority; or, as they tersely put it, "they have a divided face—the one half for the interrogator, and the other half for themselves." They never boast, and dislike hearing others do so, and but seldom lose their presence of mind under the most trying circumstances. Plucky with a cool quietness that commands admiration, they at the same time are never forgetful that their own individual existence is a matter of the first importance to themselves. As long as their strongholds are intact they defend them ably, and on several occasions have successfully repulsed assaults made by small parties of soldiers unaided by cannon; but convinced of the hopelessness of withstanding arms of precision, and disliking cold steel, they never await the onslaught of troops whose guns have previously made a breach in the defences of their fort, but scatter to take up a new position behind fresh stockades elsewhere. Cruel in so far as an utter callousness and absence of sympathy towards suffering is concerned, they are yet kind and indulgent to their children. They have a great dislike of petty wrangling, and shun the society of the quarrelsome.

They are the most sensitive of Eastern races to any disturbing influence, and many of them suffer from a peculiar neurotic complaint called *latah*, which is a disease that makes the sufferer lose all power of self-control on certain occasions; for instance, in one case the sudden use of a certain word will make the person afflicted jump and shout, no matter where he may be; in another case, a sudden exclamation and a pretence to fight will cause the person afflicted to use the same cry, and to copy the action of fighting in every particular, hitting anyone who may be near, absolutely unable to control his movements until the paroxysm is past, when, as soon as he has recovered from his momentary exhaustion, he turns and curses the practical joker whom he has been forced to mimic. This nervous disease is more frequently to be met with in women than in men, and unless you happen by chance to hit upon the subject upon which they are *latah*, you may never discover that there is anything wrong with them. On one occasion I accidentally found it out in a man whom I had known for years, often travelled with, and never suspected to be at all afflicted with any sort of nervous complaint, for several times to my knowledge he had behaved in a very plucky way. One day in the jungle I touched him suddenly on the back and said "cut"; he jumped and wildly cut the air with his parang, exclaiming "cut, cut, cut," the while, and when the paroxysm had passed, turned round and said, "Ah, Tuan" (Ah, Master), in a beseeching manner, as much as to beg of me not again to take advantage of his malady; and of course I assured him on this point, and said that it had occurred unwittingly, and that I would be more careful in the future.

Their complex nature can be better understood by studying their antecedents. The race as at present constituted in this portion of the peninsula is for the most part composed of descendants of emigrants from Sumatra who have intermarried with the aboriginal inhabitants. Notwithstanding the Mohammedan conquest of the thirteenth and fourteenth centuries, Malays still retain in their legends and mythology many traces of the Hindu influence that was previously paramount for many centuries. They are not strict Moslems, neglecting many of the observances and tenets of that religion when they clash with their own pleasures and indulgences. The fasting month of Ramadhan is kept by many only in a most perfunctory manner, and they have holy places at which they make their vows, whilst spirit legends and folk-lore enter largely into their faith. They firmly believe in the efficacy of breathing upon sick persons, as well as upon the medicine, before it is given, and in cases of illness they constantly requisition the attendance of the local exorciser. Foreign and other influences seem to have had much to do with the building up of their present temperament, and their chief characteristics can be traced to such sources.

The influence of Hindooism accounts for many of their superstitions, as well as for the fabulous tales they are so fond of repeating, and other myths and legends. Their treachery, cunning, and absolute disregard of human life is due to their Arabian ancestors, who introduced the Mohammedan religion, which is answerable for their fatalism and the looseness of their marriage ties. They owe the indulgence of their love of ease and pleasure to the productiveness of the soil, which grows enough for their daily wants without requiring any great effort on their part. The aboriginal admixture accounts for their preference to fight in the jungle and dislike to meet an enemy in the open. Their inherent taste for gambling perhaps comes from former Siamese conquests and Mongolian influences. The climate is answerable for their neurotic tendencies, and in great measure for the nervous diseases from which they suffer. Their nautical vocabulary was added to and enriched by many Portuguese terms and expressions, during the time of the ascendency of that race in this part of the world.

The youths go through a phase of strutting about in fine raiment, always ready for an intrigue in which there may be some spice of danger; for before British intervention, a *krise*—a long shaped dagger, the blade of which is often fluted and twisted, the handle and scabbard being of highly polished wood—was carried by everyone, and drawn without much provocation, and used with deadliness, although generally treacherously and when the offender was off his guard. Often the victim was waylaid, or craftily induced to go on some expedition with his would-be destroyer, who, whilst they were travelling together, took the opportunity of killing his companion.

This latter was a common method practised by the followers of a chief, when ordered to remove a person who had made himself obnoxious and given offence, or whose death was necessary to the accomplishment of some cherished scheme or to gratify some private spite.

As these people were under no absolute necessity to labour, and only did so to obtain luxuries and greater comfort, it was a difficult matter to induce them to do a good day's work; but by tact and perseverance and sparing no pains I had trained my older hands into excellent workmen, and the new arrivals would follow their example, and in time things went on very smoothly. An advance would be given to the men every Saturday evening, and after work on the last day of every month each man received any balance there might be due to him. It was always a lengthy business paying the men, and especially so if there were many who had never worked on the estate before, and were receiving their pay for the first time; for there would always be several men who, on being told the number of days on which they had worked, would appear much disappointed, and strenuously declare that the entry of one or two had been omitted. They were always quite positive that they were correct, and that you were wrong in not recording their presence on the day in dispute.

This necessitated the calling together the friends and companions, and questioning them upon the subject, and perhaps, after a quarter of an hour's interrogation, one of them would remember that the complainant had had a headache on the day in question and did not work, or had gone to the village at the foot of the hills or elsewhere. The grumbler would then acquiesce with a stolid indifference, disliking to have been found in the wrong, but without the slightest compunction for having wasted your time and kept everyone else waiting, or thanks for the careful enquiries made; however, this was better than that anyone should carry the tale of his having been cheated back to his village, to prejudice the minds of others and prevent their coming. It is marvellous how soon news spreads amongst an Eastern race, and the slightest rumour of unfair treatment would have seriously reduced the number of workmen; for unless Malays like and have confidence in the master for whom they work, they prefer to stay away and not go near him. A brusque manner, or a tactless method of dealing with them, has often proved quite sufficient of itself to cause an employer to be boycotted; and so quietly was this accomplished, that the person affected would vainly wonder why it was he could get no labourers to work for him.

The day after paying was always one of anxiety as to how many would remain, for a great exodus invariably occurred, and there was a scarcity of labourers for the next few days until more arrived, each of whom brought either a krise or spear, often both, in addition to his parang, so that the houses they occupied presented quite a warlike appearance from the number of dangerous weapons hanging and lying about. Although there were often about two hundred men living within a short distance of one another, they never once fought amongst themselves or created the slightest disturbance, which, considering their past careers, and that they came from many different states and villages, and were constantly changing, was extraordinary, and only shows how easily the Malay is affected by outside influences, and exemplifies the advantages derived from the prohibition of intoxicating drinks by the Mohammedan religion.

# CHAPTER IV.

Monkeys—Flying Squirrels and Lizards—Wild Dogs—Jakuns—Benighted—The Jungle—Birds—Wild Beasts—Leeches—Ticks—Snakes—Fish—Scenery—Coffee Planting—Cholera—Fall over Rocks—Waris Families—The Chief of Sungie Ujong—Sword Dance—Berok Monkeys—Malay attacked by Tigress—Death of Tigress and Cub—Growth of Coffee—Difficulties of Labour—Government dilatory—Abandonment of Estates.

THE dawn of each day was heralded by the weird cry of the wa-wa, or Gibbon monkey, whose call was soon taken up by others of its tribe on the opposite hillside, so that all around the air resounded with their loud whooping shrieks.

Wa-was have long arms and very short legs and tails; they are black in colour, with a white fringe of hair round their faces, which gives them an almost human look, and each has the appearance of some pigmy old man. They are most attractive and plaintive creatures, but dwindle in confinement, and seldom live for any lengthened period after capture. There is also a white or cream-coloured variety, but I never saw one in a wild state.

It is an interesting sight to come suddenly upon a group of common monkeys, and then to watch their stampede. They run up a tree and along its branches, till reaching the extreme ends they jump without the slightest hesitation right out into space, seeming not to mind and little heeding how long the drop may be to the branch they wish to gain. They fall through the air with their arms and legs stretched out, and no sooner have they clutched the bough, which bends beneath their weight, than without a seeming effort they are off again, scampering across the tree and along its branches, flinging themselves on to the one beyond.

The wa-was are of a more solitary disposition, and swing from branch to branch with their long arms, using their feet but little. Their progress is slower, and they are less nimble, but they also fling themselves from tree to tree, doing so with outstretched arms, ready to seize the branch when reached.

Flying squirrels would sometimes be seen sailing through the air, but *flying* is a misnomer, for these creatures have only the power of supporting their bodies as with outstretched legs they skim across the valley, always reaching some tree at a lower elevation than the one they started from.

Flying lizards do much the same, and when disturbed they appear to inflate themselves and flit to another tree, up which they run and launch themselves into the air once more, making short flights from stem to stem, but never, as far as I could discover, flying for any great distance.

Both these creatures have a kind of web which stretches between the limbs along each side of their bodies, forming a bat-like wing, so that when they are extended the skin becomes taut, and sustains their bodies whilst in motion and carries them along.

Occasionally wild dogs in full cry after some animal would be heard as they travelled along the hillside; but, being very shy and wary, they are seldom seen, and it was only once that I came suddenly upon one of these little creatures, which was no bigger than a jackal, and appeared as much surprised as I was at the encounter, and disappeared directly he caught sight of me.

Along the ridges of the hills travelling was fairly easy, for there was usually a track made by wild beasts moving to and fro that could be followed; and these paths were used by the Jakuns, signs of whose existence I sometimes came across, but seldom managed to discover where they lived. These Jakuns are supposed to be the descendants of the aboriginal inhabitants, and they are a harmless race of men who spend their lives in the jungle, and make their dwellings in some secluded and retired spot, where they are with difficulty discovered, running away at the first signs of an approaching stranger, being very timid, and having gleaming, restless eyes just like a wild animal's. They are small in stature, though well formed, somewhat resembling Malays in physiognomy, but having sharper and smaller noses; living upon jungle roots, rats and other rodents, for which they set traps, or monkeys and larger animals killed by the poisoned darts which they expel from their long blow-pipes with extreme accuracy. And it is fortunate that they have had a means of defence so deadly and dreaded by the Malays, or they would long since have been exterminated, as they suffered much persecution in this part of the country, and were never safe from raids should the place where they encamped for the night be at any time found out, when the men were killed and the women and children captured and sold as slaves; for it was only some while after the establishment of British supremacy that slavery and slave dealing were abolished. There were but a few representatives of this interesting tribe left in this part of the peninsula, and they were quite distinct, having a different appearance and dissimilar characteristics, from the Melanesian race who dwell in the hills further north.

Three rivers have their sources in this mountain range, and flow in different directions—the Linggi to the west, the Moar River to the south, and the Triang to the east—and I often used to make excursions and wander among these hills looking for and prospecting places in which the soil appeared richest, or scaling the neighbouring peaks where great granite boulders and steep solid cliffs of rock obstructed my progress, necessitating many a detour, and only to be circumvented with difficulty. Once, being benighted on my homeward journey and unable to find my way, I made myself as comfortable as I could for the night, selecting a nice dry sandbank in the bed of a mountain torrent for my resting-place. The night unfortunately turned out wet; there was a heavy fall of rain, causing the stream to rise and cover my improvised couch, from which I was obliged to move and clamber up the steep bank at the side by feeling my way, for owing to the pitch darkness it was impossible to see anything around me; and there I sat, wet through, in the jungle, listening to the water rushing past below me, until morning dawned and I was able once more to continue my journey.

The soil in these hills is of excellent quality and of good depth; it consists of a nice friable loam permeated by quartziferous sand. The rocks are granite, containing an unusual percentage of feldspar, and enormous boulders project through the earth along the slopes of the hills as well as on their summits and in the rocky streams.

The large jungle trees were fine and tall, being crowned with wide-spreading, leafy branches, beneath which there was a close thicket of smaller trees and undergrowth, necessitating a track being cut to form a passage—an easy matter for those accustomed to frequent the jungle; a snick here and there cutting through some obstructive sapling or branch was quite sufficient to make space enough to pass, and this was done so deftly and quickly that a fair walking pace was kept up the whole while, unless some thicker entanglement of thorns or bamboo made the cutting more arduous than usual, when a slight check would occur; for however many a party consists of, going through the jungle all walk in single file, one behind the other; thus the leading person does most of the clearing of the pathway for the rest to follow.

Birds were not numerous; that most frequently heard was the Argus pheasant, a pugnacious bird that lives much by itself, and has a loud cry that sounds like a distant coo-ey; it is very shy, but can easily be captured with traps,.for the male birds have certain spots which they frequent and strut around, showing off their lovely plumage and calling defiance. There is a beautiful small pheasant, just like a diminutive peacock, having similar eye-like marks on its feathers, and another whose reddish-brown-coloured back has caused it to be called the fire-backed pheasant. A gregarious species of quail is sometimes to be seen, the male being of a brilliant green with a red-plumed crest. Large pigeons, resembling the ordinary wood pigeon, although sometimes seen, are difficult to approach. Swifts and swallows fly about in the daytime, and in the evening the nightjar comes out and sits near the house, making a noise, like a stone skidding on ice several times in succession, with the most delightful irregularity in the number of cries it gives and its intervals of silence.

Wild beasts were fairly numerous on these hills; the tracts of elephants and seladang (*bos sondaicus*), deer and pigs, tigers and panthers, rhinoceros and tapirs were to be seen, as well as porcupine; the latter make their abode in the hollow trunk of some fallen tree, and when disturbed by hearing the log tapped at the end furthest from the hole, they rush out and scuttle away at a great pace. Leeches from two to three inches long abounded, and in wet weather the ground seemed alive with them as they stretched out their spindly bodies in the air or made their way towards you, caterpillarwise, arching their backs as they rapidly travelled along.

Should you happen to stand still, numbers of

dark brown leeches would be immediately seen crawling over the dead leaves from all directions, and sometimes a green one with a yellow stripe down the length of its body, and light brown underneath, might be observed coming along with the rest; but usually this variety remained amongst the living green leaves of the branches, and adhered to your clothes as you brushed past, occasionally getting down your neck, but more often they crawled up your sleeve and fed upon your arm. The bites from this kind were more venomous than those of the brown leeches, and the place they sucked became more inflamed, felt sorer, and took longer to heal.

After passing places much infested with these creatures, the blood would ooze through the stocking above the boot, for just round the ankle was their favourite feeding ground; and when, on your return home, you pulled off your stockings, numbers fell out, fat and bloody, whilst others were to be seen still gorging, often as many as ten or twenty round each ankle. The bites gave but little trouble directly the bleeding ceased, and disappeared in a few days unless poisoned by swamp water, which caused obstinate sores that would not heal.

To come across a place abounding in tiny ticks was equally disagreeable, for they fastened on and buried themselves in your skin, causing the greatest irritation and annoyance, and being so minute they were difficult to see and remove.

Snakes are so constantly met with as to cease to cause any alarm, and when riding along a narrow path the rider's face sometimes nearly comes in contact with one lying along a bough and waving about its head, uncertain which way to turn. A person walking through the jungle frequently encounters one of these reptiles coiled up on the branch of a shrub, and often only sees it just in time to prevent his clutching hold of it with his hand. The bright green harmless whip snake is occasionally made a pet of, but one that I had, instead of becoming tamer by handling, grew more spiteful, so I let it go. Amongst the snakes whose bite is certain death, the dreaded cannibal Hamadryad, who devours its own kind, is by far the worst of them all, for it is very savage, always moving slowly and reluctantly out of the way, and if interfered with or annoyed, not only attacks the disturber, but pursues him as well.

The rocky streams were full of pools, abounding in quantities of little fish, which, upon observing anyone approach, darted away to hide themselves beneath the stones and boulders. After a few had been caught with rod and line they became quite cunning, and were hard to capture unless snared with conical-shaped traps made of rattan tied closely together, having a concave opening by which they could enter but not return, and these were placed in spots through which the fish had to pass on their way up stream.

From the summits of some of the ridges of the hills the sea could be seen, as well as the opposite coast of Sumatra, but views were difficult to obtain owing to the height of the trees and the density of their wide-spreading tops. The far-off scenery at best was somewhat uninteresting, for there is not much variety in dense masses of forest when viewed from a distance. The wooded valleys below appeared like a sea of sober green, relieved here and there by small patches of lighter tints, indicative of the position of some village, the paler green of whose paddy fields was all that could be discerned.

Quite different again was the landscape as seen from my house looking down on the opposite side of the mountain, which was close enough to allow of my being able to distinguish the leafy top of each individual tree. The heads of some towered above their neighbours, and every one was different in shape, size, and colour, consisting of various tints of green and bronze, upon which the rising or setting sun caused fresh shades and shadows to appear, creating a constant change never wearisome to the eye.

In order to prepare the land for planting coffee the undergrowth and smaller trees are first cut down, then the larger trees are felled in clumps—a method not only saving a great deal of labour, but also safer, as otherwise trees are constantly falling while the men are at work. The usual way is to cut a notch on each side of the tree, leaving a sufficient piece uncut in the middle to prevent its falling of itself, and when a sufficient number of stems have been thus treated a large tree is selected and completely cut through, so that it may fall in the desired direction, bringing down all the smaller and half-cut-through trees with it as it descends. Then all the standing-up boughs have to be lopped and laid flat, so that the fire may more easily consume them, and as soon as the timber is sufficiently dry, and a fine day with the wind in the right direction arrives, the whole hillside is fired. This is quite an exciting event; several men with torches commence lighting the fallen timber at the top, and clamber down the hill, setting alight to different places as they pass and shouting as the dried wood ignites. They run down the steep side of the hill upon the branches and trunks of the fallen trees, often many feet from the ground, and where, should they slip and break a limb, nothing could save them, for the dead leaves crackle and the fire blazes up directly the torch is applied, and by the time they reach the lower parts of the field the upper portion is well ablaze, and the fire roaring above them. Of course, it would be less dangerous to light the fire at the lower end, but the burn would then be patchy, and the wood not so well consumed. It is a glorious sight to see the whole hillside ablaze, and the fire and sparks leaping up, whilst listening to the roar and crackle of the flames; and for days afterwards the embers glow and simmer. The next proceeding is to place pegs at certain intervals in line, for which a long rope is used; and roading and draining have also to be done, and holes cut and filled in with surface soil; and finally, when the wet season commences, the coffee plants raised in the nurseries are planted out. All these works necessitate a close supervision, and in addition to this the labourers also required to be instructed how to perform each part of the work.

To weed and keep down suckers from the coffee shrubs, which are topped between two and three feet from the ground, is all that is necessary until the trees come into bearing and the berries mature and require to be gathered. I suppose there are not many people who drink a cup of coffee, or buy the roasted bean, who know or think how many coverings it has when it is plucked ripe from the tree. If the coffee is dried in its outside shell the latter becomes hard and difficult to separate without injury to the bean, which is then of less value, as it has not so good a colour and shape. Another advantage of removing the covering at once is that the bean is much more easily dried, a great consideration in the hills when the weather is uncertain, for each evening, and during every passing shower, the coffee that is drying outside has to be replaced in the store. This building is always erected in a spot where a plentiful supply of water is procurable by gravitation, and by it the berries are carried on to a revolving cylinder, round which is fastened a copper sheeting, having rough projections or teeth, which strip the pulpy outer covering from off the bean and drag it past a bar that prevents the bean from following, and the water flowing down washes the pulp away on to a heap outside, whilst a sieve moving backwards and forwards throws to one side any berries that have escaped the teeth; but the beans themselves go through its meshes and are carried into a cistern, where they are allowed to slightly ferment, thus loosening the glucose matter that still adheres to their next covering, and making it possible to remove it by washing, after which the coffee is dried in the sun until the shell has become sufficiently brittle to allow of the beans being placed in a mill and bruised by a large wooden roller that goes round and round, and whilst it breaks the outside covering skin, or parchment, as it is called, it also removes a fine inner, transparent covering called the silver skin, but does no damage to the bean itself. These now dusty fragments are separated from the beans by winnowing, after which the latter are assorted according to their size by passing down through a revolving circular sieve of different meshes, through which they fall into receptacles below, whence they are collected and got ready for shipment by being placed in casks or bags.

In addition to constantly recurring fevers, an outbreak of cholera occurred. It was a dreadful time, demoralization at first set in strongly, and it was very difficult to persuade the men not to all leave in a body. Many did go, however, frightened that their families might be attacked in their absence, for this scourge was claiming many victims in the neighbouring villages. Others decided to stay, knowing that everything possible was being done to help them to overcome the malady, and that if they were taken ill in their homes they would not have the advantage of being physicked and medically treated.

They had great faith in my powers of doctoring, and certainly I always did a large amount of free dispensing, not only amongst the coolies working on the plantation, but to many who came for miles to consult me as to their ailments. During this outbreak I had to do all the doctoring, and also the nursing, for the patients' friends could only be got to administer to their comfort in a perfunctory way, and kept as much as possible at a safe distance; so what with trying to keep the estate work going and looking after the sick, my time was more than fully occupied.

I spent much of each day with those who were suffering from the complaint, and often took off my coat to wrap it round heated stones trying to alleviate the patient's spasms and keep his body warm when nothing else was handy; but in spite of all my efforts many of them died as I sat on the floor by their side. It was heartbreaking work at first, as case after case ended fatally, eluding my utmost efforts and every care bestowed, for no medicine seemed of any avail, and I tried many cholera mixtures of different kinds. The scare was so great that the burying of the dead became a difficulty, their comrades only taking them a short distance and placing them in very shallow graves in the jungle close to the edge of the path. I managed to maintain pretty good discipline throughout this trying time; only once did a man refuse to obey a necessary and sanitary order, remarking if he did as he was told he would surely die. However, I insisted, and he gave in, but the poor chap was buried the evening after; his words came but too true.

After a while the disease became less fatal, seeming to lose its malignancy, and gradually died away; not, however, before it had laid hold of me, and within a few minutes I was so shaky and feeble that I dared not take the ordinary cholera mixture I used to dispense to my patients, from fear of drinking an overdose, so had recourse to brandy instead, as a little more or less of that liquid did not signify, and I had just sufficient strength to pour out and swallow over half a tumblerful, obtain a blanket, and gain my bed. I was afraid of calling in aid, lest the report of my seizure should spread amongst the coolies, of whom already over twenty-five per cent. had succumbed on the estate itself, besides the numerous deaths of those who had managed to reach their homes before they had been attacked, and it was only the influence I had over them that kept them together and prevented a general exodus.

It was astonishing how quickly the disease overpowered me, and I collapsed from strength and vigour into an awful weakness, feeling utterly helpless to combat the malady. A sensation of icy coldness crept up my legs, a twitching cramp tingled in my arms and hands, my heart fluttered wildly, and I was absolutely incapable of foretelling the ultimate result of the attack as I lay helpless and alone. However, in twelve hours I managed to get about, although very limp and feeble, for the epidemic had already lost its extreme virulence, and my case was the last one that occurred on the estate. After a week's interval, during which there had been no further outbreak, and I had freely told the men we had entirely got rid of it, I had a terrible fright, being called one night to attend what was supposed to be a fresh case. On reaching the houses where the coolies lived, I found them all in a very excited state, and from scraps of conversation overheard I, for the first time, began almost to despair of restraining them from bolting, and knew it depended upon whether I saved the patient's life or not, for the coolies were becoming alarmed, declaring the place was haunted by evil spirits. I was conducted to where the sick man was lying on the floor, whilst his comrades were packing up their goods ready for an early start the next morning back to their homes. At the first glance I was relieved to see it was not cholera the man was suffering from, but, nevertheless, was somewhat puzzled with the symptoms, and no one appeared able to afford me any information. I gave him an emetic, then another, with no result, and as he was becoming very drowsy I got him up, and with assistance walked him about, half carrying him the while. At last the emetic acted, and I found he had poisoned himself with refuse opium; much to my relief he recovered, and I therefore did not lose my men as I should have done had the case terminated fatally. I was in the future to be amply repaid for all the care I took of them; it was a subject of conversation in the villages round for some time, and materially assisted the recruiting of labourers.

When the road to Seremban was sufficiently completed to allow of a horse traversing it without difficulty, I was able to go to and fro more often; and on one occasion as I was riding down the mountain path, and passing a place where some rocks obstructed the way as it circled round by a gorge, the sides of which were precipitous and rocky, my horse caught his hoof in a crevice, and being unable to withdraw it he fell forward towards the edge of the road. It was quite unexpected, as I had often ridden past the spot on previous occasions, and before I had time to collect my thoughts I found myself lying on my back, my downward course having been stopped by a large boulder about ten feet below. On looking up I seemed to see nothing else above me but feet and hoofs, for the horse having been unable to recover himself, and after giving me a bit of a start, had also fallen over the side. Scarcely had the thought of how very awkward it would be to be jumped upon passed through my mind, when I saw the horse make an effort to clear me, which he managed to do, landing by my side in a much worse place, striking and grazing himself against the rocks and stones, upon which he left his hair as he drew his hind legs over their sharp edges, and disappeared in the gully beyond. I jumped up to follow him, expecting to find he had come to terrible grief in the stream below; but a fallen tree that was lying across the gully had just caught the pommel of the saddle as the horse was passing under it, and stopped his further progress. I managed to extricate him with some difficulty, and to regain the road by a circuitous route, and was much relieved to find that although he had been badly cut and grazed he was otherwise uninjured.

The chieftainship of Sungie Ujong, like many of the other smaller states, does not descend from father to son, but from uncle to nephew, through the female side of certain families called "Waris." In addition to a chief ruler of the state, headmen to manage the different villages were elected, and invested with authority to settle minor differences and disputes, and to maintain law and order. These headmen met with ready obedience from the other villagers, unless they made an abusive use of their powers, in which case factions and disputes arose, and the discontented portion of the community would often leave and make new homes for themselves elsewhere.

These "Waris" families are the descendants of certain settlers who, having left their own tribe or village, migrated and established themselves in a new part of the country, intermarrying with the aboriginal inhabitants. They still maintain and exercise certain acknowledged rights and privileges in respect of neighbouring forests and lands, and these vested interests were fully recognized by the more recent settlers, who only owned the ground they occupied and cultivated.

The chief of Sungie Ujong at this time was called the Datoh Klana, but his official title was Klana Putra, and he resided in the village of Pantai, at the foot of the hills, until some years afterwards, becoming mad, he was sent to live in Singapore. One night he gave a great entertainment; quite a large assembly of Malays collected to watch a display of sword-dancing which took place in front of his house. It was an interesting scene as the lurid glare of many torches lighted up the fencers and the bright and varied-coloured costumes of the lookers-on, Malays from different states, who collecting in little groups discussed the fencers and their methods, whilst the rhythmic beat of many drums made an almost deafening and bewildering noise.

A sword-dance is a fascinating pastime to the Malays, who watch each movement of the players as they advance towards one another, then retreat and pirouette, then twist and twine their bodies in a snake-like fashion, imitating caution, stealth, attack, then bending, stamp and circle round, vying with each other as to who can make the most graceful movements; and as they get excited the game becomes quicker, emulation increases the pace of their movements, their breathing grows more laboured, their weapons approach each other nearer, and flash here and there so quickly that in the flickering light it appears as though they struck each other,—but that seldom happens, as they manage to control their tempers,—until one of them tired out at length gives up, and invites another pair from amongst the bystanders to come out and take their place, and give an exposition of their swordsmanship.

As a show of agility and dexterity amongst friends there is no danger in the game, but played as it was that night, before little groups from different states standing round, each man fully armed and unaccustomed to much self-control, with the memory of many former raids and feuds amongst themselves still strongly lingering in their minds, all of them desirous that their champion should excel, and each party more than jealous of its neighbours, there was an element of risk, and the smouldering fire might at any moment have burst forth with sanguinary results.

It was not long before one more hot-headed than the rest began to prick his adversary, who happened to be his own nephew, just to show those standing round that there was no fear in the village and state from which he came, and to intimate that if he was willing to pierce his own relation, how much readier he would be to plunge his weapon deeper into the body of some adversary, totally unconnected by any ties of kinship or tribeship.

A few of the older heads suggested a cessation of the games, as matters were becoming a little critical, advice with which the Datoh Klana cordially agreed, for he had probably been thinking the same for some while, but was ashamed of his own initiative to intimate that once the passions of the miscellaneous spectators were fairly aroused, his authority would not suffice to prevent an outburst. The games were brought to a close, and the various groups gradually dispersed, taking their torches to light them on their different roads, and the murmur of voices and beating of drums slowly died away in the distance. The hot-tempered fencer was invited up to where we were sitting, to keep him out of mischief, and being regaled with cigarettes and lemonade made in Chinese fashion (the latter a nauseous compound in which little filaments of stuff are generally to be seen floating about), soon became a safer and pleasanter companion after he had had a few soothing whiffs and a chat upon other subjects.

Many of the inhabitants of this village kept a

large, ugly kind of slave monkey of the Berok species, to ascend their cocoanut and other trees and gather the nuts and fruits for them. These monkeys were kept chained up near at hand, and were intensely savage with strangers; going to the end of their tether they would stretch out their hind legs to try and clutch the passers-by, if they thought they were within reach; at other times they would look at you in a defiant manner, and make a grimace expressive of how dearly they would enjoy the chance of one good bite.

When a cocoanut was wanted a man or boy would fetch a light rattan reel, on which was coiled a long cord. The chain would be detached from the monkey's collar, and the string fastened to it instead, and he would then be led towards some tree where there appeared to be a ripe nut or two, and told to ascend it, which he would do in a somewhat sulky and protesting manner, stopping halfway up, until a sharp tug of the cord and an expostulatory remark from his master compelled him to continue; for in this respect the monkey is very human in his dislike of being made to do what he is told, if it is at all distasteful to him. On reaching the cluster of nuts near the top, several tugs of the cord would be necessary to assist him to make up his mind which was the ripest and easiest to detach, and to throw down the one required. Finding a suitable foothold he would twist the nut round and round until it broke off and fell down, none too easy a task to accomplish, as its fibrous stem is tough and difficult to break. If another nut was wanted, a look of wearied disgust would overspread his face as he slowly proceeded to do as he was bid. The order to descend was obeyed with more alacrity, and the string being re-wound he would be led back and chained up, and left to take his exercise, walking to and fro as far as his tether would permit.

A tigress used to roam in the district through which the road from Pantai to Seremban passed, usually behaving very well, and molesting nobody, except when her cubs were young, and then generally two or three travellers along the road disappeared. Once an Indian coolie, who was be-nighted, lay down by the side of the path, and the next morning all that was left to mark where he had rested was a cloth he had placed underneath his head; his body had disappeared, and he was never heard of more.

On another occasion a Malay had a lucky escape as he was returning homewards with his purchases slung on a stick carried over his shoulder, amongst which was a large bottle of kerosene oil. The tigress sprang out upon him as he passed by, but jumping short missed his body and struck his bundle, breaking the bottle of oil, and then bolted, for tigers are like cats in this respect when they miss their prey. The man ran away, giving the tigress no chance of a second attempt, and leaving her to ruminate upon the difference of a good meal and the taste of kerosene oil as she licked her paws.

Whilst some Malays were hunting for game in this neighbourhood, and were beating a clump of bushes standing in the midst of a track of lalang, a tiger cub was shot by one of the party as it emerged from the thicket some distance away, and the tigress, seeing her offspring mortally wounded, turned and charged towards its destroyer. The Malay had just time to slip another cartridge into his rifle, and preserving his presence of mind and coolness, he shot the tigress just as she was about to spring.

Owing to the isolated position and flimsy construction of the houses inhabited by Chinese charcoal burners and small tin miners, they were sometimes entered by tigers; and connected with this a curious superstition and belief was current, namely, that the oldest Chinaman of the party was usually singled out from amongst the sleeping group and carried off.

The coffee bushes on the hills were commencing to repay all the trouble and labour bestowed upon them by their vigorous growth, as well as to cover the ground with their foliage. Fevers became less prevalent, good houses had been erected for the labourers, and all that was wanted was the necessary permission to import natives of India to pick the crops, for which work it was impossible to obtain sufficient coolies locally. In 1876 the Secretaries of State for India and the Colonies had both agreed to the principle of allowing natives of India to be employed in the Malayan States, and in 1878 the then Governor of the Straits Settlements requested permission for their direct importation to the native states from India. It will hardly be believed that although these protectorate states were under duly qualified British officers, it took from 1878 to 1885 before the

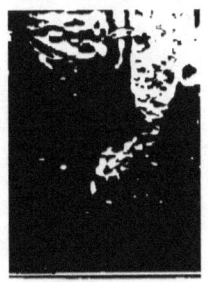

TAMILS

necessary permission to allow of this being done was finally granted.

These estates had been opened on the understanding and in the belief that there would be no doubt whatever of being able to procure the necessary Tamil labour long before the crops should be fit to be gathered; but the coffee-trees commenced to bear, and the berries to ripen, and then to fall for want of hands to pick them, and a long stretch of 360 acres of luxuriant coffee in full bearing, which had been planted and cultivated under most difficult and trying circumstances, had to be abandoned; and although nature and disease had been overcome, this industry was strangled by red-tape, and fell a victim to the seven years of protracted negotiations that took place before the Colonial and Indian Governments would finally accede to the earnest and urgent representations of three successive Colonial Governors.

Fortunately experiments in the growing of Liberian coffee in the plains were proving satisfactory, and being more favourably situated with regard to labour facilities, all that was already under cultivation could be maintained and kept up, although no extensions could be made until some years later.

# CHAPTER V.

Exploring and Surveying — Rassa — Events which caused British Intervention — Man-eating Tiger — Camping in the Jungle — Sleeping Man seized and carried off by Tiger — My Syce killed and partially eaten by Tiger — Placing Spring Guns — Alone with a Tiger — A Shot at a Tiger — Village of Lukut — Port Dickson — Cape Ricardo.

UPON the closing and abandonment of coffee cultivation on the hills, I turned my attention to exploring, surveying, and road-making, and in consequence travelled many times throughout all the native states now under British control on the western side of the peninsula, gaining a thorough knowledge of the country and acquaintance with its inhabitants. It was an arduous life, full of hardships and exposure; for at this time the country was covered with dense forest, with small villages dotted here and there, having but little intercourse with one another, and the only means of communication between them being narrow tracks through the jungle, along which only one man could pass at a time, and occasionally these paths were so indistinct as to be nearly obliterated and most difficult to follow.

The obstacles encountered in traversing and exploring the country, in order to discover the best route for a road to follow after its general direction had been decided upon, were many. The jungle was so thick that nothing could be seen ten yards in advance, and as the country was much broken up into innumerable hills and ridges with gullies between them, in which swamps and thorns abounded, progress was necessarily slow and tedious. These numerous difficulties had to be overcome before I could be thoroughly assured that the line of the future roadway was the best, and the gradients staked out the flattest which under the circumstances could be chosen.

In wet weather even travelling was very fatiguing; the tracks across or along the slopes of the hills were wet and greasy, causing the foot to slip back some portion of each stride taken; swamps waist deep in mud and water had constantly to be floundered through; everything got more or less wet and sodden; and fever often followed as a natural consequence. It was trying work journeying across such country day after day for ten hours at a time, or working in dense jungle on the scantiest of fare.

For some little while I lived at Rassa, a village within a short distance of Seremban, and which owed its existence to its having been the highest point on the river to which laden boats could ascend. My house was built on the side of a low hill by a moat that had formed part of the former defences of the fort that crowned the top of the slope, and close to the execution ground where prisoners sentenced to death were shot, a method that had replaced the Malay mode of capital punishment, which was in its turn to be superseded by hanging within the walls of jails as soon as they were erected. The original Malay system of executing prisoners was curious. A cotton pad was placed on the shoulders of the kneeling victim, and a long straight krise thrust through it into his body until the heart was reached; then the weapon was slowly pulled back, and the cotton pad both checked the sudden rush of blood and cleaned the blade of the krise as it was withdrawn.

This village of Rassa was formerly the centre of the disturbances that so agitated the country between the years 1873 and 1876 as to cause the British to interfere. A Malay of Arab descent, Syed Ahman by name, had managed to get himself elected Klana, to which office he had some claims, but was not the rightful heir according to long-established custom, and his appointment occasioned jealousy and discontent. He was strongly supported by a subordinate chief called the Banda, who unfortunately died, and was succeeded by a man who took the opportunity of making the Klana's unlawful succession a pretext for creating disturbances. Jealousy added to the Klana's unpopularity, for he was proving himself a capable administrator, encouraging Chinese miners, and there were not wanting signs that if left unmolested much longer he would become too firmly established to oust, for he had with some acumen obtained recognition by the British Government as Chief of the State, and with their help had already given a lesson to Sungie Ujong's hereditary enemy, Rembau, when that state had blockaded its outlet on the Linggi river. He had also requested the assistance of a British official to help him administer the government of the state; and it was as well that he had done so, for the Banda being assisted in his revolt by some Selangor freebooters and marauders led by one of their rajahs, equally noted for his cruelty and fighting qualities, matters became very serious for Syed Ahman, whose power was well nigh gone, and had it not been for his British adviser, and a body-guard of Arab mercenaries, he would have been driven from the state. About this time the S'trimenanti people, delighted at the prospect of humbling the Klana, who, because of his descent from the prophet Mahomed, had refused to recognize the Malay rajah of that state as his titular chief, joined the Banda and were preparing to invade Sungie Ujong.

Rassa became the centre of the disturbances, and its defences were lost and retaken by each party in succession; whilst in the neighbourhood there were over five thousand Chinese miners at work, who were with difficulty restrained from joining in the fray. The Government of Singapore becoming anxious lest there might be a repetition of the wholesale massacres of Chinese which occurred fifteen years previously, in 1860, sent troops to the assistance of the Klana to help him to maintain his authority.

The Banda and his rajah friends, after a slight and faint-hearted resistance, fled to Selangor, but being refused asylum in that country by its sultan, surrendered to the British, who, although they declined to allow the Banda to return to the scene of his former intrigues, granted him a pension which was continued to his family for a number of years.

Whilst travelling about the state of Sungie Ujong at a time when disease had destroyed large numbers of wild pigs, that form the principal food of the tigers, with one of which I had on two occasions what might have been unpleasant encounters. Tigers are not only carnivorous, but eat various kinds of food; they frequent the vicinity of durian trees at the season when the fruit is ripening, and upon hearing the thud as one falls to the ground they leave their lair close by, and breaking open its thorny covering enjoy a luscious meal. They wander in the mangrove swamps feeding upon unwary crabs, and roam along the sea-shore eating several kinds of dainty mollusca; they lurk by swampy places satisfying their appetites with frogs, of which they are exceedingly fond, but should one of them take a fancy to human flesh, its whole nature changes, and then, instead of shunning, it seeks the resorts of man. An inveterate man-eating tiger becomes very cunning and cowardly; it does not frequent one spot but travels twenty miles or more during the night, capturing its prey about the same localities but at different intervals of time, thereby increasing its own security. It is never certain where this pest will turn up next, for by the time the rumours spread of its having been seen at any particular place it has moved on elsewhere before steps can be taken for its destruction, creating fear and dismay throughout the districts it frequents. So easy of capture does it find its fresh prey, that it devours but a small portion of each victim, and does not return to finish its meal, but seeks another one many miles away the next or following day.

Travellers, and even bullock-cart drivers, wait until a company of them have assembled before passing tigerish localities, hoping by their numbers to scare the enemy. No one stirs out at night, and even in the daytime there is always a chance you may be suddenly pounced upon. The road becomes absolutely unsafe, and the tiger grows so bold that it wanders up and down in the bordering jungle, rushing out to attack sometimes a bullock cart, at other times it will even spring upon one of a gang of passing men, for numbers cease to frighten it. I have seen a small, thin, slender knife the blade of which was bent, the striker having failed to drive it home into a tiger which had seized his companion who was walking close behind him. It is fortunate that, although the man-eater grows bolder, attacking one of a band, instead of as formerly only the solitary wayfarer, it never really recognizes its own power and strength, and the ease with which it captures its prey makes it less tenacious to keep it, and it allows itself to be driven away by shouting and the flourishing of sticks, whereas formerly if interfered with it would have avenged itself upon the interrupter.

When camping in the jungle it is usual to erect very primitive little shelters, taking but a short time to build, in which to pass the night. A lean-to roof thatched with palm leaves keeps off the dew and rain, sticks placed near together make a sleeping-bench upon which all lie down in a row with their heads underneath where the roof is lowest, and their feet touch the outer edge of the structure and have to be tucked up to avoid getting wet if it rains. The sticks are so hard and uneven that at first most of the night is spent in tossing about, endeavouring to find some less irksome position, until habit teaches that this is useless, and the best way is to determine not to mind, but try and drop off to sleep with a stolid indifference to discomfort.

The lean-to roof forms the only wall, the rest is all open and unenclosed, and when the flickering glow of the fires used for cooking dies away, and the one solitary lamp with its dull glimmering light is put out, all is in darkness.

Accidents but seldom happen to parties camping out, and finding that an apparent indifference to danger increased my influence over the Malays and made them regard me with more respect, I never during all my travels carried a weapon of any sort other than a "golah," a sharp-edged chopper knife, fitting into a sheath placed inside the cloth or belt of its bearer, and thus held in position, whereas the larger kind of chopper, called a "parang," is carried in a sheath by the side and fastened to a cord encircling the waist.

At first the inky darkness of night creates a kind of awe, as you lie awake listening to the heavy breathing of some sleeping coolie, and pondering upon your seeming loneliness and helplessness should some passing beast of prey happen to select you for his supper. Habit, however, soon reconciles you to sleeping peacefully, oblivious of all thoughts of danger, and even the rustling of a dead leaf as some wild animal passes by ceases to disturb otherwise than by causing a feeble curiosity as to what it may be, for experience teaches that in this part of the world the wild animals, as a rule, are just as disinclined to make your near acquaintance as you are theirs, and the sudden start and scamper often heard intimates that your scent has reached the intruder's nostrils and frightened him away.

Of course there are exceptions, and one morning on arriving at a camp, such as described, I found that the occupants of it had passed through a terrible experience the night before. They had all gone to sleep as usual, and woke up horrified on hearing one of their number shouting for help as he was being hauled out from their midst by a tiger, who had seized him by the leg, and was pulling him out of the shelter and making away with him. The man's piercing screams vainly resounded through the trees as he was being dragged further and further off from his terrified companions, who sat huddled together quaking with fear and powerless to help, for they had no firearms; the night was dark, and as the fires had gone out they could see nothing. The cries shortly ceased, and when daylight came search was made and the partly-eaten body of their former comrade was found, about 200 yards away from camp, and carried back and buried, and at the time of my arrival the men were all getting ready to leave their camp and to build another some distance away. Several days afterwards I spent a night at this deserted camp, but nothing occurred to disturb my rest.

One of my syces also met his death whilst he was journeying along and carrying a saddle on his head which he had been sent to fetch. He was at the time accompanied by a native overseer to whom I had lent a pony, and who, having overtaken him as he was returning, had advised him to halt and wait till morning at a wayside house, as it was getting dusk, and the part of the road which they were approaching was frequented by the man-eating tiger. On my syce's refusing to do as suggested, and expressing his determination to continue his journey, the overseer, for safety's sake, made him walk on in front of the pony he was riding. The roadway was bordered on each side by scrub and forest, so that the obscurity made it difficult to follow the track, as it wound in and out amongst numerous small hills. Suddenly a dark object was seen to spring from the bank above upon the unfortunate syce, from whom but one cry was heard as he was knocked over and fell prostrate by the roadside. The tiger stood over his prey, and growling at the pony as he approached, caused him to jump across the road and start off galloping as hard as he could until he reached his stable, and it took some coaxing to get him to leave it the next morning. Directly I got on his back his courage and confidence returned, and he carried me to the scene of the seizure of the night before without any trouble, for we had been on many journeys together, and I had often helped him out of boggy swamps, from which he could not have scrambled unassisted. The poor little animal must have been terrified the night before, for on examining the road I discovered he had made, for him, a tremendous jump from quite close to where the man was knocked down by the side of the road, and I quite believed what the overseer told me as to his not knowing how he managed to stick on, but imagine fear made him grip the pony very tightly. I found two or three men waiting for my arrival, having already recovered my saddle, which had fallen several feet down the bank at the side of the road.

We followed the line taken by the tiger with its victim—picking up a portion of the man's clothing on the way—and after crossing a swamp, and proceeding a short distance beyond, we found my poor syce's body, lying face uppermost, on a ridge in the jungle. The cleanly-picked bone of the man's right leg, which had been torn off, was close by; the marks of the tiger's fangs were plainly visible at the back of his neck, showing how he had been seized and carried away, otherwise to all appearances his body was uninjured. We placed spring guns all around, which we visited the next morning to find them just as we had left them, for the tiger had not returned for another meal, and as it appeared useless to keep the body exposed any longer, it was buried where it lay. At a distance of over twenty miles from this place I had a very unpleasant half-hour as I was journeying along a jungle track, which I had to traverse in order to inspect some work going on in the neighbourhood, where this man-eater had created quite a panic amongst the workmen, as he had taken several of them away. I had ordered my bearers to go on to a camp some five miles off, intending to follow myself almost immediately and to catch them up. However, I was detained in talking to one of my employees until there was only just time left for the journey before darkness set in. I started off at my best pace along the narrow track, and at about mid-distance, as I was ascending out of one of the innumerable gullies that had to be crossed, I smelt the strong odour of a tiger, and on looking down saw its fresh pug marks on the path. Here was a nasty predicament to be in, for in all probability this tiger could be none other than the famous man-eater, which was following up my bearers, and therefore he must be between me and the camp I wished to reach.

The light was already becoming a little indistinct, and I had some distance before me yet, so there was no time for hesitation, for in these climates darkness comes on quickly, as there is little or no twilight. I drew my knife, although it was but a poor instrument for defence, and carried it in my hand. It was a time of intense excitement, peering into the undergrowth on both sides of the path, every now and then seeing the footprints of the tiger as I hurried along, not knowing at what instant I might be face to face with the beast; or perhaps having missed seeing him as I passed by some bush, I should feel a sudden blow behind as he sprang upon me. After nearly two miles of anxious walking, during which I made as much clatter with my boots as possible, in the hope that such a strange and unusual noise might scare him away, I saw in front a large tree that had fallen across the path, and remembered when last I had passed this obstacle I had taken some little while creeping round it through the undergrowth at one side. Fortunately the ground sloped down at a considerable angle towards the tree that blocked the way, which enabled me to take a short run and leap on to the barrier, from which I jumped off on to the ground below as noisily as possible, and as I landed, there was the sound of a sudden rush in the thicket close by as the tiger bounded away. There is no doubt he had heard me coming, and was crouching and waiting close to the thick entanglement caused by the branches, through which I could only have made my way slowly; but the strange sight of a man, perhaps to him clothed in an odd manner, with a large white mushroom hat on his head, jumping through the air, and whose feet made such a thud as he landed, was too much for his equanimity, so instead of attempting a capture he took fright and fled, much to my relief as I sheathed my knife and continued my journey. When I reached camp I said nothing about my adventure, as I did not wish to increase the alarm of the labourers, as they had already erected palings round their sleeping-places for protection, and it was becoming increasingly difficult to prevent their quitting this tiger-infested district and returning to their villages.

A short while afterwards I was destined to come to still closer quarters with this man-eater, and to make his very near acquaintance. I was driving to Linggi with a friend who had but lately arrived from England, and was armed with a sporting rifle; and hearing rumours, as we passed some houses by the wayside, of this tiger having been seen not far off, I borrowed a gun, after enquiring if it was properly loaded, and receiving an affirmative reply, qualified with the remark that owing to its being very wet the night before the owner had withdrawn the charge, and then dried and reloaded the gun. We had not started long before a bullock driver shouted to us as we were passing him that the tiger had just come out to attack his bullocks, but that he had driven it off, and it had gone up a small path on one side of the road.

On reaching the path indicated we left the trap and walked up it out of curiosity, and having but little hope of seeing anything, when suddenly to my eyes—which were practised and accustomed by much forest travelling to note and quickly see things that to the ordinary observer would pass unnoticed—there appeared a shade of colour unnatural to its surroundings, and on looking more closely the head of the tiger gradually became visible as he lay motionless beneath a bush almost out of sight. He was crouching but fifteen feet away, intently watching me with his head close to the ground, and waiting to spring, perhaps only prevented from having done so already by my unfamiliar white face and attire. He returned my gaze with a quiet, steady stare, never blinking nor shifting his eyes in the slightest degree.

I stood still; my friend with the rifle meanwhile endeavoured to look round my shoulder, but could see nothing. The tiger remained quiet—there seemed to be no hurry—so taking a steady and deliberate aim I pulled the trigger. The gun went off with a puff, and a sound as if it had been but sparingly loaded, and there followed the noise of a sudden rush, and then all was quiet. Upon examination I found drops of blood on the leaves where the tiger's head had been, as well as on the spot where he had landed from the tremendous spring he made. I tracked him a short distance by the twigs he had broken and the marks of his claws on roots and ground as he dashed along in his frantic flight, but soon gave up the chase and returned to the path, as we were on our way to catch a steamer at Linggi, and could not delay longer without the risk of its leaving before we arrived.

Some days afterwards, when I returned to this part of the country, I made enquiries, and discovered that the gun had been loaded with but a few pellets of shot and a little powder, and as it had been raining heavily for some days the latter was more or less damp. The owner of the gun had been pigeon shooting, for which purpose a very light charge was all that was necessary, as he always crept up close to the bird before discharging his piece; and when I borrowed it the one barrel loaded contained only what was left of his supply of powder and shot, which had become almost exhausted.

The tiger entirely forsook the district, and was

not heard of for some two months, when he carried away a Chinaman from a house about twenty-five miles distant, in daylight, and being followed up, was shot as he stood growling over his victim. He was a very old male, with but one eye; so I fancy, as both his eyes were sound when we looked at one another, that a shot from my gun must have penetrated one of them and blinded him, and this, added to the burning powder which probably scorched his face at such close quarters, would account perhaps for his not having sprung upon me.

Close to the northern boundary of Sungie Ujong is the village of Lukut, situate upon a small river of the same name, and famous as being formerly one of the principal places from which tin was exported. The foreshore has become so silted up that the village is now difficult of approach from the sea; but although it has lost its former prosperity it is still an interesting old place, where the remains of ruined stockades and defences, now almost obliterated by a rank growth of underwood, as well as the occasional discovery of some old rusty cannon or blunderbuss, testify to the lawless and uncertain times that formerly existed, when each petty chieftain was constantly at war with his neighbour, and was obliged to protect himself from sudden surprise and attack, and the few Chinese who had the hardihood to live amongst such turbulent surroundings were not sure of their lives from day to day, nor that the tin won amidst such perils would not be forcibly taken from them. At any rate, they were always certain to be compelled to pay a heavy toll for the protection of the chief in whose district they were living.

The petty chiefs themselves were careful not to make their exactions too burdensome, or too frequently to kill the goose that laid the golden egg, as the revenues they received from these industrious Chinese aliens not only added materially to their comfort and power, but were the only exactions they could levy other than from their own followers, who would migrate elsewhere should their taxation become unbearable, and seek the protection of some milder chief. This constant internecine fighting at last so crippled the power of the smaller chiefs that it became only possible for them to defend the stockaded villages in which they dwelt, and they were no longer able to afford any sort of protection to the Chinese miners, who were left to the mercy of marauding gangs of bandits and robbers, pirates and murderers, who so terrorized and desolated the country, that previous to British intervention the revenues of the district of Lukut had fallen from 200,000 to 5,000 dollars per annum, and were on the point of being entirely extinguished.

Not far from here, to the southward, on the sea coast, is the prosperous and thriving town of Port Dickson, the only sheltered deep-water anchorage near the shore between Singapore and the Straits of Klang, and which is now the calling place of steamers trading up the coast, and the outlet for the trade of the interior. Villas and houses built on the hill slopes overlooking the Straits of Malacca occupy the place of the trackless forest; there is a fine pier, alongside of which steamers load and discharge their cargoes, and what was once mangrove swamp has been filled in with earth from the adjacent hill and is now the site of shops and streets.

Further to the south is Cape Ricardo, a bold rocky promontory, having a lighthouse on its summit, which was attacked by pirates at the time of the Selangor disturbances.

A shallow flat makes many of the villages along the coast difficult of access, except by small boats, and for these this headland is a dangerous place to weather unless the tide is slack and the sea quiet, for the current races round the cliffs that rise abruptly from the sea and tower overhead. The water is usually disturbed by numerous eddies, and dashes against this wall of rock only to recoil and to be driven forward once again by the tide; and even at the best of times a small boat tumbles and tosses about as she rounds the point and turns the corner into the smoother waters beyond, that continue along the coast of Sungie Ujong until the river Linggi is reached, which near the sea is the southern boundary of the state, and separates it from Malacca.

On the narrow strip of sand which connects the projecting headland of Cape Ricardo with the peninsula there are still remains of a canal, which, when finished, was to have saved the small boats trading up and down the coast from risking the passage round the rocks; however, the intentions of the originator of this scheme were better in the conception than in the execution, and the canal was never completed.

# CHAPTER VI.

S'tul — Brennang — Samunieh — Pudu — Kwala Lumpor — Frequent Fires — The Capitan China — Secret Societies — Events which caused British Intervention — Kwala Selangor — Lombong Tin Mining — Winning, Sluicing, and Smelting of Tin Ore — Division of Profits — Miners' Houses — Shed for Dying Coolies.

ADJOINING Sungie Ujong to the north lies the state of Selangor, and in 1883 the only means of communication between the two places was by a jungle track, which some distance from Seramban lost itself in a muddy stream until the foot of the S'tul range of hills was reached. After surmounting these and descending on the other side, the valley of S'tul was passed, and amongst the few houses dotted round the paddy fields were some inhabited by men from Karinchi in Sumatra, who have the reputation of being able to transform themselves at will into tigers, a superstition firmly believed in by their neighbours, who hold them in some dread and awe.

The next inhabited place reached was the isolated village of Brennang, consisting of two or three wayside houses of the usual flimsy kind, easily built, and as lightly abandoned should the dwellers care to leave them and move elsewhere. Each house had a rough shelter for passers-by, in which hung sundry bunches of shrivelled plantains for sale, and which were generally occupied by half-naked children, who made these sheds their playground. Here the traveller rested awhile before attempting to cross the swamp, full of rank grasses and rushes, and waist-deep in mud, that stretched across his path.

Just as night was falling the river of Samunieh was reached, and in the village beyond the wayfarer felt thankful that half the journey had been achieved, and that the next day would bring him to Kwala Lumpor. Not, however, that the second day's journey was any better than the first; more tedious, if anything, was the narrow jungle path, full of holes and roots; the paddy fields of Cadjan and the river at Cheras had all to be crossed, as well as innumerable streams and spurs and swampy gullies, before the mining camp of Pudu was reached, an outskirt of Kwala Lumpor, and a settlement of Chinese miners, who were all busily employed "winning" the tin with which the valley abounded.

Kwala Lumpor is the chief town of Selangor, and the principal Government offices are located here. It is situated at the mouth of the Gomba river, a tributary of the Klang, the latter being the chief river of this part of the country. The houses of the Government officers were pleasantly situated on the adjoining hills overlooking the town, roads were in course of being laid out, order was kept by a small body of Malay police, and Mr. (now Sir) Frank A. Swettenham had lately been appointed the British Resident of the state; and its rapid development was in large measure due to the policy adopted of improving the means of communication to enable the Chinese miners to transport their supplies at a reasonable cost, and also to the encouragements to settle that were extended to the Malay immigrants from foreign states, who readily availed themselves of the advantages given.

The immediate neighbourhood consists of a fine fertile basin of flat country forming an amphitheatre, surrounded on the east by the mountains of the main range, and on the other sides by subsidiary spurs. The hills here are bolder and the valleys more extensive than further south, and these characteristics become even more marked in the state of Perak, further to the northward.

The town itself already presented all the appearances of a prosperous mining centre; the streets were littered with bricks and timber, for substantial structures were fast taking the place of the flimsy wooden houses so liable to catch fire and be destroyed. It was no unusual occurrence for a whole village, which had quickly sprung into existence owing to some great influx of Chinese miners to the neighbourhood, to be entirely devastated and laid waste by fire, a layer of ashes and a few badly-charred posts here and there being all that was left of what had been but a few hours before a flourishing little centre of trade. In the towns, of course, the destruction was on a bigger scale, and the opportunity was taken advantage of by all the bad characters to lay hands on and steal what they could; rioting and fighting also created a new danger, and made the confusion worse. The better houses were formerly built with mud walls, and over the ceiling there was a layer of earth. On the first alarm of fire, a hurried rush would be made by the inhabitants to close the doors of their shops in order to prevent their contents from being looted. The owners of the wooden houses nearest the conflagration were busily employed in carrying what they could of their goods to some place of safety. Those in the mud houses simply sat inside and patiently awaited events, in comparative safety if the conflagration was not too fierce; for although the light roofs overhead were burnt and destroyed, the contents of the shop were but slightly damaged unless the fire gained an entrance through the wooden doors or windows, in which case the building would be entirely gutted. On no consideration would those inhabitants who were somewhat more remote from the fire help to extinguish the flames or open their doors, and the only way to gain an entrance was by bursting them in. As an instance of this, I have seen the roof of a shop catch fire from some spark that had blown on to the thatch unknown to the inmates within, who obstinately refused admittance to those outside endeavouring to enter, so that they might get on to the roof and put out the flames. Shouting and hammering were of no avail, and there was nothing to be done but to break in the door with an axe, when the Chinese occupants were disclosed crouching down and awaiting events in dumb stupidity, seemingly paralyzed by the dread of being robbed should they open their doors and by the fear that the fire after all might reach them.

Then in turn house after house had to be broken into, and the inmates compelled to fetch water to throw over their roofs in order to prevent stray sparks from igniting the palm leaves with which they were thatched.

It was to prevent the destruction of property and its concomitant evils, that directly a village became prosperous and of sufficient importance, orders were given that within a defined area all the shops were to be built of brick before a certain date. This decree had been issued at Kwala Lumpor just before my visit, and accounted for the roads in the parts affected by the order being littered with building material.

The "Capitan China" was the title of the head of the Chinese community, and the position at this time was occupied by Ah Loi, a man of considerable influence and power, who greatly assisted the Government in preserving law and order. He was an old settler, and on several occasions had led the Chinese in their resistance to Malay cupidity, and during the disturbances the town of Kwala Lumpor had been three times burned down, and on each occasion it was rebuilt by this insuppressible trader, who not only had to defend himself from external attacks, but also to quiet the different tribes and societies of the Chinese when they fell out and fought among themselves. Although to an outsider one Chinaman looks very like his neighbour, they often speak so entirely different a dialect as not to be able to understand one another; and the various tribes are animated with a hostility which is only too ready to break forth on the slightest provocation, unless restrained and kept in check by superior force and discipline. The secret societies also made matters worse, for if two members of separate communities had a dispute with one another, it was not long, if they happened to belong to different societies, before they appealed to their fellow comrades on either side, and a free fight took place. As the numerous cries for assistance spread the numbers increased, for the men of each society were obliged to help their faction if called upon to do so, and all new comers were forced to join one of the societies for self-preservation if they did not already belong to any. In dealing with these societies it has been a difficult task to limit their tendencies for evil and to curb their sphere of action by legislation, and should they be suffered at any time to go unwatched and unchecked, they would speedily again grow powerful and dangerous. Some of the Chinese mine-owners kept their labourers almost in a state of serfdom, and occasionally treated them with the greatest barbarity. The smuggling of opium used to be very prevalent, and I often came across the tracks formerly made by smugglers in the uninhabited jungle, stretching between the coast and the mining districts of the interior.

The present Sultan of Selangor, whose name is Abdul Samat, resides, as he always has done, at a village near the mouth of the Langat river. In 1856, with the assistance of a powerful chief, Rajah Juma'at of Lukut, he succeeded, notwithstanding the hostility of several other claimants, in securing the chieftainship and establishing his authority. In 1863 he appointed his son-in-law, Tunku-dia-Udin, to be Viceroy over Klang and the inland districts, thereby offending his nephew, Rajah Mahdi, who claimed the position for himself, and endeavoured to assert his claims by force of arms. The whole state became involved in an internecine warfare that lasted ten years, during which time the Sultan remained quietly at Langat watching events; and eventually it was only with the assistance of a force of three thousand men, sent by the ruler of Pahang at the request of the Governor of Singapore, that Tunku-dia-Udin was enabled to defeat and quell his enemies. In the meantime the districts he had been appointed to govern had been ruined and depopulated, and the expense of the struggle had overwhelmed him in debt. Such anarchy prevailed that every Malay over twenty had at least killed one man, a life was taken for a hasty word, a jest, or a debt of a few dollars, and as often as not treacherously and without warning. The example set by the rajahs was deplorable; one of them boasted of having taken a hundred human lives, whilst several others counted between twenty and fifty; they maltreated and killed their slaves, and murdered their followers in cold blood on the slightest of pretexts. Pirates made the sea unsafe for traders; and becoming emboldened by long impunity, a gang of them proceeded to Penang and shipped as passengers on board a schooner, which they surprised and captured at sea, murdering thirty-four of its passengers and crew. The rumour of this piracy caused a search to be made for the missing schooner, which was discovered anchored off the pirates' haunts at Langat, whilst her cargo was openly displayed for sale in the shops of the town, and a large sum of specie had been already divided. Several of the pirates were discovered still on board their prize, and were arrested; a visit was paid to the Sultan, who was affable and obliging, and although personally not involved in the piracy, regarded it as a pastime and amusement which kept the unruly followers of his rajahs out of other mischief. Everything appeared to be passing off well, when suddenly a treacherous attack was made on the boat's crew as they were on the point of returning to the steamer. In consequence of this a gunboat was sent, which, in spite of a brisk fire from the fort, shelled the stockades, drove out its defenders, and a party of soldiers landing completed its destruction and burnt the town. The Sultan agreed to outlaw the rajahs implicated, but the unruly elements were only scotched, not killed, and the coast became as unsafe as ever. At last the very daring of these cutthroats resulted in a further capture, a native of Malacca, the only survivor of a party of nine British subjects, suddenly and treacherously attacked whilst at anchor off the Langat river, and who had marvellously escaped by clinging to the rudder of the boat for hours whilst the pirates looted its contents, after swimming ashore, fortunately fell in with friendly Malays, and finally succeeded in returning to his native town, where shortly afterwards he recognized some of the

ABDUL SAMAT, SULTAN OF SELANGOR.

murderers of his companions as they entered the Malacca river, and informing the police obtained their arrest, when some of the pirated property was found in the boats on board of which they were. At the request of Tunku-dia-Udin, these men were tried and sentenced by a native court held at Langat; seven of the eight captured were executed, being publicly krised. A heavy fine was exacted of the Sultan, who agreed to the appointment of a British Resident to advise and help his Viceroy, and consented to have an official stationed at Langat, so as to be in constant communication with himself. During the negotiations Cape Rachado lighthouse was attacked by pirates coming from the banks of the river on which he dwelt, and later on a piracy occurred close to the Sungie Ujong boundary. But these proved the last outbreaks by the unruly elements that had terrorized the state for so many years; and the outbreak of the Perak war afforded an opportunity of giving congenial employment to several of these restless rajahs, who, delighted at the prospect of fighting, readily joined the British troops, to whom they gave valuable assistance from their knowledge of the country, its inhabitants, and the arts of Malay warfare. Although British troops were necessary to quell the disturbances in Perak, Sungie Ujong, and S'trimenanti, the Sultan of Selangor, with the loyal assistance of Tunku-dia-Udin, managed to keep the remnant that was left of his former subjects under control and peaceable. He still lives in retirement at Langat, although now in affluent circumstances, and takes an interest in the development of the state by British officers; but is only seen on special occasions when he travels to Kwala Lumpor with all the luxury that a princely steamer and well-fitted railway saloon carriage can afford, accepting his prosperity with the same calm placidness with which he received his blood-stained rajahs, and weathered the intrigues, storms, and disputes that well nigh devastated and depopulated the country; truly an interesting man, this doyen\* of the Malay sultans, whom neither prosperity nor adversity can alter.

Langat and Klang were not the only seaboard towns of Selangor where misrule and excess ran riot, for there was a settlement at Kwala Selangor, near the mouth of the Selangor river, whose population consisted of Menangkabau, Mendaling, Rawas, and Bugis Malays, and Chinese shop-keepers, and which was a well-known rendezvous of bad characters and robbers. Fish-curing formed the principal peaceful vocation of the inhabitants, and the river was notoriously unsafe owing to the boldness of the crocodiles that lived in it, and not only fed upon the offal thrown into the water when the fish were split and cleaned, but even attacked the occupants of small boats, seizing and pulling them out of their little craft. The village itself was by no means a sweet-smelling place, for a brisk trade was carried on in drying prawns and making *blachang*, the latter being an odoriferous mass of decomposed prawns, much appreciated by Malays, who eat it as a condiment at their meals with relish

---

\* Since writing the above the news of the death of Sultan Abdul Samat has been received.

and esteem it a delicacy, apparently oblivious of its foul smell. To me it was nauseating, and I never tried to conquer my aversion beyond experimentally tasting a little on one occasion.

On a solitary knoll overlooking the village there are the ruins of a fort erected by the Dutch in order to command the mouth of the river, so as to conveniently collect the dues levied upon the imports and exports; and at the same time it was well situated for the purpose of carrying on their system of monopolizing the chief products of the country, which obliged the merchants and traders to sell to the Government all tin and certain produce obtained in the interior at an agreed-upon price, fixed considerably below the market value of the goods. On the signing of the treaty of Holland the Dutch evacuated this place for the last time, and the Malay inhabitants not only re-occupied it, but made it their stronghold from which to fit out piratical expeditions. As late as 1875, whilst the British Resident was on a visit to the place, a man was stabbed and killed openly in the street before a large number of witnesses, and it was not until some years afterwards that the unruly elements were thoroughly quieted.

The interior of Selangor, which had become depopulated during the disturbances, soon attracted Malay emigrants from Sumatra and elsewhere, who, hearing of the establishment of law and order under British officials, came over to settle and make new homes for themselves in the Malay Peninsula, and being more industrious and better cultivators than the previous inhabitants, brought much fresh land under the plough and formed new villages, with the result that now the Malay population of the state is for the most part composed of these aliens who have settled in the country.

There are two systems of tin mining pursued throughout the country by the Chinese, and these methods are called "Lombong" and "Lampan" workings. The Lombong, or open working, is the one more usually carried on, as it is in the valleys that most of the tin is found. It consists of digging, carrying, and throwing to one side the top soil to a depth varying from three to thirty feet. The first work to be commenced, when on satisfactorily prospecting the decision to open a mine has been arrived at, is to fell the jungle, pile and burn it; then the surface water has to be drained and confined to channels. An excavation is next made, the size depending upon the scale upon which the mine is being opened; usually in a new valley the commencement is but small, and the land is thoroughly tested and proved before extended operations are undertaken. A water-wheel, or engine and pump, are placed in position; the hole in which the water collects is kept dug out at a lower level than the workings, so as to keep them dry and free from water and to enable the miners to dig and carry away the earth, which they do in small oblong baskets, the side handles of which are connected by a length of stiff rattan, through which a carrying-stick is passed. The miner then lifts his load and places the stick on his shoulder, having a basket suspended at either end, which is kept from slipping off by a knob or projection at the top of the stick. He then runs up ladders at a great pace, steadying each basket with a hand to prevent their swinging about and spilling their contents. These ladders are ingeniously simple, and made from the long, slender trees cut from the forest close by; and when steps have been scooped out the miners are able to run

up and down them, carrying their loads, if they are not placed at too steep an angle. The men carry their full baskets up one ladder, and when they reach the surface empty them at some little distance and return by another ladder, to find that their comrades at the bottom of the mine have already filled fresh baskets for them, and discarding the empty ones they take up full ones in their place and commence the ascent again; so that there is a constant moving succession of coolies going up and down, for whom the men working in the mine itself are busily employed preparing their loads, so that they shall not have to wait and waste their time. The soil removed usually consists of several feet of ordinary earth, then a beautiful white clay, and on these being taken away the tin-bearing sand is exposed to view. This sand is then carefully sampled, and small portions of it are washed now and again in a kind of open wooden dish to discover whether it contains any ore. Directly prospects are obtained, the sand, instead of being thrown away as heretofore, is piled up in a place allotted to it. These tin-bearing deposits vary considerably in thickness, from a few inches deep to several feet, and usually consist of sand and stones, although sometimes large waterworn boulders are also to be met with.

A long wooden trough, or sluice, through which a stream of water flows, is then prepared, and charged with sand and stones, which are raked backwards and forwards with a long-handled species of hoe, the larger stones being collected and thrown to one side, whilst the lighter ones and the sand are carried away by the water, but the tin ore being of a heavier specific gravity remains in the sluice, and this process continues until the quantity of ore accumulating makes it necessary to turn off the water. The ore is then collected and put into a bucket, and the work commences anew. Many feet below this quartzose sand another layer is constantly discovered, and when this proves to be the case the tin sand at the lower level has usually a better percentage of tin ore mixed with it than is found in the upper strata. Before smelting, the ore has to be washed again, and cleared of all impurities as far as possible.

The Chinese method of smelting the tin ore is in cylindrical-shaped furnaces made of clay, round the outside of which sticks are placed perpendicularly, and close together, being held and kept in position by bands. In the centre, and down through the middle of this structure, there is a hollowed-out space in which the fire burns, being kept alight by fresh supplies of charcoal thrown on the top, where the tin ore is also placed in small quantities, and whence, melting, it trickles down through the burning charcoal and runs out at a small aperture at the bottom of this tube, falling into a pan dug in the ground and lined with clay, from which it is removed by ladles and poured into sand moulds, where it cools and solidifies. These moulds are made by passing a wooden block, shaped to correspond to the size of the ingot required, into damp sand.

Should the results of this first experiment be satisfactory, fresh houses are built, more men obtained, and another paddock, or excavation, is opened on a larger scale; and this is continued as long as sufficient ore is met with to cover the cost of working, or until the deposits have been exhausted. In places these deposits are fairly regular, in others most uncertain; very rich in some spots, but close by nothing is often found, and what is called the tin stream has disappeared entirely. If the mine is a prolific one, its owner usually does as much of the work as possible by contract, or by giving daily wages to his miners; should, however, there arise doubts as to the success of the venture, an arrangement is made whereby each coolie, according to the number of days he works, has a share in what the mine produces, so that if there is a loss it shall be well distributed.

There is besides a salutary custom, that should the advancer of the mine suddenly cease giving the usual supplies, thus necessitating an arrangement being made with someone else, the new advancer, upon the raising and sale of the tin ore, receives payment for everything he may have advanced before the man he succeeded has any claims at all. This rule is necessary to prevent the sudden and arbitrary withdrawal of supplies, and the consequent abandonment of the mine before the wash dirt, or tin-bearing sand, is reached and the ore saved. It also guards the miner from being deprived of the results of often many months of labour and hard work, and recognizes the principle that unless an advancer is prepared to see the result of his venture through to the end, for better or for worse, and has well calculated the cost beforehand, he had better devote his energies and capital to some other branch of trade.

During the progress of the work the owner supplies what is requisite, and this he does much to his advantage, retailing his goods to the mine at a greatly enhanced value, so that should the tin ore obtained be only sufficient to satisfy his account, he makes a good profit. The more successful the mine, the greater luxuries and the larger credit does he allow the miners, who increase the variety and excellence of their food, as their enjoyment in great measure consists in living as well as they can afford to do, sending a portion of their earnings to their homes in China, and gambling with the balance. For on pay-day the mine owner obtains permission from the gambling farmer to enable him to allow his miners to gamble on their own premises for a certain number of days, and during this period he looks forward not only to regaining possession of some of the monies he has disbursed, but of lending his men further sums which usually return to him as well. After the festivities and jollifications are finished, the men once more return to a spell of hard-working industry.

The houses in which these miners live are of simple and primitive construction. A long, high-roofed building, thatched with attap-palm leaves, whose sides are made either of the same material used more sparingly, or split logs placed close together; but whichever method is adopted, plenty of daylight peeps through, causing these sheds to be quite light inside, although entirely destitute of windows. There is usually only one entrance, which is closed at night by a rough plank door. The interior is broken up with benches and sleeping places, and in a conspicuous place there hangs a list of all the labourers, and daily the head man marks an entry against each name, recording whether its owner has been to work or not, as well as keeping voluminous and methodical accounts of what he has received and issued to his men.

A hollow wooden gong beaten with a stick is

the signal for commencing or leaving off work, and tapers which burn for a certain time are lighted, so that there shall be no tampering with the clock—when there is one—or deception as to the number of hours worked.

A little shelter, the roof of which is just large enough to cover a mosquito net that hangs down, being fastened at the top to the four posts which support the structure, reminds the passer-by that death is ever present; for the Chinese miners have a superstition against allowing their comrades to die in their houses, considering it a sure precursor of misfortune. In order to prevent this, as soon as they judge recovery very doubtful, and death to be close at hand, they carry the sick man out and put him in this little shelter, always ready and waiting for a new inmate, and here he is left alone for death to overtake him. These shelters are so small that during the showers and squalls which are so frequent, the rain splashing up from the ground bespatters and saturates the sick man's couch, and the mosquito net that surrounds him becomes dripping with moisture, whilst the chilly cold of the early dawn makes his last moments replete with misery and discomfort.

# CHAPTER VII.

*Gambling houses—Hua-Hoey lotteries—Lampan working—Superstitions regarding tin ore—Malay Pawang—Dwellers around mines—Malay wood-cutters; felling, sawing, and squaring of timber—Buffaloes at work—Charcoal burners—Buffalo carts—Reverberatory furnaces—Alluvial deposits, and the lode formation of tin and gold.*

In all villages of sufficient size there are public gambling houses where Chinese miners congregate and play. These gambling houses are under the control of the "farmer," the representative of a syndicate, who, in consideration of a fixed payment, is granted by the Government the exclusive privilege of erecting gambling houses and permitting play within them, as well as in any other houses for which he may grant permission for short periods. This system is simply a relic of former times, before the era of British protection, when every means of increasing the revenue was greedily seized upon, and would ere now have been discontinued, with other debasing practices, were it not for the large sum accruing to the Government from the sale of this monopoly.

These gambling dens have a most pernicious and demoralizing influence; they openly entice the passer-by to try his luck, and allure the weak-minded to their ruin, as well as being the fruitful source of much misery and crime. Within are to be seen little tables placed about the room; a croupier is in attendance at each, around which, of an evening, stand groups of excited Chinese, anxiously watching the result of the spin, or waiting in eager expectancy to hear what number is called, which will settle the fate of the stakes they have deposited. As the croupier pays his losses and rakes in his winnings there is a hum of conversation and much animated gesticulation, succeeded by a breathless, earnest silence as the gamblers once more crowd around the different tables, those behind pressing forwards, and, as it were, striving by their very wishes and the ardent intensity of their hopes to induce the number they long for to turn up; and their haggard, dubious faces betray the eagerness of the emotions they are striving to subdue. As the groups grow larger the heat becomes intense, and the odour from so many panting, perspiring, and unsavoury human beings, closely crowded together in so warm an atmosphere and confined a space, becomes intolerable, and the stench sickening. The large amount obtained by the Government is only a portion of the monies taken from these ignorant and uneducated miners, and the continuance of this injurious and debasing system, and the direct encouragement of this vice, is most discreditable to British administration.

There formerly existed a system of gambling, prevalent in the colony as well as in the native states, called Hua-Hoey, which was really a lottery, the tickets representing thirty-six different kinds of animals, and all stakes on the winning beast received thirty times the wagered sum. As coloured pictures were all the stock-in-trade requisite, this species of gambling afforded the unscrupulous an easy means of defrauding and swindling the credulous. Trickery and cheating took place at the drawings, so that the animal upon which there were fewest tickets was frequently made to win. Although the traffic was illegal, the difficulties of detection were great, and in 1885 the evils arising from the increasing numbers of sharpers in Penang became so disastrous and far-reaching, that a numerously signed petition was forwarded to the Government, drawing attention to the pernicious trade, and requesting that stringent measures be taken for its suppression, as its dissemination amongst all classes was creating much misery and unhappiness, besides ruining many. Not only did clerks rob their employers, and coolies steal the goods entrusted to their care, to enable them to place a stake upon an animal they fancied, but women also acted as the agents of the promoters of these lotteries, and going about persuaded others of their sex to gamble, edging them on by spurious lotteries and a little success at first to venture larger sums, the loss of which caused them to sell and pawn their jewellery, to deceive and to be dishonest.

As I have already mentioned, the other system of mining pursued is called lampan, or hill-mining, which in respect to its uncertainty is similar to valley workings, for some hills contain tin ore, whilst close by others are destitute even of a trace of the metal. The ore is found sometimes amongst a regular and defined narrow stony streak, some distance below the surface, at others it is distributed throughout the whole soil of the hill; in fact there is no rule, and I myself have seen it right on the surface and amongst the roots of the trees; but these signs are no guarantee of its existing in sufficient quantities to repay the workers, as a few yards away the earth may contain none at all.

The method adopted is to cut a watercourse to conduct the water from the nearest available stream, so as to utilize its force to sluice and wash away the hillside, when the lighter particles are carried off by the current, and the heavier ones with the ore left behind. It is a much less expensive and laborious way of obtaining tin-ore than valley mining, and is much in favour with Malays, who have numerous small workings in the hills, to which they repair when the necessity of earning a little money arises; and these mines often descend in the same family for several generations. Improved communication, however, has brought them within easier reach, and they are rapidly passing into alien hands, to be systematically developed and opened up. There seems to be absolutely no rule with regard to these tin deposits, and it is entirely a matter of chance whether the strike turns out a rich one or not. Hills and valleys that have proved unprofitable and been abandoned by one set of miners, when reopened after the lapse of several years by others have given satisfactory results, and this very uncertainty in the distribution of the mineral accounts for the innumerable and wondrous stories that obtain currency.

There is a strong belief amongst the Malays that the tin ore grows, and no matter how you may argue this question with them, they will, although politely agreeing with you, still retain their opinion that such is the case, and bring forward many instances of their own experience to prove that this theory is correct. Formerly, when the ore was smelted and yielded poor results, it was popularly supposed to be young, and not sufficiently matured, and this used to be a constant complaint; now it is not so frequently heard, education has spread, and the miners have discovered that very often such bad results have been caused by too great a proportion of hematite or wolfram mixed with the ore. Both are very similar in appearance when in fine particles to tin ore, and being of somewhat the same specific gravity they remain behind in the sluices, and can only be separated from the ore by careful hand-washing in smaller sluice boxes or pans ; and unless this is done before smelting their presence makes the tin ore form a conglomerate, instead of trickling down the furnace in a molten state and flowing out into the pan below.

These particles of wolfram and hematite are largely distributed throughout the tin-bearing lands, and to the uninitiated present much the same appearance, in fact often only testing or assay will finally decide the question. I have known an instance of a would-be tin miner, with more pluck than experience, returning delighted to his friends with the tale that he had walked knee-deep in mud and tin sand mixed, only to find by the bitter results of practical working and money lost that an abundance of wolfram is no criterion of the presence of payable ore, and besides giving much trouble when too plentiful, it is rather a bad sign than otherwise when met with in large quantities.

Of course the vagaries and perversity of spirits enter largely into tin-mining folk-lore, and are greatly relied upon by the ignorant to explain away many of the curious phenomena and startling uncertainties so frequently met with in this industry in the Malay Peninsula, which the cleverest geologists have only accounted for in a general way, and wherein the practical and experienced local miner, rendered cautious and wary by many a mistake and failure, is a far safer pilot and guide than the best of theories or the wisest of savants. No greater offence can be given to a gang of miners than by descending their mine with boots on and an umbrella opened overhead, as it is popularly supposed that such a proceeding is an insult to the presiding spirits, who, out of revenge, will make the tin ore disappear. So firmly rooted was this superstition in the early days of British protection, that the mere presence of a European in proximity to a mine so equipped was disliked and resented, and his nearer approach would cause all the miners at work to utter a warning cry in order to stop the intruder's advance; now, however, so many Europeans are connected with the industry, whose advent has done something towards breaking down many barriers of superstition, as well as having had a civilizing effect upon the miners themselves, who have much changed for the better, for instead of looking upon the white man with disdain and hostility, they have begun to fully recognize and appreciate the many benefits and protection obtained by his presence in the country, and have themselves become quieter and more law-abiding.

There is in each district a Malay who has gained some considerable local reputation as a prophetic dreamer, or Pawang, a sort of general adviser and mediator between the spirits and the miners. He is consulted on all occasions, decides on what spot a commencement should be made, and assuages and propitiates the spirits by the slaughter of a buffalo or some other means. He constantly visits the mines in which he takes an interest, receiving small gifts now and again, so that his influence may be for good, and not malevolent, and mixing so constantly with the Chinese he picks up a smattering of their language and is generally an opium smoker. He is constantly called in to give his advice, or by his incantations to exorcise some fancied evil sprite who, by his wickedness, is causing disaster; needless to say these men make the most of their prophetic successes, and their many failures are accounted for by every conceivable and ingenious method of argument, the blame for misfortune being attributed to the miners having done some act which occasioned the spirit's wrath, or omitted some necessary deed or offering. An intimate knowledge of the district enables the

Pawang to shrewdly guess the most likely places for tin to be found, and long habit makes him very wary of expressing a decided opinion, whilst all is covered by the plausible sentence, "God willing, your venture will turn out well," with which he glibly encourages the hesitating, and which he is never tired of reiterating.

A few Malay squatters invariably build houses and take up their residence in close proximity to every fresh Chinese mine that proves successful, or any new village commenced. The women occupy themselves and obtain a fair livelihood from re-panning and re-washing the "tailings," or refuse heaps of sand, after the Chinese have saved what they can, for owing to the large quantities of tin-bearing sand that have to be put through the sluices it is impossible to prevent the loss of a certain proportion, and there is always a considerable quantity of light ore carried away by the water, sometimes owing to careless or unskilful washing, for tin-washing is quite a trade, and good Chinese washers are valuable acquisitions to a mine. This re-washing of the heaps of "tailings" is quite an industry; it is not entirely relegated to Malay and Chinese women, but is also followed by aged Chinamen past the prime of life, who no longer having sufficient agility to carry baskets up the ladders, nor the strength for hard manual labour, have built small houses for themselves in which two or three of them live together and cultivate a small plot of ground adjoining, and generally possess a pig or two in a sty close by. In the Larut district in Perak a small colony of Siamese were thus employed. It is a desultory sort of pursuit, and one of its attractions is that those engaged in it can choose their own time for going to work. In the mornings, long after all others have gone about their daily tasks, the Malay women may be seen starting off in twos or threes to some stream that is flowing from the mines, carrying under their arms large open wooden dishes somewhat hollowed out in the centre and about eighteen inches in diameter. Standing in the streams, these women scoop up some gravel from its bed and commence washing it in their pans. They are very dexterous, and a few swift movements backwards and forwards, combined with a peculiar twist, is quite sufficient to get rid of a large portion of the lightest matter. The stones are picked out and thrown away after having been cleaned should there be any clay adhering to them, and then the residue is carefully manipulated and gradually allowed to fall over the edge of the pan, which is held and rocked on the surface of the stream, so that its current may facilitate operations when necessary, until all that is left is perhaps a thimbleful of tin ore, which is carefully put into a discarded tin or palm leaf; perhaps, more often, an old bit of rag, or the corner of the washer's sarong does duty instead. A fresh scoop is then made and the process continued, the searchers wandering about these streams, sometimes successfully, sometimes otherwise, till after a few hours they grow tired of their work and return home with their winnings, the value of which varies from ten cents to one dollar, according to their luck.

The aged Chinamen go about the same occupation in a different way, and usually confine themselves to the old heaps of refuse or tailings, which they wash over again in small portable sluice-boxes, easily carried from place to place, and fixed near a pool of water, where, whilst one fills the box with sand and washes it, his comrade supplies him with water by throwing it up with a scoop attached to a handle into a small and quickly prepared reservoir. This scoop is either made of bark or more usually of an old kerosene oil tin, and the water is used over and over again as it is always returned to the pool.

The Malay men find plenty of work and occupation, when required, in clearing the forest, cutting and drawing timber, building houses and sheds, as well as in the many little odd jobs constantly necessary about a mine. They are far more expert in the use of the axe and parang, or chopper, than the Chinese, and seem never to tire when so engaged. The axes they use are of the lightest description and peculiar in shape, being fitted on to a thin pliable handle, so that instead of using the axe with a strong muscular swing, and causing it to bury itself in the wood by the force of the blow, merely the wrist is used, and the axe flicked against the tree, the springiness of the handle making it chip a little piece out each time of striking, and a quick succession of blows in a short while eats through the largest trees. These wood-cutters, in order to save themselves all the extra labour and cutting they can, especially when the tree is large, erect a staging often ten to fourteen feet off the ground, so as to be above the spot where the stem is augmented in size by the large buttress-like projections ending in huge roots, which are mostly surface feeders, and therefore inclined to spread. The tree is made to fall in the desired direction, first of all by cutting it nearly through on the side where it is to be felled, and then a similar cut is commenced a short distance above at the opposite side.

When the tree is ready to fall this scaffolding becomes a dangerous place on which to stand, so the wood-cutter clambers down as fast as he can and runs to a safe distance, from whence he watches the results of his labours. Generally the first indication that one of these enormous trees is about to fall is a slight shivering and unsteadiness of the leaves above, then a quiet, gentle inclination forwards, to be immediately followed by a cracking sound as the portions not completely cut through commence to strain and break; then the tree's momentum increases, slowly at first as its branches force their way through the neighbouring boughs; then leaves and broken and torn limbs fly about, and there is a roar of sound, followed by the crunching noise of the branches being shattered underneath as the tree strikes the earth with such a mighty force that the ground around shivers, and the huge tree itself gives one shuddering rebound and then lies still beneath the swaying branches of the neighbouring trees that swing backwards and forwards, shedding a shower of leaves which for some little while continue to drop with a rustling sound.

The sawing of the trees into planks is always done by Chinese, the work being too laborious for the ordinary Malay, who dislikes so monotonous and continuous an occupation; should he, however, require planks for any purpose, he obtains them by splitting the tree with wooden wedges into lengths, trimming these rough and uneven slabs into shape by adzing. In the course of time he manages to hew them into very tolerable planks, but they all differ somewhat in width, as the most is made of the material at hand. He also squares small trees into beams and rafters, dragging them out of the jungle with the aid of a buffalo, and leaving behind quantities of chips and shavings to mark the spot where he has been at work.

These buffaloes vary very much as to the loads they are able and willing to draw, for they have obstinately stubborn wills which resist every species of persuasion should they consider themselves overloaded. Consequently a strong and well-disposed beast is a great acquisition to anyone engaged in this trade, and they are not only expensive to purchase when compared with others, but their owners dislike parting with them if they can avoid it. The buffaloes are either white or black; the former have a sort of flesh-coloured skin with coarse and rough prickly white hair, and dull, lazy-looking pink eyes and pale-coloured hoofs and horns; they are ugly and of clumsy appearance, very slow and ungainly in their movements. The black buffaloes, however, do not appear so awkward as their colour is less noticeable; they are supposed to be hardier, and when sold for slaughter fetch a slightly higher price, as their flesh is thought to be better eating; but I myself could never discover any difference, the meat of both was equally tough and stringy unless rendered more palatable by being wrapped up in a leaf of the papaya, which has the property of making meat thus enclosed tender in a very few hours. The harness is of the simplest kind, and only consists of a wooden yoke that fits over the buffalo's neck, having a notch at each end, over which is slipped a ring made of rattan that is attached to a shaft or long stick, the ends of which trail on the ground, and are cut so as to leave a branch a little distance from the end, which is chopped off not too close so as to form a fork; and into these forks a cross-stick is placed and tied, and this rude sleigh-like contrivance is ready for the log, which rests on the cross-piece of wood, to which it is firmly fastened to prevent it from slipping off.

The buffalo driver walks in front, giving an occasional tug at the leading rope attached to a ring passed through the nose of the animal, which follows slowly behind, stopping every now and then to regain its breath, for if the log is heavy and the track rough, progress is made by a series of spasmodic and strenuous efforts. Should the track along which the timber is hauled be much used and the ground be at all soft, sticks are cut and thrown down crossways at intervals that they may prevent the ends of the shafts and the logs from cutting into the ground and rendering the path impassable during wet and muddy weather.

Charcoal burners commit great havoc and destroy

many of the best and finest trees annually, being especially partial to the varieties whose timber is the hardest and most durable, as it is from these the best charcoal is obtained. The tree is felled, and the trunk-end for several feet is covered with earth and clay and ignited, and when sufficiently burnt the charcoal is collected and carried away in baskets, and placed under cover to prevent its getting damaged by the rain. Fresh earth and clay are thrown over several more feet of the log, and this process is continued until the whole tree is gradually converted into charcoal.

The Chinese employed in this trade carry the baskets long distances, often a day's journey, to the nearest road, mine, or central depôt. The life led by these men is lonely in the extreme, going their rounds and visiting the trees that are burning; solacing themselves with opium, they generally present a thin and attenuated appearance, and their skin becomes of a pale and sickly hue owing to living continuously in the deep shade of the jungle, where it is usually moist and damp. The carrying of the loads is done by younger men as yet unpractised in the burning, or the tin-smelter sends his own men to take the baskets down to where he is able to send a cart to fetch them. Formerly nothing but buffalo carts were utilized for this purpose; now bullock carts have somewhat taken their places, because along the hard roads the buffalo is but a poor beast for draught, going at a snail's pace, extremely susceptible to heat, so much so that the Chinese drivers often hang a broad and long piece of white cloth over the animal, completely sheltering it from the sun. This sheet is attached to two long sticks which, fastened to the cart, stretch horizontally over the buffalo's body. A scoop is also carried, so that every advantage may be taken of any pools or streams met with on the journey, to cool the beast by throwing water over him. A pleasing trait in the Chinese character is that they are uniformly humane and careful of the animals owned by them or of which they have charge, and it is no uncommon sight to see a Chinese carter patiently waiting by the side of the beast he is driving until it intimates its willingness to proceed. They never overwork nor overdrive their animals, which are consequently always sleek and fat, showing unmistakable signs of the care bestowed upon them.

To lessen the destruction of fine forest trees, the Government gives every facility for the exporting of the tin ore, and now large quantities are yearly smelted in reverberatory furnaces in the neighbourhood of Singapore, where the coal used can be discharged from steamers lying alongside of the works, and the business has become a very lucrative one for those concerned.

The alluvial tin deposits have proved themselves richer, extending over a larger area, than was expected; but they are also being exhausted at a quicker rate than was at one time supposed possible; and as the wave of discovery and the rush to new fields passes onward the valleys become a desolate waste of mounds and heaps, stagnant pools and ponds, where the hoarse croaking of many frogs replaces the sound of busy human life that formerly prevailed.

The rapid development and advancement of the Malay States has been entirely due to the wealth of these alluvial deposits, for they have supplied the means for supporting an efficient Civil Service, enabling good roads to be made and railways constructed. But these very facilities help and assist the process of exhaustion, and it will not be many years before what has happened in other parts of the world, where placer mines have been worked, will come to pass here.

In certain districts a proportion of alluvial gold is found mixed with the tin ore, and in several instances the lode formation of the gold has been discovered and worked with satisfactory results, the cheap Indian and Chinese labour materially aiding and placing the industry in a most favourable position when compared with other gold-producing countries. Should the formation continue to reasonable depths, of which there are many indications, then the Malay States will enter the ranks of gold-producing countries with every prospect of success, possessing advantages only to be equalled in India. Tin lodes have also been discovered, and are being worked remuneratively, but reef-mining is at present in its infancy, and only the future can determine its ultimate success.

# CHAPTER VIII.

Communication in Selangor—Forest—Rattan—Journey to Klang—Timber—Night in the jungle—Woodcutters—Kwala Lumpor: its central position—Resident-General—Leaving Kwala Lumpor—Travelling northward—Limestone hill and caves—Soil—Wild animals—Rogue elephant—Former denizens of the jungle—Camp—Insects—Scorpions—Horse leeches—Crossing pass—Ulu Yam—Benighted on horseback—Bathing—Sunset—Remains of Siamese tin-workings.

IN 1883 the only other egress from the State of Selangor besides the river routes was by a primitive and roughly constructed earth road between Kwala Lumpor and Bukit Kuda, which was very steep in places, with so many ups and downs as to appear somewhat like journeying over a tempestuous sea. On both sides of the road was dense jungle, the large trees of which nearly met overhead, consequently there was no varied scenery along the route, nothing except an unending vista of forest, beautiful in its way, yet somewhat monotonous. Tall, giant trees towered overhead, amongst the forks of whose heavy and wide-spreading branches grew enormous stag ferns, very striking when seen nestling so high up, with their long green fronds hanging down, overlapping the withered brown leaves underneath. Some of these forest trees had stems upon which the dark brown bark grew rough and crinkled, whilst on others it was of a greyish hue, smooth and glossy-looking, and here and there might be descried a trunk spreading out with several wing-like projections as it neared the ground; and beneath the mighty monsters grew other trees of smaller girth, and beneath these again still smaller ones, and saplings of various sizes, down to the newly sprouted seed sending up its tiny shoot, trying to force its way in life, and either strangled at the outset—killed by the dense shade and tangled growth amidst which fate had placed it—or perhaps, more fortunate in its surroundings, able to struggle upwards with thin attenuated stem and scanty top, its efforts seemingly bent upon endeavouring to rear its head high enough to obtain its share of the glimmering sunlight which, although blazing bright and strong above, only penetrates the dense mass of foliage with uncertain, feeble, and flickering rays. Amidst this tangle of boughs and branches, the home of orchids and lichen, huge ropes hang down, sometimes dangling overhead, at others rooted in the ground, and growing up. There are quantities of these parasites, varying in thickness from a piece of string to a chain-cable, and of many varieties, from a species that when cut exudes an excellent rubber, to another from which water trickles to slake the thirst of the traveller, who holds the dangling end over his open mouth, into which the water drops. Flowering plants are conspicuous by their absence, although now and again the solitary bloom of a ground orchid or other shade-loving plant may be descried, as well as the grape-like clusters of the fruit of the attap palms, and various fruits and berries.

The vegetation of the swamps differs considerably, being dependent upon the depth of water, mud, and other influences. The trees are smaller, and grow from a tangled pyramid of roots; their timber is always soft and of little value. A dense mass of impenetrable thorns takes the place of undergrowth, and it is in places such as these that the rattans are collected, and cut out of the thorny shell-like covering which is peeled off, as only the inside is of any use. These rattans grow in thick profusion, twining and twisting amongst the thorns and bushes, many yards in length, with nearly a uniform thickness throughout, raising their heads and growing upwards until, overcome by their own weight, they fall down and entangle themselves in still more inextricable confusion.

There were about sixteen miles of uncomfortable travelling along this road, so bad as to be impassable for carts in wet weather, and only practicable in the dry months for those lightly loaded. The journey was very hard on the poor little ponies, who often were forced to make great efforts to drag the conveyance to the top of the hill, and were then compelled to exert all their strength to prevent the vehicle from running upon them as they descended the other side. As it was, they were only able to accomplish quite short distances, and it was necessary to change them several times during the journey. Here and there a freshly broken cart by the side of the road bore witness to the struggles that had taken place when it stuck fast in some deep rut, and it is upon such occasions that the training of the bullocks is put to a severe test, for they are coupled by a yoke or cross-piece connected to the pole of the cart by means of an iron pin, which, passing through both pieces of wood, is kept in place by a nut at the bottom, thus allowing the yoke to freely move backwards and forwards. The oxen are fastened and kept in their places by two wooden pins, which, passing through holes in the yoke, hang down on each side of the bullock's neck, and in order to prevent the cart from tipping up, or the bullocks from slipping out their heads, a piece of string is passed round their throats, and its ends secured to the yoke. The load also has to be carefully balanced, so that there shall be just sufficient weight on the bullocks' necks to enable them to utilize their full strength, and to prevent the cart from tilting backwards; for should the burden on their necks be too oppressive they soon tire, and lowering their heads allow the yoke to slip over their horns, and are only prevented from entirely ridding themselves of it by the cord encircling their throats, which often becomes so taut as to nearly choke them. It is always difficult to get the best of cart bullocks to work in unison, after they have failed once or twice to move the load to which they are attached, and the driver has a hard task, twisting their tails, prodding them with a sharp stick, shouting and abusing them; for immediately they find the cart cannot be moved, one of them is sure to give way and back, which allows the other one to go forward, the cart turns to one side, and the bullocks place themselves in such a position that

## JOURNEY TO KLANG.

the driver has much difficulty in getting them right again before making another endeavour. During these struggles the cart works backwards and forwards from side to side in the soft mud, sinking deeper at each unavailing effort, necessitating some of its load being removed unless there is plenty of assistance at hand to help in pushing the wheels round. Some drivers

have a cruel and odious practice of making a raw place on the bullock's back, and with a pointed stick prodding this open sore—a barbarous method; usually, however, the animals are well cared for, as if not they are unable to work, and especially is this the case with the fine white species imported from India; whilst those from Siam cost less, do less work, and require but little attention. The terminus of the road from Kwala Lumpor to Klang was the small village of Bukit Kuda, a most uninteresting place, where every house was a resting and refreshment place for travellers, and did quite a lucrative business. Hot and dusty wayfarers were lounging about on the seats outside the shops, resting in the shade of the verandahs, eating or chewing betel, or smoking. Coloured syrup in glasses, sugar canes, plantains, sweetmeats, and other eatables were displayed upon the small counters, which were drawn up at night, and served as shutters to the windows within which the shopmen sat and gossiped with their customers outside. A few weary-looking bullocks lay in the road, and a pony was being led about to get dry in the sun, having been bathed in the Klang river, which at this point is tidal. A small steamer (when not broken down and useless) plied between this village and the port called Klang, some distance further down the river, and up to which place trading steamers from Singapore and Penang were able to come to discharge their cargoes.

The strength of the tides is considerable, and there must always be a dangerous undercurrent as well, for anyone falling overboard from the deck of a steamer is usually sucked under and drowned, and his body is not recovered. During spring tides the water rushes up or down between the somewhat narrow banks, fringed on each side with mangrove trees, and the traveller, if he is proceeding by a rowing boat, has to wait until the current flows in the desired direction, as it is useless trying to stem the stream in a boat of this description. Klang itself consisted merely of a few houses and

Government offices built on a swampy flat surrounded by hills, one of which reached down to the water's edge, and upon it a fort had been constructed and armed with guns to command the river. It was also an uninteresting place, the abode of many sandflies, these being most annoying and maddening tormentors, and only kept out by the finest mosquito nets; they are irritating to a degree, and although I could sleep comfortably with mosquitoes buzzing round and sitting upon my head and face, if the other little pests were about, nothing but covering myself over so as to effectually prevent them from biting would allow of my obtaining any rest or peace at all.

Klang has greatly increased since these days, and the country round has been opened up and converted into gardens, and a resident population has caused it to become quite a settlement. The railway now joins Kwala Lumpor and Klang, and is even extended further down the river to its estuary, where there is a large basin of water perfectly protected by islands and land on every side, into which large steamers are able to come and discharge their cargoes; higher up the river turning is a difficulty, the bends are sharp, and the depth of water insufficient for ships other than small coasting steamers.

On one occasion, upon arriving opposite Klang on a dark murky night, with a strong tide running up, the anchor was let go, and the ship commenced to swing round and had already got broadside on to the stream, when her stern caught in a sunken tongkong or sailing schooner laden with bricks, and at the same time her forepart dragged on the anchor chain, which, instead of being clear of the bow, had got underneath her keel. Fast fore and aft, broadside on to the current, which was flowing strong, she began to heel over to a dangerous extent, so much so that the captain awoke me to give me a chance, as he termed it, should anything happen, since I was the only other white man on board besides himself. There were close on 200 passengers, and matters looked so serious that the question of sending them on shore arose, only to be negatived on consideration, for had they become frightened and crowded on the wrong side of the steamer they would have caused the very catastrophe we were anxious to avoid. The water could scarcely be seen moving along the ship's sides, but the swishing of the current as it tore past was plainly to be heard, and brought to mind how little chance there would be of surviving if anything went wrong. There was nothing else to be done but turn in again and continue one's broken slumbers, hoping for the best, and on awaking next morning I found the ship had gradually been lifted off the obstacle, against which she had struck, by the rising tide, and was lying quietly at anchor as if nothing had occurred.

The country along the banks of the river in this neighbourhood is for the most part low and swampy, necessitating a thorough system of drainage before planting. In places this has been done, and the cultivation of various products has replaced the former rank vegetation and thick jungle.

The forests contain but a small quantity of the

best class of timber, but the inferior kinds are fairly plentiful, whilst there is an abundance of useless varieties. It is this inequality in value that has prevented any export timber industry from growing and the successful working of saw mills, for there is no means of transporting the larger and finer specimens, once the few trees adjoining any navigable stream have been cut down; and even then the harder woods will not float, and it is necessary to fasten them to those of a lighter and softer species to prevent their sinking. It is cheaper to have the tree sawn into planks or scantlings by Chinese sawyers on the spot where it falls than to make any endeavour to transport it to some central factory, an impossibility should the log be overweight for a buffalo to drag, whilst the scarcity of merchantable woods effectually prevents the utilization of any other motor power. A gentle, undulating country, whose soil contains somewhat more sand than usual, is the kind of locality liked by the harder varieties of timber, of which perhaps the best and finest is the chingei, which is cut down by Malays, split in two, then the solid trunk is adzed and hollowed out and made into boats, which last for many years. There are several species as durable and more so, but they do not grow to the same size, nor are they so easily worked, with the exception of the merbau, which has a smooth bark, and runs the chingei with its thick coruscated bark hard for supremacy; for tool handles nothing can approach the tough, long-fibred penaga, whilst for Chinese carrying-sticks mengapus is best. Sea-going craft are usually constructed of a hard yellow wood called kulim, which grows in the coast districts, and has the property of resisting many kinds of marine insects, besides being very durable and easily worked. Rengas, a dark red wood, makes excellent furniture and takes a good polish; but it is troublesome to shape unless kept for a considerable time, owing to its sap having the unpleasant properties of causing pustular eruptions on the skin of any person it comes in contact with. I have often seen men with their faces so badly swollen that they could hardly see at all for several days from incautiously or unknowingly cutting a rengas tree, and getting the sap on their skins; even touching its leaves will cause some inconvenience and puffiness. Some Malays profess to be proof against the irritant and poisonous qualities of this tree, and to be able to cut it down without feeling any ill effects; but in such cases the man is always careful to anoint himself well with oil before setting about his task, which appears to be the real reason of his immunity.

Of the softer woods the many varieties of miranti are amongst the finest, and its colour ranges from a dark red to almost white, the former being much superior, having often when cut in the hills at an elevation of over 1200 feet a flowery grain nearly equalling the famous satin wood of Ceylon; whilst jelutong, with its dark smooth bark, grows to a great height, and exudes a milky substance when cut; its timber is very soft and of poor quality, but it is popularly supposed to be less inflammable than other kinds of soft wood, and is much used for making clogs and coffins.

Journeying one evening between two wood-cutters' camps my guide lost his way, and, night coming on, there was nothing to be done except to sit on the root of a tree and wait for morning. There were four of us altogether—my comrades consisting of Malays from Singapore; and, unaccustomed to such experiences, they were filled with much dread of wild beasts, especially the rhinoceros, and took very unkindly to the situation in which they found themselves. The distress and fears of these men would have been rather comical had it not been for a steady and continuous downpour of rain the whole time, in which we were compelled to sit patiently, as it was too dark to move about. Everything was soaking wet, and ten unpleasant and chilly hours had to be passed before daylight enabled us to continue our journey once again. The next morning we found ourselves within a quarter of a mile of the place we had endeavoured to reach, and getting a boat we were soon in the main river, where the sun dried the clothes on our backs whilst breakfast was being prepared.

Owing to the convenient and central position of Kwala Lumpor, which, since the opening of the railway between it and Klang, has been brought well within twenty-four hours of Singapore,—a journey which is now accomplished with every comfort that a good steamer can afford—it has been made the headquarters of the Resident-General, an officer responsible to the Governor for the proper administration of the native states. He supervises the Residents, and, whereas formerly each state had land rules and regulations peculiar to itself, and which were constantly being materially altered and changed so as to meet the opinions and ideas of each new Resident who took up his appointment, now progress is being made under an eminently qualified officer, Mr. H. Conway Belfield, with a view to the unification of the laws and regulations relating to the land; and this is also being carried out in other departments, and the system of judicial administration especially is being remodelled and placed upon a more equitable and consistent basis.

This process of unification and solidification has come none too soon, for the revenues of these states are now quite capable of sustaining the burden of the expenditure necessary during the next few years for the completion of the railway system on the western side of the main range, and for the development of the eastern districts less favourably situated with regard to means of communication. At the same time the fact cannot be lost sight of—that as the alluvial deposits of tin get worked out in certain districts, there follows a very serious diminution of revenue from those parts affected, which has hitherto been made up and concealed in the general expansion of the total revenue caused by the opening up of new fields and the continually improved facilities of communication.

But what is happening in detail will assuredly before long have disastrous results on the revenue as a whole, for agriculture alone could in no way supply the equivalent to the taxation obtained from the tin-mining industry, and these alluvial deposits are now within measurable distance of being exhausted along the western coast; and then the mining population will have to turn their attention to the undeveloped eastern side of the mountains. Before this takes place it is to be hoped that the permanent cultivation of some agricultural products will have extended sufficiently to enable this certain loss of revenue to be in some measure recouped, and that the nomadic habits of a considerable portion of the Malay settlers will not cause them to abandon their holdings and migrate elsewhere, following in the wake of the mining industry.

During the early years of the decade, 1880 to 1890, the country between Kwala Lumpor in Selangor, and Kwala Kangsar in Perak, the headquarters of the Resident of that state, was entirely unopened up, there were no roads to speak of, and the journey consisted of a difficult and tedious tramp through the jungle. Leaving Kwala Lumpor and travelling to the northward for a few miles towards the hills that encircle this portion of the country, the village of Batu was reached—a few scattered houses alongside a fordable river, across which on the other side could be seen rising from the forest-covered plain, and standing isolated by itself, a picturesque white limestone hill. This hill is famous for its fine cave whose narrow entrance is situated a little way up the hillside, and almost immediately opens out into a broad, high-vaulted space, at the apex of which there is a small aperture admitting just sufficient daylight to change the darkness into a sombre gloominess, through which comes the rustle of many wings as colonies of disturbed bats fling themselves into space, flit hither and thither with sudden dashes, seeking safety in flight; so that by the time the intruder's eyes have become somewhat accustomed to the semi-darkness, he thinks himself alone, and feels but a pigmy as he looks up at the roof above and shouts, only to hear his own voice reverberating with a hollow, deadening sound and echoing back to him, having frightened a solitary and belated bat that has been hanging in some darker and more obscure corner than its companions, and quickly disappearing, it leaves nothing but insects of various kinds behind, which placidly continue their pursuits undisturbed and unalarmed by the unusual sound of a human voice. The floor beneath is largely composed of guano, but not in sufficient quantities to be of any commercial value; and exploring still further, a smaller cavern is discovered, from which narrow, damp, and clammy tunnels lead on into the hill, and whose roofs are composed of thick greyish masses of pendant stalactites.

Around these limestone hills the soil is especially good, and vegetation is luxuriant on either side of the cool bright stream that meanders through the forest, full of little minnows, which dart hither and thither; along its banks the tracks of many animals show that this is one of their favourite localities, and the especial haunt of the seladang, the bison of the Malay Peninsula, a magnificent species of wild cattle, known to have measured as much as seventeen hands, or five feet eight inches at the shoulder, and possessing wide-spreading and very sharp horns. They are exceedingly fierce and dangerous when wounded, charging without hesitation the intruder of their haunts, and most difficult to approach in the thick jungle, through which it is no easy matter for the tracker to move silently without treading upon some of the many dead twigs that bestrew the ground or shaking some small sapling as he creeps along. Being extremely wary, these animals move off at the slightest noise, and when once disturbed and thoroughly aroused the sportsman had better give up the chase for that day. With luck, and the wind in the right direction, the tracker may perchance come upon one of these fine creatures lying down and resting, or asleep after its early morning feed, and as it rises and starts round to see what the unwonted sound may be it exposes itself to view, and affords the sportsman an opportunity of getting a shot; but he must not delay, as the seladang dashes away once its curiosity is satisfied, or the scent of the intruders reaches its nostrils, and travels a long distance, not returning to the place from which it has been disturbed for some days.

A rogue elephant was a constant frequenter of this neighbourhood, and well known to the inhabitants owing to the malformation of one of his feet, which was smaller than the others. He was very wicked, and caused the locality he haunted to be shunned by all, and when I first passed through it I found the small jungle path had not been traversed for some time by human beings, and there was plenty of evidence of his having but lately been there. Elephants are usually harmless, but a rogue is dangerous in the extreme to follow, for should he discover that he is being tracked he silently waits for the sportsman in some dense thicket where he is with difficulty seen, and rushes out unexpectedly upon him. This is just what occurred to a party who were following up this particular rogue through the jungle, having already obtained one shot at him, and were endeavouring to get another. The elephant stopped, awaiting his pursuers in a swampy locality full of thorns, through which it was difficult for the tracker to make any progress at all, and suddenly without any warning he rushed out and charged upon those following him, who were unable to move out of his way owing to the entanglement of the undergrowth. As it happened the person upon whom the rogue rushed was the late Captain H. C. Syres, who was subsequently Commissioner of Police for the protected Malay States, a well-known sportsman and excellent shot, famed for his coolness and nerve, whether shooting big game or allaying the turbulence of a Chinese mob. Owing to the denseness of the jungle the elephant managed to get to such close quarters before it was possible to lodge the contents of an eight-bore in his body, that one of his tusks struck a sapling so near to the captain that on stretching out his gun at full length the end of the barrel touched the splintered tree which the elephant had split as he turned to fly. The party spent the remainder of the day following his tracks, but they never came up to him again; and fresh trackers sent out the next day to continue from the place at which they had left off, after proceeding some distance lost his trail entirely. It was but a short while ago that news arrived that this gallant sportsman, who possessed such numerous trophies of his skill, had met his death whilst on a shooting expedition on the eastern slopes of the mountains. A wounded seladang charged and tossed him in the air, and hurt him so severely that he succumbed to the injuries he received.

Flourishing coffee gardens and macadamized roads have now taken the place of the primeval forest, and the seladang has been driven from his haunts. The grunt of the frightened wild pig disturbed at its meal is no longer heard, the rhinoceros has abandoned its wallow. The large shady trees are gone beneath which the elephants used to sway their trunks in ceaseless motion, and over whose tops the flapping of the hornbill's wings was heard, or the hoarse cry of the bird as it rested amongst the topmost boughs or searched for the fruits and reptiles upon which it fed. The weird cry of the Argus pheasant has ceased to echo through the woods, nor does the stealthy tread of the many jungle cats (so destructive to the smaller animals) startle the timid mouse-deer from its resting place. The python no longer crawls amongst the rocks or waylays its prey, nor does the tiger spring and seize its victim by the neck, or howl by night, silencing the barking elk, which, startled, fled away, whilst all the denizens of the forest quaked with fear and became instantly quiet at the sound of the dreaded roar, which was all that then disturbed and broke the death-like stillness of the jungle.

Crossing this fine alluvial flat, the track emerged into an open space and lost itself in the tangled growth of the coarse and many-jointed buffalo grass, which creeps and spreads, covering the ground wherever it obtains sufficient light to enable it to grow. Across this open space was an abandoned house—our resting place for the night—and alongside of it were the ruins of another one, which had been demolished and levelled to the ground by an elephant which had taken up his abode in the vicinity, and had scared away the occupants who had made it their temporary home.

The floor of the remaining house was raised several feet from the ground, as is usual with all the Malay dwellings. The steps were broken and had fallen into decay, so fresh ones had to be made; but this took only a short while to accomplish, for a few sticks tied together with jungle rope cut close by made a sufficiently good ladder up which to climb. Dirt and dust, spiders and insects, had held possession of the house for some time, and there was a musty smell of decay pervading it all. A branch plucked from a neighbouring tree served as a broom to sweep away most of the former through the interstices between the rough, uneven sticks on to the ground below. The cobwebs and spiders remained undisturbed overhead, and no attempt was made to drive out the many insects that had their dwelling in the nooks and corners, or the harmless armies of ants crawling along and up the sides in ceaseless moving phalanxes without a break in the long dark line of the travelling throng. Should you happen to cut this advancing multitude in two, then a sudden commotion takes place, the ants hurrying and scurrying to right and left, seemingly panic-stricken for an instant; but the disorder is only momentary, they soon return to their ranks, picking up the dead and wounded on their way, methodical even in this, for should one of them lift up his fallen comrade another soon comes to his help, and the two carry the burden between them, regaining their place in the ranks, which are quickly re-formed, and all signs of the recent tumult effaced as the procession marches onward. These ants forage everywhere in search of food, creeping through the smallest crevices, and if any jam or tinned milk comes within their reach they crowd to it, smothering and drowning themselves in their anxiety to get their fill; and the preserve presents but an uninviting appearance with a layer of dead ants on its surface. The only way to prevent this is to surround the tins with water, over which the insects cannot pass, and it is usual in all houses for the legs of the sideboards and cupboards in which sugar and such-like things are kept to rest in saucers filled with water.

But the most baneful insects are scorpions and centipedes, and though I have escaped being bitten myself, several of my men have at times been invalided; for, as is well known, the bite of both is very painful, causing the part affected to swell and become tender for some days. On several occasions these insects have been found amongst my bedding in the morning, when it was shaken out preparatory to being rolled up for the journey, and once I discovered a scorpion underneath my pillow as I felt for my watch, which I had placed there overnight.

A few small branches laid on the flooring made a somewhat more level sleeping-place upon which to spread our mats, whilst dead bits of stick were collected for firing, and soon the rising smoke betokened that food was being cooked, and it was time to have a bathe—a frequent necessity in this climate; so picking my way barefoot to a tiny stream flowing through a swampy bottom hard by I plunged in, luxuriating in the cool water after the long march. My enjoyment was destined to be of but short duration, for a sharp bite on one of my legs startled me, and I commenced to scramble out, but not before another bite hastened my efforts; and on gaining the bank I found two large horse leeches, nearly six inches in length, fastened on to my leg. Pulling them off, the blood still continued to flow as I returned to the house after my unpleasantly curtailed bath, where my meal, for which I was more than ready, awaited me.

A soothing pipe whilst darkness was coming on, a last cup of tea, and then to bed, being careful to tuck the mosquito net in securely under the mat all round, after which it took but a short while to fall asleep, for I had to rouse myself by half-past four the next morning and see that the men who had to light the fires and cook the food did not oversleep themselves, and delay our getting a good start at the first peep of dawn and directly it became light enough to see; because a short while lost at daybreak might cause a late arrival after the day's journey, and give but little time in which to make preparations for the night.

After the morning meal, which only differed from that of the preceding evening in so far as then I ate half of one of the small fowls of the country hot, whereas now I ate the other portion cold, a plate of rice and a small piece of dried fish as a relish, followed by a cup of cocoa or coffee, and I was ready to creep into the still wringing-wet clothes of the day before, which there had been no means of drying. It was useless to think of putting on a dry change of raiment, for in a short while it would again have been wet through, soaked with perspiration, and consequently I should only have had two wet suits instead of one. The early dawn always felt more or less chilly, and dressing in sodden clothes was usually accompanied by unpleasant fits of shivering.

Soon we were wending our way along the spur of the hills we had to ascend, past the dangerous place frequented by the rogue elephant. The path became more overgrown, and the track rougher; large fallen trees blocked the way, retarding progress, as they had to be crossed, for the ground was too steep to admit of laden men going up or down in order to get round the obstacle, so with as little delay as possible a foothold was cut in the log, and sticks placed on either side to enable the men to climb over it.

The path as it approached the pass became almost precipitous, and so slippery in wet weather as to be very difficult of ascent. The loaded coolies clambered up this portion laboriously, careful of their foothold at each step they took, and using their toes to clutch the ground. The descent for a short distance was equally bad, and had to be negotiated even more cautiously, but it is amazing how a barefooted man will manage to walk in perfect safety where a booted one has to use a stick with which to steady himself. Habit and use make their feet become almost like additional hands; they are able to pick up money or sticks from the ground, they seize and hold any object they may require to keep steady whilst they are working at it, and in climbing ropes they grasp it between the first and second toe, instead of swarming up as we do. They take the greatest care not to tread on thorns, for notwithstanding that the soles of their feet have a thick and hardened skin, thorns readily penetrate, and have to be pulled out; or if they break off, as they often do, leaving their sharp points in the flesh, they require to be extracted, and it is a very usual sight to see the carriers after a rough day's journey performing this operation, and cutting the thorns out of one another's feet.

After some hours of descent the valley of Ulu Yam is reached, a fine stretch of paddy fields, and a village inhabited by immigrant Malays from Sumatra.

Some years afterwards, when a six-foot road had been cut contouring the hillside, I was benighted whilst riding down it on a little black pony. There was a high bank on one side, and a steep drop on the other, and it was so dark that I could see neither, so there was nothing to be done but sit quietly on the pony's back and trust entirely to his guidance. It was the first time we had been on a night journey together, and the poor little beast was nervous and terrified. Fearful of walking over the edge of the path he kept constantly smelling the track, whinnying and crying with fear, and although I had often heard horses when badly hurt shriek out with pain, I had never known them do so from abject fear before. Some of the little wooden bridges across the numerous gullies were slightly rotten, and these he crossed with nervous trembling; and on the edge of one he stopped, so dismounting I lighted a match, to find it broken down, but as the ravine was only some five feet deep we managed to scramble over, and finished our journey safely.

After that night's experience we always seemed to understand one another better, and a mutual liking and confidence was established, so that no place was too difficult for the pony to try and negotiate if I went first, for if he came to grief he knew I should somehow help him out. I was very sorry when he died; he was a picture to look at, and made a beautiful wheeler in a tandem, but nothing would persuade him to go properly in single harness; he would rear, throw himself backwards, jib, try and shake himself free of the harness, and failing that start off with a bound, gallop a short distance, and go once more through the same performance; but with a leader in front no pony could go better or more pleasantly; he had the best of manners, and most delicate of mouths, and in saddle was as game as possible.

The house of the Orang-tua, or recognized head of the cluster of dwellings in Ulu Yam, was situated close to the path, and was our halting place for the night. We were made welcome, mats were spread, and bits of news interchanged. At the back of the house was a nice clear flowing stream with gravelly bottom, nearly three feet deep. As I walked into the water I saw a long, thin, attenuated water snake, that had been disturbed by my intrusion, swiftly wriggling itself across to the other side. There was no fear of my bath being disturbed by leeches here, for they only swarm in muddy places; nothing more disquieting than the nibbling round my legs of a number of little minnows, which, attracted by my white skin, came to examine and try whether it may not be something edible, and amused me by the persistency of their efforts.

On my return to the house after bathing, it was with feelings of contentment that I ascended the ladder on to the verandah, for the accommodation was comfortable and luxurious when compared with the night before; and sitting down on the doorstep the look-out was bright and cheerful, for the setting sun, throwing a last beam of light across the brown, watery paddy fields, that had been so lately planted, lighted them up with just one warm parting flash of radiance before its golden orb disappeared below the horizon, leaving an afterglow of colours in the heavens to tinge the wavy clouds with brilliant sheens of splendour, gradually deepening in tint to a glorious crimson, which was slowly lost in darkness. One of my bearers had found he possessed mutual friends and relations with my host, and they sat up late together discussing them and chatting.

The next morning saw us all once more on the move; skirting alongside the paddy fields we commenced a hot and dreary journey to Ulu Selangor through grass and scrub, for all the intervening country had been cleared of its forest growth and abandoned, after a crop or two had been taken from the land. Crossing a river about mid-day we travelled on, reaching in the afternoon the low ridge of hills on the far side of which lay the village where we intended to camp for the night.

This ridge was covered by a dense growth of bamboos, and was interesting from the fact that it contained signs of a former Siamese occupation, the record of which would have been lost had it not been for the numerous round shafts which had fallen in and were nearly filled with earth, and amongst these the track wound in and out, threading its way between them as it traversed this honeycombed hill. The mining method adopted by these Siamese adventurers, in probably the eighteenth century, required the assistance of two men, one of whom was employed in excavating a circular hole of sufficient dimensions to enable him to work within it. As he dug out the soil under his feet he put it in a basket attached to a cord, which his comrade drew up, and throwing its contents to one side returned it to him. When the ore-strata was reached he not only sent up to the surface what there was in the shaft itself, but undermining as far as he could all round he scooped up everything that was within his reach, and this all had to be carried some little distance to a neighbouring stream in order to separate the tin ore from its surroundings. Alternate notches were cut in opposite sides of the shaft, into which the miner, by sticking his toes, was able with the help of a bamboo pole, or by pressing his elbows against the walls, either to gain the surface or to lower himself without much difficulty, for these holes were seldom much over twenty feet in depth.

Being unable to cope with the water in the flats, these Siamese emigrants confined their attention to higher places, where, by sinking shafts at regular intervals, they systematically extracted and scooped out all the ore-bearing strata of the ground in which they worked; but they must have been satisfied with results which would be totally insufficient nowadays to have made their method worth while in the poor land in which they worked.

# CHAPTER IX.

Ulu Selangor—Destroyed by dam bursting—Trade—Kalampong—Ulu Bernam—River—Mountains—Herd of elephants—Kwala Slim—Crossing swamps—Kwala Galeting—Death of the only Europeans in this district—Fish-hook ants—Trollah—Crute—Small-pox—Sungkai river—Kwala Lepis—Catching wild elephants—Jungkau—Tapah and country round—Hanging over precipice—Sakais.

THE original village of Ulu Selangor was built on a low bank by the side of the Selangor river, at the highest point where it was navigable for the small boats conveying the imports and exports of the district. At the back of it stretched away a long valley, in the upper portion of which a high bund had been constructed, confining many acres of water of considerable depth, which was utilized by the miners in the neighbourhood.

This dam had been in existence for very nearly a hundred years, and the villagers had ceased to realize the dangerous situation they had selected for their houses, until one wet, dark night, succeeding an unusually rainy day, the cry was raised that the tank was bursting. Some hurriedly ran to higher ground, but many, hardly crediting the intelligence, remained in their dwellings rather than face the storm outside, whilst others lingered to collect as much of their goods as they could carry away before abandoning their homes. Fatal delay, for the bund had broken, and the opening, small at first, soon widened, letting loose an avalanche of water that ramped and tore down the valley, levelling everything that opposed its passage across the intervening space, and, rushing on the village, swept it and all its inhabitants out into the river; then, dashing against the opposite bank where the ground was steep and high, the waters recoiled and eddied, tossing shattered houses, animals, and human beings about in tumultuous confusion, whilst the current pressed and carried them on in its downward course.

A few houses that stood on a slight eminence were all that escaped being destroyed, and the valley above bore witness for many months to the torrential flood that had passed over it. The bushes and tall grass were still lying flattened to the ground, and where the bund should have been a wide rent gave entrance to what had once been a lake, but was now a stretch of quickly drying mud, where a few fish lingered and hid in the slimy bottom. The village was rebuilt on higher ground, and being connected with Kwala Lumpor by railway, it has become a flourishing little centre of trade, and substantially built brick houses have taken the place of more temporary structures.

Its inhabitants do a considerable business with the neighbouring state of Pahang, as it is from here that the road starts that leads over the mountains to the mining district of Tras and to the gold mines of Raub; and it was the base where supplies were collected for one of the forces that were sent to put down the disturbances that broke out shortly after a British Resident had been imposed upon the Sultan of that state.

The sole mark left to remind the traveller of the disaster that once overwhelmed the place in its early days is a grassy mound, the grave of the District Officer, the only white man who was in the village at the time of its destruction, and whose body was recovered some distance down the river.

The Malays in this neighbourhood had been almost exterminated during the many internecine fights, for they had commenced by helping the Siamese to conquer Perak, and before the effects of that expedition had disappeared they began fighting among themselves, which was more destructive still. Those lower down the river prevented any merchandise from passing up or down, and took to piracy directly the Dutch, in accordance with the Treaty of Holland, 1824, withdrew from the fort they had constructed at the river's mouth. The most terrible anarchy prevailed, and traditions of murders and horrible cruelties were still current among the poverty-stricken remnant left in the interior.

The scenery in the neighbourhood of the Selangor river is uninteresting, the whole country round being broken up with numerous little hills and valleys, and these had to be crossed on the journey towards Bernam, the first part of which was dull and uninteresting until Kalampong was reached, where there had formerly been quite a considerable mining settlement; but the houses were already falling into decay, the population having mostly left owing to the rich discovery of tin which had once attracted them having become nearly exhausted. The last portion of the journey, notwithstanding the flatness of the country traversed, was a tedious and trying walk, along a path much cut up by the buffaloes which were employed to drag provisions for the miners over this narrow way, rendering it muddy and slippery in wet weather, and rough and uneven to walk upon when dry. The village of Ulu Bernam is situated in a beautiful and broad valley through which the Bernam river flows, the boundary between the states of Selangor and Perak, and its inhabitants were foreign Malays, who appeared prosperous and well-to-do; their houses were nicely built, and the turf between them was kept closely cropped by the many goats and buffaloes that roamed at large, whilst here and there a clump of bamboos broke the uniformity of the level sward.

Tied to the river bank were a few small boats, whose owners were lazily lolling under the shade of the removable roofs—made from leaves of the nipa palm sewn together—they had erected, and resting after their two weeks of hard poling up the river. The children were disporting themselves in the river itself, laughing and shouting at one another with gladsome exuberance of spirits; higher up a group of women were vanishing behind the bank round a bend in the stream, in order to seek a more secluded bathing-place; and across the water the curious bleat of the cow buffalo could be heard as it called to its calf, and emerging from a path leading to the woods came several buffaloes, which having done their day's work were being brought by small boys perched on their backs down to the river, into which they were driven, almost disappearing as they lowered their bodies until nothing but their heads were visible above the water. In the far distance the dark bold outline of the Slim mountain range, six to seven thousand feet in height, formed a fitting and picturesque frame to this pleasant landscape, where the air was pure and balmy, and where only happiness seemed to reign, and contentment appeared the lot of all.

Whilst travelling along the foot of these hills in the direction of Ulu Slim, I unexpectedly came across a herd of elephants standing in a bamboo glade; and as they were not aware of my presence, I sat down and was interested in watching these huge beasts in their wild state, oblivious of the prying eyes so intently gazing on them and observing their every movement. They stood a little distance apart, all facing one way, swinging their trunks from side to side, or flapping their ears backwards and forwards, otherwise motionless, solemn and silent. They were not more than thirty yards off, and I left them undisturbed, more fully convinced than ever that shooting these useful animals was but poor sport, for they are dull of sight and not over quick at hearing, being largely guided by smell, so that the tracker is often able to get quite close up to the unsuspecting beast, should the wind be in the right direction. The principal danger is that when a herd is disturbed and thoroughly frightened its members rush panic-stricken in all directions, and there is the chance that one of them, terrified by the report of the sportsman's gun, may in its mad career accidentally knock him down, and do him an injury as it dashes past.

Shooting elephants, unless a licence has been obtained, is wisely prohibited, so that as long as they stay in their haunts, and do not come forth and destroy the crops and gardens of the villagers, they are left in peace. These herds frequent certain feeding places and districts, wandering to and fro for many miles, being often joined by tame elephants that have broken loose and been lost by their owners; but when this is the case these runaways can always be detected, for the wild ones raise their trunks and feed upon the young shoots of overhanging trees, whilst those that have once been in captivity tear up the creeping grasses that grow in the open glades as they pass along, in addition to eating the foliage, for they are less fastidious, and have acquired the habit of eating the common grasses that grow so freely in the neighbourhood of villages.

There was one especially famous elephant which had a malformed foot, and was well known in many districts, as he used to travel from the western coast, adjoining the Straits of Malacca, right over the range of mountains into the territory of Pahang. On one occasion, when walking alone in the jungle, I came upon his tracks, and whilst stopping to examine them I was considerably startled by hearing him trumpet within a few yards of where

I stood, and being in no wise anxious to break in upon his solitude I moved quietly on and left him undisturbed. He had the reputation of being a sacred elephant, and never did any injury, so that his visits were not unwelcome, and he was popularly supposed to be the hallowed and reverenced elder and leader of his herd.

Native shikaries have a clever dodge while hunting game of finding out from what quarter the wind is blowing, for in the forest it is often faint and imperceptible. They lightly scrape one of their nails with a knife, obtaining a fine white dust, which falls but slowly through the air, and is easily affected by the slightest breath of wind there may be, and clearly indicates from what direction he must approach his quarry, so that it may not scent his presence.

Leaving Ulu Bernam, our next day's march was to Kwala Slim, a spot where the two rivers meet on their way to the sea. The track followed the course of the river the whole way, through alternately flat and swampy jungle. During the journey we passed the Berang river, whose brown-tinted and effluvial waters gave evidence of the unwholesome and malarial nature of the country through which it flowed, and crossed it by means of a large fallen tree that stretched from bank to bank. Malays but seldom suffer from giddiness, and are very expert at walking along logs and trees, and even should the bridge oscillate with each step taken, as often happens, they appear in no wise disconcerted; most of them can swim, and although their method is entirely different to ours, resembling more the actions of a dog than a man in the water, they manage to get along at a fair pace. I usually made the syce, if he was anywhere at hand, swim with my pony when crossing a river, in order to save myself an unnecessary wetting, should there be a bridge or any other means by which I could get over. Upon one occasion, when my pony was being taken across the Berang river, he got bogged in the muddy bottom just as he was trying to clamber out; so I sent the syce to lift his tail and took the end of the reins myself, and although all that could be seen of the man was just his face above the water, the pony managed to gain firmer ground without much difficulty. When a horse gets fast in the mud it is no use dragging him by the bridle if after a plunge or two he cannot free himself, for he only sinks deeper into the mire; better far go to his tail and lift it, so that the animal may obtain a leverage to assist him successfully to extricate himself from his difficulties. If there be two persons, one should hold the end of the reins out in front as well, this will assist him still more; and it is marvellous through what bad places a pony accustomed to be bogged will manage to pass helped in this way. One of my ponies would cross any morass, provided it was free of roots, that I myself could struggle through; and when unable to proceed any further by himself he would wait until we came to his assistance, and not till then would he make any desperate plunges to free himself from the clinging mud.

By the evening I reached Kwala Slim, a dreary, remote spot by the side of the river, whose banks were liable to be flooded, and with the whole country round it periodically suffered from inundations. Here the officer in charge of this district lived, and on inquiring for him I was told he was suffering from fever, but he shortly came out, having just risen from his bed, looking dreadfully ill and weak. The excitement of seeing a fellow-countryman and hearing his own language made him more cheerful, and by the time he went to bed he seemed somewhat improved.

Early the next morning I started for Kwala Galeting, a river that flows into the Slim at the foot of the main range of mountains, and on arrival the headman of the village came to tell me that there was a European ill a short distance away who had ordered a boat to take him down the river that morning, but he had not arrived. He was a planter from Ceylon who had commenced a coffee plantation in the hills near this place, not realizing what the difficulties of transport were and how little chance there was at that time of ultimate success. Taking some men with torches to light me on my return journey, I started off to see him, and found him in bed suffering from his daily recurring afternoon attack of ague and fever, but the shiverings had ceased. He informed me he was going down country the next day, and that some work he had wished to see finished before departure was just completed that afternoon. To enable him to leave the first thing the next morning I went and inspected what had been done, and offered to stand by him and start him on his journey if he wished it. He said it was not necessary, so I lighted the torches I had brought and returned to camp thoroughly tired out. The next morning I left on my way to Trollah, and being so accustomed to an attack of fever myself and to see others suffering from it, did not anticipate the reply I received, on reaching the end of my journey at Kwala Kangsar, to my inquiry if any news had been obtained of the only two white men I had met on my journey across Perak, and was shocked when I heard that they had both died a few days after reaching more civilized parts, showing that they had delayed their departure too long; a not infrequent mistake, and one easily made, for after the first few attacks of fever the patient ceases to realize how the poison is sucking away his strength and vitality, and expects to shake it off as he has already succeeded in doing so often before.

Few people used the track that led to Trollah and the places beyond, for during the next two days' journey I did not pass more than a few inhabited dwellings. The track was over steep, abrupt hills, tiring in the extreme, and very hard work for coolies carrying heavy loads. I usually walked on alone some distance in front of my men to save the tediousness of waiting whilst they were passing difficult places in the path, over which they were obliged to proceed slowly and cautiously. A little off the track was a hot spring, smelling strongly of sulphuretted hydrogen, where I often had a deliciously warm and refreshing bath, and never passed without drinking its waters. It was a favourite place for wild beasts to come down and drink, their tracks in the vicinity being numerous, and a little distance further on a tiger's lair was close to the path; but he never molested me nor any other travellers that I was aware of, although on many occasions I knew that he was lurking in the neighbourhood as I passed by.

What struck me most as I sometimes sat and rested on some fallen tree, was the absolute stillness all around, the barking of a deer being but seldom heard, no birds singing, and as a rule nothing broke the still monotony and dreariness of the jungle, at most only the rustling of a leaf, caused by some dark-coloured lizard running over it; or sometimes, if you remained motionless, a lovely orange-breasted woodpecker, or a black one with scarlet head and crimson crest, would afford you an opportunity of observing it flit from tree to tree, hopping up and continuously tapping the stem of each one in its search after the insects upon which it preys; or perhaps you might be startled out of your reverie by feeling a sharp prick on your hand as you carelessly placed it on the rotting log upon which you were sitting, and upon examination would find a reddish ant attached to it, known amongst the natives as the fish-hook ant, on account of its having two hooks on its back shaped like fish-hooks. These hooks are exceedingly sharp, but of what use I could never discover, for once caught fast in any object the ant would hang supported by them, powerless to extricate itself from its dilemma.

Other kinds of ubiquitous little ants were always

in evidence, hunting around in search of food, very vicious and pugnacious, for I have often watched them pursue and capture larger ants that have strayed into their neighbourhood. It was curious to observe the anxiety to escape the larger insect showed, when it found itself being surrounded by these tiny little creatures not a quarter its own size; it would run in every direction, only to be met and turned back each time it attempted to break through the gradually closing circle. At last it was laid hold of by one bolder than the rest, and the struggle began, the large ant appearing not to retaliate, and only striving to get away, until at last, becoming overpowered as its captors increased in numbers, it gave in and allowed itself to be dragged away without making any further resistance.

At Trollah the only accommodation was a house that was rapidly falling to pieces, and the roof was in such a wretched state that daylight was plainly visible through, and it afforded but scant protection should rain happen to fall during the night; some little while afterwards nothing remained of this dilapidated shelter, necessitating a forced march to a hamlet situated at Crute, which could only be gained before dark by leaving Kwala Galeting at the first peep of dawn and after a long day's journey of continuous hard walking without a rest. Just before reaching Crute the worst swamp on the whole route had to be crossed, which was wide and often up to the neck in depth.

Once when arriving at this place at a time when small-pox was raging with particular virulence and decimating the few inhabitants in the neighbouring villages, the parents of a child came with their little one, and crying, placed it in my arms to discover whether it had the dreaded scourge, in the hopes that a white man might effect a cure where all the native remedies had failed. Small-pox was a disease in attending to which I had had no experience; however, if I had told them I was ignorant of the subject they would not have believed me, so the only thing to be done was to try and diagnose the case. After an examination, during which all the occupants of the two houses had come to look on, I handed the child back to its father and pronounced it not to be suffering from small-pox, but from fever; so dosing it with some simple remedies, I gave the parents some quinine to use when I had gone. Everybody seemed pleased and delighted with what I told them, but it was with some trepidation for my reputation that when stopping here on a future occasion I made inquiries after the child, and was relieved to hear it had quite recovered.

During the journey I am now describing I passed by this place, and spending a night at a primitive village alongside of the Sungkai river, which I crossed the following morning, reached Kwala Lepis, or Bidor as it is now called, the same evening, where I found excellent accommodation for the night in the house of the headman of the village.

Alongside of the dwelling was a high platform, from which the elephant trappings were put on the animal's back; they were of the crudest kind, consisting of a few old sacks, then a skin, and on the top of this the panniers, made of rattan, were placed and fastened.

It is curious that in Selangor, and further south, although tame elephants are mentioned as having been in use in Malacca when it was captured by the Portuguese in 1511, now all traces and records amongst the people of the former use of elephants as beasts of burden have been lost in that part of the peninsula, although in portions of Perak elephants are still fairly numerous, being principally owned by the chiefs. The words of command used by the mahouts are of Siamese origin, which shows that the custom of elephant training was introduced into the peninsula from Siam.

The catching of these animals used to be a more lucrative affair than it has recently become. Formerly the chief only had to requisition each village headman in his district to supply so many men, who worked for weeks without pay, often even having to provide their own food as well. As this system of forced labour has been abolished, the chiefs now are obliged to pay the men employed, so that the expense of capturing elephants has greatly increased, and there is always some risk that after all the preparations have been completed the herd may move off somewhere else, and refuse to be brought back.

The method adopted is to build a kraal or enclosure in a valley near some favourite locality much frequented by the herd. As soon as the enclosure is completed, numbers of men are required to drive the forest to try and force the elephants to take the desired direction. The animals soon become frightened, and often break away through the line of beaters, and have to be refound before the drive can be recommenced on the following day, unless they have gone too far, when the beaters go back to their homes, to await news of the return of the herd to the neighbourhood of the kraal. Should the drive be successful,

which seldom happens on the first day, and the members of the herd enter the narrow entrance of the enclosure, it is immediately closed and securely fastened. The now captive elephants trumpet loudly, and rush round the kraal making a great noise, charging the fence, and trying to break through the structure, which has been made of trees securely lashed together and strengthened by numerous supports on the outside. On the inside sharpened bamboos are placed at intervals in order to ward off the elephants' attacks, and men keep guard day and night, walking along a platform on the top of the fence, and at any attempt on the part of the animals to break out they drive them back with spears. After some weeks of captivity and starvation the elephants become sufficiently quiet to allow themselves to be shackled, and are then one by one led away harnessed to a tame elephant; but in order to prevent the wild one becoming too obstreperous or unruly on the way ropes are fastened to its hind legs and allowed to trail behind, so that they can be quickly wound round some tree close to the path, and speedily render its struggles futile and its efforts to escape abortive. The elephants are thus conducted to strongly made, although temporary stables near some stream, and are securely fastened, so that they can do no damage. They now receive the best of treatment; the sores caused by the chafing of the ropes are attended to, their keepers wash them, scrub their backs with cocoanut fibre, feed them, and do all in their power to tame and reconcile them to their new mode of life; for their object is to get them quiet and docile as quickly as possible, a process that takes two to six months, according to the disposition of the elephant, which also has to be trained to carry burdens; but it takes another year or so before its back becomes sufficiently inured to carry heavy loads, and its feet hardened enough to stand much travelling. An elephant is only able to work for a limited number of days at a time, for its feet soon become sore and tender if overworked; and since the extension of roads, and improved facilities of transport, their usefulness has greatly decreased, and their value fallen fifty per cent. The best of them can carry half a ton of tin, although only a quarter of a ton of rice can be loaded on their backs, but an ordinary elephant will only transport half these weights, travelling at the rate of a mile and a half an hour, and often less should the track be at all bad and hilly.

But to continue my journey. The track after leaving Bidor to the north became wider, the bushes on each side being cut back somewhat in order to prevent their interfering with the loads carried by the elephants; but the way itself was no easier for foot passengers, rather the reverse, for these animals when going along a path always tread in the same spots, causing each footprint to become a pool of water, and the path itself gets so churned up, and what is left of its surface so greasy, that it is by no means easy for the pedestrian to avoid slipping into some of the many holes with which it is cut up.

Passing through the Jungkor Valley, famous for its alluvial gold deposits, and adjoining which the lode has been discovered at Bukit Mas, where it is being worked, Tapah was reached, then consisting of but a few tumble-down huts close to the river. Now this place has become the head-quarters of the district officer; it has its club, cricket ground and hospital, and is a good example of a small district station, with perhaps still a somewhat notorious and evil reputation for the insalubrity of its climate, and is connected with the railway by a few miles of excellent cart-road, and equally good roads branch from it in several directions. Upon the hills around are the officers' quarters, and a wooden suspension bridge crosses the river, a fine piece of engineering at a time when only small boats could ascend the river, making the transport of heavy iron material impossible and necessitating the use of timber, which could be locally supplied.

Black cobras, which are scarce in other portions of the peninsula, are frequently to be met with. The country in the neighbourhood is very much broken up and distorted; small steep hills surround the town, preventing any free current of air from circulating and driving away the malarial fumes which arise during the night. Away to the north-east the Tapah river has its source, high up among the distant mountains, over which the eagle soars, and where numerous rivulets wind in and out amidst the stunted undergrowth before falling over steep precipices into the valley below, where, being joined by numerous other torrents, they form one river which rushes down, confined by the steep hills on either side, and is often unfordable for several days at a time during wet weather, when it carries huge trees along in its current, and dashes and splinters them against the large boulders that bestrew its bed and obstruct their progress. I spent nearly a month amongst the higher ranges of these mountains, where the sides of the hills are so abrupt as to make travelling difficult and dangerous; many places of sheer rock had to be crossed on bridges, and such bridges! a few frail, slender sticks with a hand-rail that gave to the slightest pressure, whilst the sticks beneath one's feet danced up and down, supported only by equally thin saplings fixed into some chink in the rocks. The slightest slip, or the breaking of a rotten stick, and the person crossing would have been precipitated two or three hundred feet over the sheer cliff, and death would have been a certainty.

I have seen natives, who will usually walk over anything, stop and turn round, and beg not to be made to cross—a request I always acceded to, for I never forgot how I felt the first time I went over one of these frail structures skirting the side of the cliff, with overhanging rocks above and a precipice beneath. On arrival at the outer side I could go no further, and after a rest returned, and gaining sounder ground sat down, for my legs seemed to have lost their use and to give way beneath me; however, the next time I had to negotiate this same place I did so without difficulty or hesitation, as I had by then become more accustomed to these dizzy heights, and walked with assurance over the most dangerous of these tiny bridges. Perhaps what made matters worse on my first attempt was, that earlier in the day, whilst passing over a slab-rock that was at a steep angle, and had been made slippery by water trickling over it, I had lost my footing and fallen down and slid on its smooth surface, but just as I was going over the edge of the rock my fingers caught in a crack, and I hung with my legs dangling in space, until a comrade who happened fortunately to be with me came to my assistance and helped me up with the aid of a stick, thus, perhaps, saving me from a nasty drop, and probably a fatal accident; for if I had been alone it is quite possible that in trying to regain my footing I should have lost my grip and fallen down the slippery precipice, over which most of my body was already hanging.

Whilst sojourning in these hills I lived in a hut built on a razor-like ridge by the side of a steep escarpment which a landslip had made; until one night the wind rose and shook this flimsy structure so much that I left it and built fresh quarters in a more sheltered spot.

The hills in this part of the country are inhabited by several tribes of Sakais, who are descendants of the aboriginal inhabitants of the Malay Peninsula, and are a pure, unmixed branch of the Melanesian race, being quite distinct from the Malays, and having skulls that approach the Negritos of the Philippines in form, and not differing widely from the Papuans of New Guinea. They appear to have no tradition from whence they came, and are unlike the Jakuns, who have a legend that they came from the north. The latter are altogether a smaller race, and have long straight hair, whereas the former are shock-headed, and their hair is black or russet-coloured and wavy or frizzy. They are lithesome and athletic looking, walking up the hills at a great pace, or creeping through the jungle with amazing facility and dexterity. If seen at a distance they usually dart away, for their first instinct is to hide

SAKAIS WITH BLOW-PIPES.

whilst the stranger passes by. I have often tried to find out where they were concealed as I walked along, but I was never able to catch a glimpse of them, although they disappeared but a short distance off. They are ignorant, not being able to count up to more than three, but they can reckon three sets of threes, and by this method can calculate up to nine, which is their limit. They have no actual religion, but possess a firm belief in evil spirits, and a case is recorded of their actually killing a member of their tribe whom they imagined to be possessed by one, in consequence of numerous cases of sickness and death, and the person chosen to carry out the sentence was the suspected man's own brother. They have faith in good and bad omens; the latter appear to become very persistent if there is any work for which some of them may be required. They are independent and unsociable, only obeying their chiefs; and so little do the various tribes intermingle that they speak a different dialect and do not understand one another. They roam at large amongst the hills with only a strip of bark as clothing, and a blow-pipe in their hands, trapping and eating any kind of animal; snakes, mice, and monkeys are to them equally tasty. They look forward to the season when the wild durian ripens, and clear small patches of forest where they plant paddy and gourds and yams, living in wretched hovels and not caring to improve their miserable mode of existence. They are dirty in their habits, and their bodies are full of vermin; they have no sense of decency, and were formerly very little better than the wild animals amongst which they dwelt. They owe their continued existence to the protection of the mountains, amongst the tops of which they lived, safe from the marauding Malay, who considered a Sakai's life of no more value than a dog's, and would kill one as readily and with as little hesitation, being only warded off by their dread of the poison-tipped darts they

expelled from their blow-pipes. They make a rude sort of music of two or three notes by blowing with their nostrils through a primitive kind of flute made of reed or bamboo. The women wear rude ornaments, follow their lord and master through the woods, carrying the camp furniture, and clothed as scantily as he is himself, and when captured they and their children were formerly sold as slaves. Finding that their persecution has ceased they have, to a great extent, left their homes amongst the higher crags and come down and settled in the lower valleys, where the soil is more fruitful and the climate warmer.

The ubiquitous and pushing Chinaman has penetrated into their haunts, and has already commenced to teach them the wants of civilization and the delights of opium smoking. Living somewhere near their settlement, he gradually gains their confidence, so that in time all the bartering is done at the little shop he has constructed in the jungle, where he lives solitary and alone. His compatriots at intervals carry him what he requires, returning laden with tin ore, which the Sakais have collected in the hill streams, or fowls, which he has persuaded them to rear, or pumpkins, or damar—a resin that is found amongst the roots of the trees, many of which are impregnated with this substance, so that they burn readily—or the incense wood, most valuable and difficult to procure, and all of which he obtains in exchange for some necessity he has taught these wild men to require. After a while he takes a Sakai woman to wife, thus cementing his connection with the tribe, the members of which will deal with no one else, and he thereby becomes their medium of intercourse with the outside world, much to his own advantage.

## CHAPTER X.

Chanderiang—Night at Malay Miners' Camp—A Sikh Policeman and his Prisoner—Kwala Dipang—Sungei Rya—Ipoh—Gunong Meerut—The Sensitive Plant—Coolies' Loads—Kwala Kangsar—The Regent—Sir Hugh Low, G.C.M.G.—The Perak War—The Perak River—A Journey Down—Birds, Fish—The Sultan—Road to Thaiping—Charged by a Rhinoceros—Seladang—Herd of Wild Pigs—Pass in the Hills—Bukit Gantong—Events which caused British Intervention, and the Perak War—Slavery.

NOTWITHSTANDING the previous digression, I only stayed at Tapah whilst a boat was obtained in which to cross the river, and reached Chanderiang the same day, and being anxious to push on with my coolies we started for Kwala Dipang with a guide, who vehemently protested against leaving at so late an hour, and said it would be impossible to reach any house before it got dark. But I was obdurate, not knowing what was ahead, and insisted on setting out. After we had gone a short distance the guide deserted and left us to find our own way, and it indeed looked as if he was going to be right, and that we should have to spend the night alongside of the track in the forest. Night came on, but a bright moon overhead just enabled us to follow the path, but with difficulty. Still we struggled on, and fortune favoured us, for we espied a light glimmering in the distance, and cooied and cooied again. A figure appeared on the threshold and directed us how to ascend the steep approach to the place where he was standing, and on arrival we discovered that it was occupied by several Malays, who had come out for a few days to wash for tin in the hills. We asked for shelter, which was readily given, although space was scanty, and there was but little room, which were minor inconveniences to what we might have encountered had we discovered no habitation. The inmates, who had never been close up to a white man before, were greatly interested in watching and noting every detail of my toilet and manner of eating, being surprised at my knowledge of their customs, and unable to suppress their wonder at the whiteness of a European skin, and astonishment at being able to see the veins in it.

An amusing episode occurred whilst travelling many years afterwards along this portion of the journey between Chanderiang and Kwala Dipang. I had driven to the former place, and wished to rejoin the cart road at the latter, and as over this intervening twelve miles a good bridle path had been constructed, the journey was much easier and less fatiguing than it used to be.

I had started to walk across the hills, and overtook on the way a Sikh policeman escorting a Malay prisoner, who was a noted housebreaker and thief. As we walked along my servants and the policeman entered into conversation; pedestrian feats formed the subject of their discourse, during which another Malay joined the party. The policeman became somewhat boastful of his prowess, and I could hear from the contemptuous way in which the Malays were answering him that his bragging disgusted them, and offended their sense of good manners and politeness. I was getting tired of the conversation, so quickened my pace in order to leave the man and his prisoner behind; not a bit of it, the policeman, after all his vain-glorious talk of how much better he could walk than anyone else, seemed unwilling to be distanced, and determinedly kept up. There were four miles of ascent in front of us until the gap at the top of the hill was reached, and as we tramped along I heard the prisoner expostulate and declare he could not travel at the pace we were going, but the policeman was too intent upon not being left behind to pay any attention, and, changing place with his prisoner, told him to catch hold of his belt and follow along, so as mile succeeded mile they both kept up, the sikh striding on, and the prisoner running behind; at last the top of the hill was gained, and the descent began. Now came my opportunity; although the lithe and long-legged policeman was able to keep up with me during the ascent of the hill, I knew that I could distance him now, and made every effort to do so, for in front lay a long stretch of level ground without any shade, which I did not want to traverse at a tearing pace in the middle of the day. I soon began to hear the clattering of feet behind, and knew that the policeman had also commenced to run, and was more than ever intent on not being left behind. Unfortunately for him, in his emulation he entirely forgot his prisoner, until a rustle was heard some distance back, caused by the prisoner making a dash into the jungle, and when we both turned round there was no one to be seen. The Malays had been distanced, and the prisoner had escaped. I laughed, as the policeman, instead of at once pursuing his prisoner, fumbled in his pouch to find a cartridge. He then fired in the air, and disappeared into the wood where the prisoner had vanished, and presently I heard a shot or two in the distance.

After a little he returned to beg me not to report him, as he was due for a pension very shortly, and started off once again in search of his charge. In the meantime the Malays overtook me, and we completed the rest of the distance in comfort, and I saw no more of our sporting policeman. The affair was no concern of mine, and I was rather amused at the man whose unwillingness to be beaten had absorbed him so entirely and made him oblivious of his duty. Some time afterwards I made inquiries, and heard the prisoner had not been recaptured, and probably never would be, as his first arrest had taken three years to accomplish. The story the policeman gave the authorities of the escape was a very pretty one, but the particulars of it were absolutely devoid of truth; but no doubt he is now enjoying his well-earned pension, and his Malay prisoner was saved from a long term of imprisonment, probably owing his life to this incident; for some Malays are like various wild animals, in so far as when deprived of liberty and freedom they pine away and die, and sentences which to a Chinaman mean many years of plenty to eat, contentment, freedom from anxiety and care, to a Malay signify encagement, from which he only emerges to be carried to his grave. Early in the morning we left the hospitable Malays, who had done their best to make our night's lodging as comfortable as possible, parting the best of friends, and to their farewell of " May thy journey be prosperous," I returned the usual reply of " May thy tarrying be peaceful," and we continued our ascent until the pass was reached, on the other side of which was a high plateau of very productive soil, amidst limestone hills, through which we commenced a gradual descent to Kwala Dipang, a small village on the banks of the Kampor river. Crossing the river, we traversed a fine alluvial flat to Gopeng, where there was already a considerable Chinese settlement, notwithstanding the difficulties of transport, everything having to be carted over a road very similar to the one from K. Lumpor to Bukit Kuda to a spot on the Kinta river that was accessible to small steam launches and fair-sized cargo boats. This village has grown into considerable dimensions, notwithstanding its having been twice gutted by fire.

On this occasion we only stopped to buy a few necessaries, and continuing onward, crossed over some low hills that separate this part of the country from the large Kinta valley, into which we descended; and crossing the Sungie Rya river we reached the village just as the cool breeze of evening was succeeding to the stifling heat of the day, and were accommodated in the guest house of the Datoh of this part of the country, who, directly he heard of my arrival, descended from his picturesque house, with its high-peaked gable ends and a verandah, having on one side stores of paddy, whilst on the other side its numerous inmates were apparently lazily lolling about, but in reality alert, and ready to carry out their master's bidding with willing obedience.

I found in the Datoh a fine representative of the old-fashioned, courteous Malay chief, amiable and friendly, having the prescience to recognize the benefits of British rule, to which he had given his cordial adhesion and co-operation, so different in this respect to some of the other chiefs of higher degree. He was wealthy withal, the owner of elephants and buffaloes, rice fields and mines; his house was situated on the bank of a beautiful river, looking on to the high white cliffs of a limestone hill which, rising abruptly out of the plain, broke the monotony of the never varying expanse of green.

Journeying from this place to Ipoh there was nothing to indicate what a future lay in store for the Kinta valley, a portion of which we were then traversing, and Ipoh itself was a straggling, uninteresting village, alongside of a river difficult of access for cargo boats. A few Chinese shops had been erected, and were apparently languishing for want of trade; there was no one to be seen about, and a deadly air of dulness and quietude prevailed, which were left behind without regret, as, passing on, I halted for the night at the foot of the Meerut range of mountains, separating this district from the valley of the Perak river. Some years afterwards the mines in Larut becoming less productive caused an exodus of many of those employed in them to Kinta, where fresh discoveries of tin were constantly being made; and soon its broad valley, was dotted with mining camps, alive with hurrying Chinese, and resounded with the creaking of many water-wheels, as revolving, they turned a drum rotating an endless wooden chain, on each link of which was a bladed piece of wood that, running in a trough placed at a slight incline, brought a continuous stream of water to the surface. The village of Ipoh leaped into sudden notoriety, owing to rich finds of tin in the adjacent country, and a town sprang up of mushroom growth only to be burnt down and rebuilt, but this time with bricks and mortar, as befitted so wealthy and rising a place. Owing to the river proving an unreliable and uncertain means of transporting food for such large numbers of men during a portion of the year, when through an insufficiency of water cargo-boats might be unable to ascend, and in order to prevent the risk of a scarcity of provisions, a railway was constructed to a point lower down on the Kinta river, which was navigable for boats all the year round; and this railway has since been connected with its southern portion, thus bringing Ipoh within easy and direct railway communication with Teluk Anson, the port of Lower Perak. Ipoh was not destined for long to be the terminus of the railway, as immediately on the completion of this section it was further extended to the northward.

Shortly after starting the next morning we commenced the ascent of Gunong Meerut, over three thousand feet in height, by a track leading up one of its spurs, and made more difficult from having been used in wet weather by elephants, whose feet had sunk deeply into the ground, breaking up the path and making it harder for my coolies, who, already tired out and exhausted by our continuous and arduous journey, slaked their thirst in the muddy pools thus formed as they struggled up the hill.

From the top of the ridge there was a glorious view, although seen with difficulty through the trees; on one side was the broad Kinta valley we had just left behind, with now and again a glimpse of the rivers as they wound through undergrowth which partially obscured them from view; to the eastward white limestone cliffs bordered the level plain and stood in the foreground of a jumble of hills and valleys, behind which long, winding, forest-clad slopes were crowned with rugged and precipitous rocks; whilst in the misty distance the dim and shadowy outline of still higher mountains could be faintly seen. The view to the northward was obstructed by a continuation of the ridge on which we stood, but away to the westward, across the Perak river valley, was Gunong Bubu, standing out with its rounded top 5450 feet in height, and connected with the Thaiping Hills by one of its many oblique slopes, which stretched in various directions. After a short rest, during which my Chinese coolies smoked their long-stemmed pipes, the small metal bowls of which require to be refilled at every two or three whiffs, we commenced the descent to the Perak river, reaching its banks at the village of Kwala Menerang, some distance below Kwala Kangsar. The path from here followed the bank of the river, along which houses and villages were scattered, and wherever the ground was uncultivated it was covered with the brown, heather-like sward of the sensitive plant, a weed that readily spreads, and whose leaves curl up and droop directly they are touched by the feet of every passer-by, leaving a faint grey trail for a little time to indicate where he has passed along until the leaves unclose again.

On reaching Kwala Kangsar my men gave relief to their feelings, and showed their delight that the journey had come to an end by throwing themselves down on the grass to rest directly they had set down their burdens. We had had a long and difficult march of eleven hours of honest, solid plodding every day; and I went over the same journey on many subsequent occasions, both in fine and wet weather, in connection with the exploring, laying out, and making of the main trunk road of the Malay Peninsula, from Kwala Lumpor to Kwala Kangsar, until the route was so well known to me and my coolies that I used to go on ahead, feeling assured they would turn up shortly after my arrival at the next camping place, and I was never disappointed. My followers were of the fewest, as I was generally accompanied by only two Chinese coolies, both picked men, and when not taking long journeys with me they enjoyed well-merited rest. No expedition seemed too long, no hardship I could endure too severe for them. At the end of a day's journey, though tired, they were always cheerful, spread my simple couch, did the little cooking requisite, and in a short while had a meal prepared. Each man carried his load slung on a stick, at one end of which hung my canteen, containing cups and plates, knives and forks, cooking pots and frying pan, all nicely packed in a round, covered, galvanized bucket, the top of which made an excellent basin, and the lower part could be utilized for fetching water; at the other extremity was the bedding, wrapped in a waterproof sheet. Mine consisted of a pillow, rush mat, blanket, and mosquito net, and theirs was similar, with the difference that it had to suffice for both of them.

The second man's load was composed of a basket containing a few tins of cocoa, milk, and meat, the latter only used when fowls were unobtainable, a lantern, oil, and a day or two's supply of rice—all slung on one end of his carrying-stick; and on the other end two changes of clothes and boots for myself, wrapped in waterproof coverings, and the same for my attendants, as well as a fowl that was to be the evening's meal, and which can be very easily and quickly prepared if it is skinned instead of being plucked, and then fried.

One of the prettiest views in the Straits is obtained from the verandah of the Residency at Kwala Kangsar, where Sir Hugh Low, G.C.M.G., lived when British Resident of Perak. The house stands upon an isolated knoll overlooking the Perak river, up whose beautiful valley an uninterrupted view is obtained until the river itself appears a mere streak or is lost to view in the mountains, their lofty peaks towering above the subsidiary ranges which follow the course of the river, and confine the valley for the greater portion of its length; in the garden in front of the Residency humming-birds hover over the flowers, sucking the nectar, but scarce ever resting on the bloom itself; and at the back there is an orchard of orange and various kinds of fruit trees.

On the opposite side of the river dwelt the Regent of the state, who had been appointed in place of the deposed and exiled Sultan Abdullah; and along its banks dwelt a large population of Malays, broken up into factions under different chiefs, who were at first intolerant of the restraints and regulations of the more settled system of government that succeeded the Perak war.

It was a matter of no small difficulty to amalgamate so many discordant elements into a homogeneous whole; but Sir Hugh Low was more than equal to the task, and it was owing to his firm and just treatment of the inhabitants that disturbances did not continue to break out, and that the Malays settled down to more peaceful occupations. He was most successful in his treatment of the chiefs, many of whom were difficult to manage, believing it to be far better policy to err on the side of liberality, with regard to the sum allotted to each in exchange for former rights and privileges, than by parsimony to create a disaffection ready to break out into hostility on small pretexts, and to subdue which would have been far more expensive than the little extra allowance that changed disloyalty into loyalty, and unrest into peaceful contentment.

Nothing illustrates the peculiarities and temper of these chiefs better than an anecdote told by Sir Hugh of a chief who happened to be sitting on the bench, with him and several other chiefs, whilst one of his own tribesmen was being tried for murder. The evidence was so clear that, with one exception, they all agreed upon a verdict of guilty. When the recalcitrant was asked his reasons for his opinion of the man's innocence, he replied: "What do I care for evidence; he belongs to my tribe."

By tact and prudence, fearlessness and a generous sympathy, Sir Hugh Low made friends of the people whose destinies he so successfully guided; and the wisdom and foresight of this conciliating policy was soon apparent in the advance and progress of the country.

During the Perak war of 1876 the Malays in the neighbourhood of Kwala Kangsar, as well as down the Perak river, offered some resistance, sheltering themselves behind earthworks and stockades, inflicting loss upon the troops whenever they attempted to rush their strongholds without first of all bringing their guns into action, with the aid of which, however, the Malay defences were easily captured. The officers and men who fell during the fighting in the neighbourhood lie buried in a small and well-kept cemetery at Kwala Kangsar, close to the Perak river, which is here four to five hundred feet in breadth.

This river is by far the largest and finest of any on the western side of the main range of mountains which separate the watersheds of the Malay Peninsula; it rises in the hills bordering on Petani, whose distant peaks are hidden from view by a series of high precipitous spurs reaching down to the river's edge. As is natural, there are many myths and fables connected with it recounted by the Malays who live along its banks. One accounts for there being no crown amongst the Sultan's regalia, namely, that a former Sultan whilst leaning over the side of the boat in which he was sitting lost his crown, which dropped from his head and immediately sank, eluding all the efforts of his followers to recover it by diving.

The river is liable to sudden floods, when the waters have been known to rise so high that persons boating over low places in the roads close to the river were able to catch hold of the telegraph wires and pull the boat along by that means. The overflow has but little current, spreading across the adjoining lowlands until the river falls sufficiently to admit of its returning to its proper course. The waters in the river itself flow swift and strong, and are so deep that persons poling against the stream are unable to continue their journey, and have to tie up until the freshet has abated. At other times of the year there is so little water in the river that men can easily walk across the greater part of it, and it is full of sandbanks, which are a great hindrance to those travelling if at all in a hurry, and especially so at night. Poling up the river on these occasions the deeper channels are usually followed, but sometimes in dry weather a passage has to be scooped in the sand to allow the boat to pass, and frequently the men have to get out and wade about in search of some feasible passage through which they can drag the boat over the shoals into the deeper water beyond. Travelling down the river is a delightful experience; the paddlers finish each stroke by knocking the handle of the paddle against the side of the boat, and it is their object to do this all together as the boat glides along, passing village after village, whose inhabitants are to be seen moving about, sitting on the banks, or bathing. The sound of many voices, all repeating the Koran together, intimates that the religious education of the youthful part of the community is not neglected; and at night the beating of drums and the flitting backwards and forwards of many lights amongst the cocoanut trees as the native dwellers beneath move to and from their neighbours' houses, pleasantly indicate the sociable evenings they enjoy. The hoot of the owl mingles with the weird and plaintive notes of the Æolian-pipes, made of lengths of bamboo in which holes of different shapes and sizes have been cut so as to emit musical notes of changing timbre, and as the wind rises and falls so does the melancholy music they give forth. The village children delight in making these uncanny-sounding contrivances and placing them in the tree tops exposed to the lightest breath of air, so that there may be an almost continuous wail of varied cadence.

As the rising sun lifts the veil of mist from the river's surface the people emerge from their houses to bathe, the women drawing water for the morning meal. There is a wide expanse of nature's glories

—crags and cliffs and wooded slopes as far as the eye can reach. At certain seasons snipe flit quickly overhead on their way to some feeding ground, and plover circle round, disturbed from one of the islets which they frequent. Sandpipers skim across the water, and in the vicinity of the river's banks there is more bird life to be seen than elsewhere in the Straits. Teal frequent the secluded pools, and the white-tailed sea eagle ranges high up in the air, from whence come the paraquets' shrill cries as they hurry by. The magpie-robin frequents the propinquity of the habitation of man, and in the adjoining scrub, where the dark brown-bodied and black-hooded jungle-crow hops from branch to branch, the nest of the weaver and tailor-bird may be found. In the open a flight of ortolans swarm from bush to bush, the king-crow hawks in mid-air for insects, and flies with a jerky, spasmodic motion, quivering its curious tail, consisting of two long pliant feathers, each terminating in a small black disc. Dragon flies flit about in the sun, a blue-breasted quail rises from the rank grass and whirrs a short distance off and settles again, a painted snipe gets up out of a muddy hollow and flies away with owl-like flaps of its wings. In the paddy fields, buff-backed herons that become nearly white at certain seasons are plentiful, and upon the top of some dead tree a flock of mynas chatter. Around the village dwellings sparrows hop about, and honeysuckers search for insects amongst the clusters of nuts pendant from the tall cocoanut trees. A lovely white-breasted kingfisher may be seen perched on some branch overhanging the shining water, and bee-eaters, with their rich dark chestnut heads, having body feathers of bright green and blue, which present a burnished appearance in the sun as the birds sit resting awhile from their quest after food.

The river itself contains many kinds of soft-fleshed, bony fishes; the tapa fish, which frequents the deepest and darkest pools, the much prized kelaban, and many other varieties are captured. Occasionally fishing excursions are got up, when men, women, and children turn out, and dynamite cartridges are exploded in the deeper holes, the holiday-makers lining the shallows below and picking up the dead fish as they float past; or perhaps the picnickers poison an adjacent stream with a decoction made from the root of a plant, the juice of which has the properties of causing all the fish affected to become stupefied and rise to the surface; but this method is a most destructive one, for it entirely clears the places where it has been used of every kind of fish, killing both large and small. Lower down the river the high mountains of the interior are lost to view, and smaller hills take their place as bend after bend is passed, until even these disappear; and after passing Passir Salak, where the British Resident (Mr. Birch) was murdered in November, 1875, the vision is limited to the fringe of cocoanut trees that line each bank, or the scrub growing down to the water's edge. As soon as the tidal influences are felt, the soil of the banks changes from a nice light sandy shade to the dark mud colour of the lower alluvial lands, and the river broadens and Teluk Anson is reached.

On the death of the Regent the present enlightened Sultan, His Highness Idris Mersid-el-Aazam, was installed in 1889, and he resides at Kwala Kangsar, where a fine residence has been built for him by the Government. He takes an intelligent interest in the progress of his country, and has a thorough knowledge of judicial procedure and the dispensing of justice, having formerly occupied a position analogous to that of Chief Justice with us. Before any material change in the laws or regulations of any state can come into operation, it has to be approved by the State Council, which is composed in each state of representatives of the Chinese, the principal Malay chiefs, a European official, with the British Resident to advise the Sultan, or head of the state, who presides. In Perak, of course, the Sultan occupies the position, and fills it most worthily, for he has a keen perception of right and wrong, as well as possessing the courage of his opinions.

The northern portion of Perak was inhabited by Siamese in the twelfth century, and became tributary to Acheen in the seventeenth; but the only ostensible relic of the latter occupation is the wooden border of the grave of an Atchinese princess in the vicinity of Thaiping.

From Kwala Kangsar to Thaiping is a pleasant drive along a fine valley, at the head of which, a little distance to our right, is Gunong Pondok, an isolated limestone hill, with white precipitous cliffs, whose sides are so steep as to be capable of being scaled only on one side, and the top is covered by small stunted trees, amongst which wild goats are said to roam. The marble found here is quarried and broken up, making good road metal, and when burnt a capital lime is obtained.

Whilst prospecting in the range of mountains that rise beyond this curious limestone hill for land suitable for the cultivation of coffee, I had proof why the rhinoceros is really so dreaded by the Malays, who have firm notions regarding its viciousness, of which I had become somewhat sceptical, for on the few occasions I had disturbed one, it had invariably made off immediately upon my approach, and disappeared. However, my dubiousness received a rude awakening, for on one occasion as I was climbing up hill with some Malays we suddenly roused one of these beasts, which rushed away ahead of us. I commenced to talk, but was begged to be quiet, for when a rhinoceros is in the vicinity Malays maintain the strictest silence, endeavouring to pass by as quietly as possible. We could hear the animal moving about in front of us some way off, and then down the hill it came charging in our direction. Owing to the density of the jungle we could see nothing, but listened as it rushed past close to us, and then we heard it stop, having made a wrong shot, and lost our scent, for these beasts are not over quick of vision, being mostly guided by their sense of smell and hearing. We hurried along up the hill, not waiting to give it another opportunity of returning to the charge, and at last I obtained convincing corroboration of the report prevalent amongst Malays that this animal is very apt to viciously attack intruders on its haunts.

On the left rises the solitary mountain Gonong Bubu, 5450 feet in height, a landmark for many miles round, and on its slopes various experiments were being carried out in the cultivation of different products suitable to the soil and climate.

Away on the lower spurs of the hill, whilst exploring the route of a road, and as I was struggling through some high grass, and had just reached a bush standing by itself, I was surprised by a large seladang, roused from its slumber, springing up and rushing away from a spot but a few feet off, and so close that it shook the leaves of the shrub against which I was standing; but so seldom is game to be met with in travelling, that I had ceased to carry firearms with me, for the chances are that when a sudden opportunity of using a gun does arise, you are either unprepared or it is being carried by someone else at the time. There was a fine herd of these beasts in this part of the country, and I often came across their tracks, but never got within such a short distance of one again, for they are very wary, and I have known of a week being fruitlessly spent in a vain endeavour to get a shot at one of them. On another occasion further away, whilst staking out a line of road, a herd of wild pigs disturbed by my men took fright, and as a river prevented their escape on one side, they came dashing across the path. No sooner had one crossed about two feet away from where I was standing, than I was startled by another one galloping by close behind, and others were to be heard coming on through the thicket towards us; but they were so intent on running away as not to take the slightest notice of any one of us, nor to heed our presence, for they rushed straight on

amongst us, passing unpleasantly close to our legs, and turning neither to the right nor left to avoid us. Some of them were quite near enough to have injured us badly as they went by, had they been so disposed. Wild pigs are coarse, ill-conditioned, lanky-looking creatures, of a dirty, dark, tawny brown, with black bristles on the mane, and they make lairs for themselves by collecting lalang grass or reeds or attap leaves, and beneath this heap they creep and sleep, and the vicinity soon becomes infested with tiny ticks. The pigs are very dangerous to dogs when brought to bay, ripping open and terribly gashing any that may be venturesome enough to come within reach of their tusks, and they are most destructive to newly-planted cocoanut groves, not only rooting up the nut when first put in, but destroying trees of a considerable size, thereby making it necessary to keep the fences around the plantation in good order and repair for several years.

The road to Thaiping rises over a pass in the range of hills that separate the valley of the Kangsar from the fine paddy fields of Bukit Gantong, the village where the former chief of this portion of the country had his residence, close to an artificial lake covered with beautiful lilies and full of fish. Fruit trees were plentiful on the hill slopes, and from here the road passes through many villages on the way to the fine alluvial flats of Thaiping.

As events that happened in this district were the immediate cause of British intervention in the internal affairs of the state, and as its chief was amongst those implicated in the murder of the first Resident, which deed led to the Perak war, a short account of both will not be out of place.

The chief, whose name was Nga Ibrahim, ruled the district of Larut, occupying the position of adviser to the Sultan, or "Mantri," by which title he was usually distinguished and addressed. He was the son of a simple Malay trader, Inche Jaffar, who coming from Sumatra had settled in Krian, and being a man of energy and strong character, was appointed to the subordinate position of headman of his immediate neighbourhood. He improved the district placed under his charge to such an extent, and the revenue he remitted from it to the Sultan was so satisfactory, that his authority was extended to Larut as well.

Shortly after his appointment tin was discovered in a stream. Chinese miners began to be attracted to the district in yearly increasing numbers. The revenues he received from these industrious Chinese soon made him the richest and one of the most powerful chiefs in Perak, and he was held in high favour by the Sultan of that state because of the sums of money he sent him. He preserved law and order, and so successful was his rule, and so many opportunities did the district of Larut during his lifetime afford to the Malays of making money and obtaining an adequate livelihood, that it became quite a saying amongst the inhabitants beyond the pass, that once any of their number crossed it they found it so comfortable on the other side that they never returned.

His son, Nga Ibrahim, succeeded him in 1852, and not only received a grant of the whole of Larut from Sultan Jaffar, which gift was afterwards ratified by Sultan Ali, but was appointed Mantri, and became absolute ruler over this portion of Perak.

The Chinese so rapidly increased in numbers that he gradually began to lose control over them, and in order to keep his position sided with one of the factions, a fatal error on his part, for by it he lost all their respect and his reputation for impartiality. These two factions were composed of Chinese who came from different parts of China; they were very jealous of one another, and cordially detested each other. The side the Mantri joined was composed of Kehs, called Go Kwans, or five-district men, and belonged to the Hye San society; whilst the opposing faction were Macaos, called See Kwans, or four-district men, and belonged to the Gee Hin society.

After a while the Mantri, finding his allies were not so powerful as formerly, turned in favour of the Macaos, and drove the Kehs from the country. The latter made preparations to return, and war was declared, several hundreds of fighting men being specially brought down from China for the purpose, and after a determined struggle they were successful in re-establishing themselves, in spite of the fact that the Government of Penang gave its moral support to the Mantri, and prevented the export of arms and ammunition to his adversaries. The Mantri, who frequently visited Penang, where he had a fine house and was well known, finding he was unable to keep order, prevailed upon a British officer to enter his service, who notwithstanding considerable opposition on the part of the Indian Government, managed to recruit a hundred Sikhs, whom he brought back and took over to Larut to try and maintain the Mantri's authority. Unfortunately about this time Sultan Ali died, and the Mantri, who had become so rich and wealthy, besides being by nature ambitious, shifty, and weak, induced other chiefs to join him in making

## THE PERAK WAR.

an elderly chief, who was not the lawful heir, Sultan, in the hopes that at his death he would be powerful enough to seize the succession for himself. This wrong action led to much trouble, as the rightful successor joined the Kehs in their desperate attempts to conquer the opposing faction supported by the Mantri; and so not only were two Chinese factions at war with one another, but the Malays themselves became divided, and took opposing sides in the quarrel. The district of Larut was transformed from a prosperous mining camp into a series of fortified and stockaded villages, whence issued gangs of marauders, robbing and murdering in every direction. The Kehs having obtained the command of the sea, maintained a blockade of the coast, capturing the Macao boats, and cutting off their supplies. Trade became so disorganized that both sides were on the point of starvation, and the Kehs becoming desperate, took to piracy and murder, indiscriminately robbing any trading schooners they managed to secure, and even attacking them in the vicinity of Penang. The shallows along the coast prevented their being chased except by rowing boats; these were no match for the light piratical craft which glided safely over places covered by but a few inches of water, and disappearing up the numerous inlets it was impossible to follow and capture them. This was the state of affairs at the end of 1873, and during the next year the British Government at last decided to interfere and put down these disorders, which were becoming an intolerable nuisance, and very harmful to the trade of

Penang. The Chinese readily assented to arbitration, and surrendered; the warfare ceased, and the imported fighting men were sent back to China; the British officer in the pay of the Mantri became Assistant-Resident at Larut, and his body of Sikhs formed the nucleus of the present fine police force. The faults of the Mantri were condoned, the succession to the Sultanate was decided in favour of Abdullah, and he was appointed in place of the newly-created puppet Sultan Ismail, who fled to the jungle. Mr. Birch, the first Resident, resided in Lower Perak, but within a year the ex-Sultan Ismail, Sultan Abdullah, the Mantri, and all the chiefs who had formerly been at feud with one another, were already joining in a last effort to uphold the unbridled use of their authority, and before two years were completed the protection afforded to some escaped slaves was the event that lighted the spark of insurrection, and occasioned the murder of the Resident, which the Perak war avenged.

The chiefs implicated in this cold-blooded murder were tried and condemned, and several of them were hanged; the Sultan Abdullah was banished, the ex-Sultan Ismail was allowed to reside in Johore under the surveillance of the Sultan of that state, and the Mantri, who formerly had fought against Sultan Abdullah and owed the retention of his position entirely to British help,—for at the time of their interference his fortune had been dissipated in trying to quell the disturbances, and he himself had become indebted for very large sums of money,—was also banished, as he was found to be involved in these intrigues, and to have plotted against the representative of the power to whom he owed everything. Rajah Jusuf, the next heir to the Sultanate, was appointed Regent, and Mr. (now Sir Hugh) Low, who succeeded Mr. Birch in the responsible post of Resident of this turbulent country, ably continued the good work of abolishing slavery, so bravely undertaken by his predecessor, so that by December, 1884, it was entirely done away with, and the last slave was free. Sungie Ujong had already set the example in 1879, and Selangor in 1880, but the many powerful chiefs of Perak were more difficult to deal with. The Regent was made Sultan in 1886, and I can well remember the entertainment he gave at his house in honour of the event, but at the time he had become so weakened by a lingering illness that he was only able to receive the congratulations of his assembled guests reclining on a sofa, and he lived only a short while in which to enjoy his new dignity and long-wished-for title.

## CHAPTER XI.

Thaiping—Introduction of Pumping Machinery—Orderly Behaviour of Chinese miners—Outbreak of Secret Societies, punishment and stampede—Hospitals—Rhinoceros visiting a ward—Sanatorium—View from the hills above Thaiping—Return to Thaiping—Tamil festival—Churches—Town Life—Government Offices—Theatres and Plays—Storms and Lightning—Malay running amuck.

THE town of Thaiping—the Chinese for "everlasting peace"—a name given to it at the termination of the disturbances in its neighbourhood, is situated at the foot of a range of mountains rising abruptly from the plain, and surrounding it on all sides were the many tin mines that have made it famous. This tin field, which had been the scene of so much disorder and lawlessness, had once more become a populous and prosperous mining camp, but its progression was restricted and limited by the difficulties experienced in keeping the mines free of water. Work had often to be suspended for days together on account of the workings becoming flooded out. In dry weather it was owing to an insufficiency of water to drive the water-wheels, and in wet weather water percolated into the mines more rapidly than such primitive pumps were able to deal with. It was at the initiative of Sir Hugh Low that the Chinese miners imported proper pumping machinery, driven by steam power, to supersede the antiquated water-wheel, thereby revolutionizing the industry, and causing it to be no longer dependent upon the uncertain supply of surface water, nor hampered by the wetness of the season. The introduction of engines and machinery enabled mining operations to be extended over a greatly increased area, for which large numbers of labourers were required, and a great influx of miners ensued, resulting in immediate prosperity. The Government treasury began to fill; the valley became the scene of a vast activity, owing to the regularity and extensiveness of the tin deposits.

To keep order in the states and amongst the various sects of Chinese miners, in addition to Malay police, a fine body of armed Sikhs, recruited from India, was organized by Captain (now Lieutenant-Colonel) R. S. F. Walker, C.M.G. Lately this force has been divided, part still carrying out the ordinary duties of police, while a portion has become a purely military force, which, under the name of Malay Guides, form a unit of the troops available for the defence of Singapore should the necessity arise.

Nothing has been more remarkable than the spread of order and respect for the law amongst the Chinese miners, and this is in large measure due to the excellence of the police force. Only once has there been any serious rioting and violence against the constituted authorities of a dangerous nature, and it was suppressed so severely and so thoroughly that the lesson then learnt has never been forgotten. I have often been struck with the manner in which a large mining camp of many hundreds of Chinese has been controlled and kept in most complete order by half a dozen Sikh police. But it is entirely due to the knowledge that there is an overpowering force in reserve which could be brought up within a short time to severely punish any violence offered to its representatives, and to instantly repress such an outbreak. Whenever any weakness or hesitation is shown by those in authority in dealing firmly with the Chinese, it always acts as an incentive to increased rioting and tumult. Secret societies gave a considerable amount of trouble at one time, culminating in Kinta in a faction fight, which, unless speedily suppressed, might have spread to other portions of the district, for many rumours of a coming general rising of antagonistic societies were circulating through the different mining camps. The officer in charge was equal to the occasion, and immediately left for the scene of the disturbance, accompanied by a European police officer and some Sikh policemen; and after quelling the rioting and arresting many of the rioters, proceeded to inflict summary punishment upon them, and soon the police were busily engaged in the task of flogging the ringleaders, picked out from a large batch of prisoners standing round. After a while it seems to have suddenly occurred to some of these that, as they were left unguarded, they might as well make a bolt for it instead of awaiting their turn to be flogged. No sooner had this bright idea seized them than they acted upon it, and then commenced a regular stampede of

## HOSPITALS.

flying Chinamen. The disturbances had ended, punishment been inflicted, and laughter at the ludicrous incident replaced the faction cries of but a short while previous; for a Chinaman is easily amused, readily giving way to risibility, and once his fancy is tickled and he commences to laugh, he forgets all else; whilst this summary method of punishment indicated to the miners elsewhere the advisability of keeping quiet and behaving themselves, and there were no more outbreaks.

The geographical position of Thaiping (but eight miles from the nearest port) was a great factor in its advancement, and it was connected by a good cart road with Matang, where small steamers could reach, and in addition soon afterwards a railway was constructed to Port Weld, where larger steamers were able to enter and discharge their cargoes on the wharves alongside. Sickness was very prevalent amongst these new and un-acclimatized Chinese immigrants, to alleviate whom the system of state-supported hospitals was introduced, and has since been extended throughout the native states, till in each district there is an efficient staff of dressers and assistants under qualified doctors, fine and airy wards, where the patient is given a liberal and generous diet, suitable to his ailment, is well attended to, and made most comfortable. Paupers receive free treatment, and of others a small sum is asked.

In addition to these central hospitals, the employer of indentured Indian labour is obliged to have a duly-qualified dresser, medical inspection, and hospital accommodation on the estate itself.

Nothing is more illustrative of the uncivilized surroundings amidst which these hospitals first arose, than the appearance one evening of that shy and seclusive animal the rhinoceros, which, entering at one end, walked calmly through one of the wards, passing between the beds of the astonished patients, and departed through the opposite doorway without harming anyone or doing any damage. This was a most extraordinary occurrence, for the rhinoceros shuns the habitations of man, is more or less solitary, and its ferocious character would lead one to expect that it would have injured or maimed someone during its passage through the hospital ward; probably it was too much astonished by the strangeness of its surroundings to care about anything except an endeavour to discover the nearest way of escape.

Not alone in hospitals did Thaiping lead the van of civilization in the native states, for on the old town being burnt down fine broad streets were laid out, shade-giving trees being planted at intervals along the sides, good macadamized roads were constructed, and after a while kept in a repair that would put to shame many a London thoroughfare. An efficient supply of bright, sparkling water was brought from the neighbouring hills, substantial houses of brick were erected, and the town was well lighted and policed. The health of European officers was not neglected, for a sanatorium was made by building several bungalows on the high hills at the back of the town, where many an invalid has since been restored to health; and on these hill-tops, where a magnificent view of the surrounding country is obtained, I first met the clever and able State Engineer, Mr. F. St. G. Caulfeild, to whose initiative and skill the state of Perak owes so much.

From the summit of these hills the town of Thaiping can be seen situated in the plain below; bayonets flash in the sun as the police go through their evolutions on the parade ground, for daily drills are in no wise neglected, and have their place in the curriculum of police duties, whilst straight rows of barracks indicate where their quarters are.

The green of the acacia trees that line the streets intermingle with the red-tiled houses of the traders, forming a pleasing contrast of colour. The sombre shingle roofs of detached dwellings mark the houses in which the Government officials dwell, and dwarfed figures in white, running to and fro on the green and well-kept cricket ground, bear witness that this national game has found a home for itself in this foreign land, where inter-state and colony cricket matches are regularly held, creating a healthy emulation amongst its devotees, who after each innings discuss its events over cooling drinks in the club hard by, where billiard tournaments are held, and where there is a good library of books and the latest papers can be read, and which is the scene of many small dances; and here the Queen's birthday is always commemorated by some entertainment, when the excellent band of the Sikhs performs and further enlivens the scene.

The jail stands out by itself, and beyond are the grey granite rocks, where some of its inmates accomplish their daily task of quarrying stone. The Government offices and hospital buildings can also be descried at opposite ends of the town.

The boom of the midday gun is distinctly heard as the sound succeeds the puff of smoke already seen to issue from the fort situated on a small hill, where ammunition and gunpowder is stored, whilst a short distance away, on another hillock, the Union Jack floats over the house inhabited by the British Resident when in Thaiping.

Around the town pools of water glisten in the sun, and grey sand is all that now remains to mark the spot that was once alive with miners and dotted with the houses in which they dwelt; further away the brown-coloured roofs of a cluster of sheds show where fresh discoveries have been made, and are being busily exploited and worked. Beyond this again is the race-course, where annual meetings are held which the Sultan attends in state, accompanied by a mounted escort and followed by several carriages full of retainers. Capital sport is provided, and as the colonies of Selangor, Sungie Ujong, and Kinta all have their gatherings, there are plenty of opportunities for those so disposed to indulge in their love of racing.

A little to the westward the smoke of a steamer is seen as she goes up the narrow inlet that leads to Port Weld, winding her way in and out, for the coast line all along has a fringe of mangroves with many tortuous channels, bordering on long mud flats, which intervene before the deep water beyond is reached. And the outline of the train appears as it travels along a narrow straight clearing in the forest and passes over the swamp that lies between Thaiping and the port.

In the distance is the island of Penang, and beyond again the coast of Sumatra, where the Atchinese have resisted the Dutch for nearly thirty years, fighting for their country and their freedom, whilst nearer to us lies the district of Krian, formerly one vast morass, now colonized by Chinese, Malays, and Tamils. To the northward, Province Wellesley, a portion of the colony, can be seen, and beyond to the north again the peaks of the Kedah hills come into view, over which country Siam exercises sovereign rights. Turning to the eastward we gaze across the valley of the Perak river, looking towards the fine, bold range of mountains that divides the peninsula in the far distance.

The air is cool and crisp, clouds begin to appear and gather round, a mist blows up, obscuring the distant view, and we look down on a vast blanket of dense vapour from whence torrents of rain pour down upon the Thaiping valley below (which boasts the heaviest rainfall in these parts), whilst we are dry above the clouds, and going indoors enjoy the unwonted treat of sitting in front of a cheerful wood fire. Taking one last look round outside, before retiring for the night, we find the mist has cleared, numberless stars are shining brightly overhead, and gazing down we see the outline of the streets of the town irradiated with lights, and the nine o'clock gun booms forth, bringing with it memories of the past, when owing to the unsettled state of the country no one was allowed abroad without a light after that hour was passed.

The most striking contrasts of beautiful scenery can be seen in Perak in one day by leaving Kwala Kangsar at daybreak, just as the morning sun is rising over the mountains, endeavouring to light up the many crags and ravines that sombrely surround the Perak valley, and its rays have commenced to brighten the green of the paddy fields and to dry up the last night's dew, whilst a shining beam of light glinting across the river warms the fortunate dwellers by its banks, as they sit at their open doors or lounge about amongst the cocoanut palms at the water's edge. But by the time the traveller reaches these hills above Thaiping the day is drawing in, and looking down on the valley below he sees the semi-darkness deepening, for the sun has already sunk below the horizon of the dwellers there; but at the altitude to which he has ascended there is a length of view and expanse of unobstructed vision that enables him still to watch the effects of the disappearing sun as it throws a last flicker of golden light from the edge of its fiery shield, illuminating the sky afar off with glorious rays of colour, yellow and purple, tinged with green, harmonizing with the distant sea; then a beautiful crimson afterglow tints the fleecy clouds lining the horizon, and gradually deepens in tone until absorbed and lost in the darkness of the approaching night.

Descending these hills, and passing an experimental coffee and tea garden on our way, where roses grow and bloom profusely, we reach the plain below, and near the quarry, where the stone-crusher was once busily at work, meet numbers of Tamil coolies dressed in their best, and the women bedecked with flowers; for it is a festival, and they are on their way to the shrine, situated at the foot of the hill, to which they are bringing offerings of fruit and vegetables, and around which they spend several happy hours, sitting, chatting and chewing, or munching hard pieces of sugar-cane, the women buying sweetmeats, scented essences, and soap from the itinerant vendors, who do not neglect this opportunity of driving a thriving trade.

In the distance, overlooking the valley, stands the Roman Catholic Church, and further on alongside the road is the Anglican Church, its graveyard already much besprinkled with the tombstones of many a young man stricken down in the heyday of youth, or British official who, after spending the best years of his life in the service of the State, has failed to gain his pension, and now lies buried here.

Soon the busy town itself is reached, the inhabitants of which are employed and occupied in various ways. The bustling merchant is superintending the loading of a hand-cart with bright shining slabs of tin; stonemasons pick away at granite blocks, hewing them into shape; the baker's assistants are kneading dough: but turn away, do not wait and watch them, for if you do so you will not eat your bread with relish, as you will see them fill their mouths with water and blow it out in a showery spray over their handiwork. On an open spot bullocks may be seen lying with all four legs tied together, for that is the method adopted to keep them quiet whilst they are being shod, as the animal's hoofs would soon wear away, and it would become lame by travelling on the hard roads were it not for the little metal plates that cover each division of its cloven feet. A little farther on is a horse tied between four posts, to one of which a leg is tightly fastened, for the farrier is careful of himself, and should the horse be restive he ties him up securely before commencing to shoe him. Sparks fly out of a Chinese blacksmith's shop as he shapes an iron bar, and steam rises with a hissing sound as he plunges the red-hot metal into a bucket of water close by. A carpenter is planing a plank, and his mate is adzing a post into shape, and a wheelwright is fitting some spokes to a hub. The tinsmith is busy making teapots, which hang in rows outside his shop. The market is crowded with miscellaneous goods, and the noisy cackling and quacking of fowls and ducks mixes with the hum of the bargaining throng. A diseased-looking Chinaman issues forth from a medicine shop, where innumerable nostrums and specifics are sold; and next door a pasty-looking compatriot is watching an opium dealer weighing out his precious mixture. Opposite a cloth merchant displays in his window many-coloured silks from China, and European made stuffs; and adjoining, a rice dealer is measuring his grain.

A procession of Chinese may be seen coming down the street, on their way to their highly-gilded temple ornamented by curious heads of strange device and dragons guarding every cornice. A discordant music accompanies the beating of gongs and cymbals, a blue-coated priest in velvet cap struts along between banners held aloft by officials in conical-shaped hats with scarlet tassels, and behind a motley crowd of Chinamen carrying more banners and offerings of the most varied description—meat, fruits, and pigs cooked whole; and amidst such incongruous surroundings the Chinese belle of the town sits aloft, bedecked in jewels, upon a car covered with festoons and garlands of flowers, whilst a less fortunate female companion follows riding astride a quiet horse. After the procession has gone by the gaping crowd disperses, and the Mohammedan Malay quietly wends his way up the few steps leading to the large stone pond, in order to wash his feet before entering his mosque to pray.

The curio collector has already bought up nearly all the old Malay silver, but the click of the Malay silversmith's hammer is still to be heard as he sits at work punching out some pattern for a silver box; but the quality of his art has not improved, although he looks very wise sitting over his work, wearing huge goggle-shaped spectacles that have tortoise-shell rims. Tamil workers are fashioning armlets and bangles of gold and silver, and a Chinese jeweller is pondering over some intricate and troublesome bit of mending, and his companion is covering some article to be embellished with thin gold-leaf; these latter craftsmen work sitting at tables, whilst the former nationalities squat upon the floor.

A Chinese barber is shaving the head of a customer previous to dressing his hair by plaiting amongst it long threads of silk, so that it is difficult to know where nature ends and art begins in his glossy pig-tail; and his comrade is cleaning the ears of a compatriot, using long horrid-looking implements that make you wonder, not that the Chinese are invariably deaf, but that they can hear at all. Shoemakers are busily at work making shoes of soft yellow hide, which look nice, but become sodden in the first shower of rain.

A jinricksha-coolie whisks his fare out of the way of a coming vehicle driven by a Sikh, who howls at him as he passes by for being on the wrong side of the road, and anathematizes him by calling him "a cursed pig," forgetful that he himself has but little control over the horse that he is driving, for he sits on a footboard close to the horse's tail and his legs dangle down over the sides of a shaft, whilst his passengers sit in a little covered-in cart, the hood of which is so low that they have to creep in, and the only way out is over the driver's seat on to the step below. Should the horse kick, the syce slips off his seat, but the fares cannot move, and are compelled to sit in the midst of a shower of splinters.

Chinese, Malay, and Tamil school-boys wait and play about until their master arrives and opens the door of the building in which their lessons are taught, for the education of the masses is not neglected, and in all Malay settlements the village headman sees that the male children attend the vernacular schools established at convenient centres.

Peons sit in the verandahs of the Government offices pulling the punkahs that make work endurable for the hard-worked officials inside, who listen to all comers, no matter what their nationality might be, with the same ready courtesy and attention. A crowd sits silently in the Supreme Court awaiting the verdict; whilst in the police court the intelligence of the magistrate is sorely taxed endeavouring to sift a grain of truth from a peck of lies, or listening to a Tamil talking a patois and slaughtering his mother tongue, which is the most highly organized of the Dravidian languages. A policeman leads a quarrelsome Chinaman by his pigtail to the station, followed by a throng of idlers who cause the lazy pariah dog that lies basking in the sun to get up and slink out of the way. Overhead a few vultures may be occasionally seen circling high up in the distance.

As evening comes on all classes of Chinamen walk about the streets, through which it is not easy to drive, for they never get out of the way until the last moment, when they give a lurch that just saves them from being run over. The gambling house is crammed, and even outside groups of Chinamen stand about in the hopes of at last getting within to try their luck. The individuals of this crowd come from many districts in China, and not only speak dialects unintelligible to each other, but follow different vocations and trades as well. The miners are principally Kehs and Macaos, the shopkeepers Hokkiens, the market-gardeners Teochews, and the Hylams domestic servants.

The Chinese wyong or play commences, and now and again a general laugh shows that the audience appreciates it, although to a stranger it is monotonous and lengthy, apparently a constant repetition of the same music and the same gestures hour after hour. The Tamils also have their show, but it is in the open air by the side of the road, where an old man beats a tom-tom, whilst a young woman poses herself and dances; but on festival days plays go on all day long, and many take part in them—women in gorgeous clothes, men dressed up as animals; a constant dialogue is kept up, and at each hit or witty saying the listeners standing round laugh, and the tom-tom players emphasize it by beating a deafening tattoo and yelling a cry of approval.

The Malays indulge in a similar relaxation, and trained troupes travel round, giving entertainments. The band sit round in a half-moon shape, and beat their hollow drums, also carrying on a sing-song conversation, emphasizing its witticisms and rhymes, but more melodiously and with less noise than the Tamils, whilst women with long golden nails fastened to their fingers gesticulate and delight the audience with the grace and rhythm of their movements; and at the finish one of them bends backwards, and is ready to pick up dollars with her mouth out of a basin full of water.

There are heavy downpours of rain, and storms are frequent, when the lightning is most vivid; but the dwellings are seldom damaged, although on one occasion, when I happened to be in the Government offices, they were struck, and we all felt the shock as the electricity ran down the wall of the room. On going upstairs it was found that the desk and seat usually occupied by the Assistant Resident had been struck and damaged, though, fortunately, he was not there himself at the time.

Thaiping possesses an efficient fire-brigade formed of members of the police force.

Whilst standing in the verandah of a house in the town, I was a spectator of a Malay running amuck not far off. He was pursuing a woman with a krise in his hand, and as they ran down the street the inhabitants shouted, armed themselves with sticks, and joined in the chase. I picked up a stick and rushed out likewise, but before anybody could reach him he had overtaken the woman, who was now clinging to a verandah post, paralyzed with fear. The man commenced to plunge his krise into her quivering body. It was a sickening and brutal sight to witness, for at each stab all the poor woman did was to writhe and cling still faster to the post. By this time the street was alive with men armed with any weapon that came handy, and the avenging crowd was drawing near, eagerly anxious to strike the murderer down; for the man who runs amuck gets no mercy from his compatriots, who beat the life out of him without compunction or hesitation. When the Malay turned to face his pursuers he saw a bristling array of sticks and paddy pounders (the latter large enough to dash his brains out without much force), and cries of "Knock him down!" resounded on all sides. The man's heart failed him as he approached the advancing mob, so he brought the tragedy to a close by cutting his own throat just in time to save himself from being knocked down; and falling to the ground he spun round, wallowing in his blood, with the gaping curious crowd around, none of whom were inclined to touch him or render him any assistance. The police carried him and his expiring victim away to the infirmary, where he managed to defeat the ends of justice by tearing off his bandages and bleeding to death.

Some people entertain a spurious sentimentality respecting amuck runners, but amongst the Malays the man who does it is looked upon as some wild beast—a fit subject for extermination—and there is no false feeling of commiseration or pity for him. Amuck-running is generally the outcome of brooding over some actual or fancied wrong, until a morbid desire of venting his spleen gains such an ascendency over the Malay that he becomes tired of life, and not only endeavours to satisfy his spite, but to leave a trail of unoffending victims of his vengeful folly.

## CHAPTER XII.

Leaving Thaiping—Journeying on Elephants, their Obedience and Sagacity—The Kurow River—Nearly drowned—Ijuk—Wild elephants—Salamah—Attacked by Wasps—Red ants—Elephants wander, and start delayed—Ascent of Gunong Inas, a disagreeable night—Descent—Janing—Shooting Rapids on the Perak river—Bruar—Kwala Plus—A Thunderstorm—Ipoh—A Coffee Plantation, Death of Manager, typical of many others—British sense of duty.

THE State Engineer having decided to make an expedition before finally settling upon the routes to be followed by several of the principal roads, we made what were to me luxurious preparations for a somewhat lengthy absence, procuring several elephants to carry ourselves, our servants, a tent, and provisions. Leaving Thaiping and travelling northward, our first halting place was at the house of a European who was living in the jungle, supervising the opening of a tin mine, and where we passed rather a melancholy night, as he was suffering from a severe attack of malarial fever, and before leaving the next morning we made all arrangements for his being carried into Thaiping.

Elephant-travelling in this country is a slow mode of progression, for the animal's pace rarely exceeds one and a half miles an hour, and during the whole journey you are never still, for at each step taken you see-saw backwards and forwards with a jerky motion. Immediately the kneeling elephant perceives that you are clambering into the rattan baskets which form the panniers it commences to rise, often without the word of command, and before you are properly seated, so that unless you hold on tightly you are liable to slip off over its tail.

The mahout sits on the elephant's neck, with his legs behind its ears, and in order to make his seat more secure he puts his feet inside the cord that encircles the animal's neck, and to which a large wooden bell is attached, stuffed with grass to prevent it from constantly clanging. It is remarkable with what obedience the elephant will either remove an obstructing branch or instantly comply with the word of command, when told to be careful of something to the right or left, generally emphasized by the driver's tapping the tree with his goad as he reaches it, to give his charge warning that unless it proceeds with caution it will strike the panniers in which the rider is sitting, cramped up for want of space, and unable to dangle his legs over the basket with any degree of safety owing to the narrowness of the path.

I have never seen an elephant fall down, but when traversing slanting and slippery ground it walks with the greatest caution, and when crossing swamps puts its trunk into the tracks made by others of its kind which have previously passed over the place, gauging their depth before placing its foot in the same spot. Should the swamp have been uncrossed by elephants before, they are very

ELEPHANT AND RIDERS.

timid and dislike facing it, especially so if there are many small roots sticking up, for they are afraid of these getting between their toes and wounding them, and each time the mahout drives the goad into their foreheads to urge them on they cry out and bellow. When the descents into the ravines are too steep to walk down, they stretch their forelegs in front and their hind legs out behind and slither down, and their method of ascending is equally uncomfortable, for they jerk and toss the rider about as if he were merely some light feather on their backs.

Amongst the elephants that accompanied us was a baby one, which followed its mother, running loose by her side; but if it happened to cry out, as it sometimes did, she would get into a terrible state and rush to its assistance, knocking up against anything that came in her way. On one occasion the little one got bogged in a swamp and could not move, until its mother came to its assistance and helped it along. Another time the young elephant, being unable to get over a tree that had fallen across the road, stood up with its forelegs upon the log, and its mother lifted and pushed it over from behind. It was a wicked, mischievous little animal, and the drivers always tried to keep it away from our vicinity whilst its mother was being loaded each morning. Elephant-drivers are rather looked down upon by their fellow-countrymen, but their calling is not without danger, for the seemingly sagacious beast, which appears so quiet and steady, is liable to take fright and bolt, as well as to sudden fits of frenzy, during which it often kills its driver, notwithstanding that he may have treated it kindly and looked after it for several years.

We traversed a sparsely inhabited and uninteresting country, crossing the Kurow river, in which some years later I and another man nearly lost our lives. On that occasion we were a party of five, and were inspecting the surveys of a cart road the Government contemplated constructing by contract. Our carriers had gone forward by another route, and on nearing the village at which we had arranged to pass the night we found our way barred by an affluent of the main river, which was in flood and flowing swiftly as there had been heavy rains. One of our party not only was unable to swim, but, unaccustomed to travelling in the jungle, had encased his feet in high jack-boots, and was carrying a revolver in a holster as well. The only way to reach camp without making a long detour was to swim across this stream, so two of us—I being one—seeing that the landing place on the opposite bank was lower down, and that the current would help us along, proposed to take the non-swimmer across by supporting him between us, and it was agreed that he should hold on to our backs and clutch the shoulder nearest to him. Taking off our coats, we gave them to a comrade to carry over and commenced the passage. All went well at first, until an eddy in the current caught our legs and forced them underneath us. The non-swimmer's jack-boots filled with water and weighed him down, and during our struggles he let go of the man who was assisting him on the down-stream side, but fortunately he kept his grasp of me, using his free hand to hold his pith helmet on his head. We alternately went under water and came up again to the surface, but in a little while, his efforts to raise himself becoming weaker, I managed to get out of the swirl, and my vest tearing at the shoulder from the strain put upon it, relieved the weight and freed my arm, enabling me to swim more easily without being dragged under at each effort my companion made to gain the surface. However, he behaved like a brick, never attempting to clutch me, but simply hung on, although during most of the crossing he was under water, and his hand holding on to his helmet was all that was visible above the level of the stream. Two of the party, who had already got across, joined hands and held out a stick, which I caught hold of, and we were soon pulled safely on shore. My companion naturally was very exhausted, being obliged to sit down and rest as he was half drowned, and I also felt queer and tottery for a few moments.

We all crossed safely over, but the State Engineer, seeing us in difficulties, had plunged in to our assistance, and in so doing had lost his hat, in which he had securely fastened his gold watch and chain. As the helmet was still floating around in the eddy, and had not as yet been carried out into the main river, which was quite near, I swam after it and brought it to shore. Someone produced a welcome flask, out of which we had a pull all round, and walked on to camp, where we found our coolies had already arrived, and we were soon enjoying our dinner, with the exception of my companion, who had not fully recovered from his immersion.

There is always some uncertainty every morning, when elephants are used for transport in this country, as to when a start will be made. They are shackled and turned out into the jungle to seek food and forage for themselves during the night, as no provisions are carried for them. In their search they often wander a considerable distance from camp, notwithstanding the hobbles on their legs, and although the mahouts start at daybreak to track up the animals, it is always some hours before they return with their charges, whose footprints they can always distinguish, even should the shackles by some mishap have been got rid of. The bell which clangs at each movement of the elephant is a great assistance in ascertaining its whereabouts, and saves the tracker many a long detour in his search.

One of our camping places for the night was in the valley of the Ijuk river, where we arrived rather late in the evening and after it had become quite dark. During the latter portion of the day's journey we had been unable to see the way at all, but the darkness did not appear to incommode the elephants in the slightest, and all went well until they smelt some wild ones in the vicinity; they then became very excited, and wanted to trumpet. Their drivers were apprehensive lest they should suddenly break away, or be charged by those at large, and they became unremitting in their endeavours to urge the elephants forward and to keep them quiet. We reached camp without mishap, but the next morning our elephants were difficult to catch, and one of them had been beguiled away for a considerable distance by her wild companions.

The next day's journey to Salamah was up and down a series of low spurs that separated the water-sheds of the Ijuk and Krian rivers; and whilst we were travelling along, the passing of the elephant ahead of ours disturbed some wasps in a nest that hung down from a branch just overhead. All we could do was to catch hold of the first suitable thing and wrap it round our faces and necks to save them from being stung, and when we had run the gauntlet we turned round to watch the same thing happening to those who followed. There are many kinds of wasps which make these nests in the trees of the jungle, and I have often been badly stung when unable to turn aside whilst engaged in surveying. The slower and less you move the more likely you are to escape without being molested, but it is rather trying to remain quiet or stationary with numbers of vicious little wasps flying and buzzing all round, for every now and again one will rush and sting you, and if you but lift your hand before having completed your work it necessitates your clearing out altogether, for they will then all attack at once. Sometimes you are compelled ignominiously to take flight and run in order to save yourself; but should you come across a nest of large hornets, it is advisable to keep at a respectful distance, for their sting is most painful, often causing fever, and persons badly stung have frequently died from the effects.

Red ants are also disagreeable little creatures, and equally annoying when a line is being cut through the jungle. They make their nest with the aid of leaves, usually selecting the branch of a small sapling or shrub, and are especially fond of the undergrowth which springs up after the virgin forest has been destroyed. They construct their nests most cleverly; some of them take a leaf hanging on the tree, and hold it together with their feet so as to enable others to do the sewing by carrying a grub that emits a thread of silk backwards and forwards, fastening each stitch to the leaf with their antennæ, and as soon as the grub's silk-producing powers are exhausted they change it for a fresh one, and continue until several leaves are securely held together by a strong web. They are of a reddish colour, turning up and bending their bodies over their heads in the same manner as an earwig, and seizing hold with their sharp, pincer-like tails. They smell strongly of formic acid, and swarm in certain localities, and never cease to torment and molest as long as you are in their neighbourhood.

The leaves and shrubs are alive with them, and every sapling the men cut down disturbs a fresh lot, who go determinedly on the war path. They climb up your legs off the cut and felled branches lying on the ground; they cling to your coat as you brush past the bushes on which they swarm; they get into your hair, inside your clothes, and bite whenever they can obtain a hold, the effect of which is irritating beyond measure rather than very painful. The natives at work suffer the most, for they get bitten on their bare legs and between their toes, and whilst they continue cutting with one hand, the other is busily employed in brushing these little pests off their bodies.

The officer in charge of the district lived at the small village of Salamah, which we reached the same evening, crossing a level plain, where the Chinese appeared to have already exhausted the tin ore it once contained. As my friend had some business matters to attend to we spent the next day here, during which I visited a supposed tin lode that had been recently discovered in the neighbourhood, and where a shaft was in course of being sunk along its course. It did not look to me at the time a very promising venture, and shortly afterwards work upon it ceased, but not before a considerable sum of money had been expended.

The next morning everything was packed and we were ready to start, but the elephants failed to appear, and it was not till late in the afternoon that one of the mahouts returned with the tale that they had spent the whole day tracking up their charges, and had only managed to capture them after a long hunt, and that the same flighty female which had previously deserted at Ijuk had once more wandered off a long distance after its wild companions. As it was then too late for a start we waited till the next day, and travelled in an easterly direction towards the hills, halting in a village at the foot of the range that separated us from the valley of the Perak river, which we wished to reach. As the path across the mountains was too steep for the elephants to climb, we sent them round by a different route, and engaged carriers to transport all that we required to take with us for the next week. Our first day's march brought us to a beautiful torrent half-way up the mountain, and we built our camp by the side of a dark, deep pool, in which we bathed, finding the water very chilly. Recommencing the ascent early the next morning, we reached the summit of Gunong Inas, 5861 feet in height, the same afternoon, after a long, tedious climb, and so steep that, had our coolies been anything but lightly laden, they could not have followed. Near the top I found several specimens of the wild coffee—a plant not often met with in the Malay Peninsula, and I had only observed it growing in one other locality; the stunted growth bordering on the summit was covered with the long, trailing vines of various kinds of pitcher plants; but the peak itself was bare of trees, only lichen and dwarf shrubs grew between the numerous sharp-edged granite rocks.

Shortly after our arrival a mist blew up, shutting out the distant view, and it commenced to drizzle just as our laden coolies began to arrive. It was time to look around for some dry place in which to pass the night, for, owing to the dearth of sticks and palms, building a camp was out of the question, and so we broke up into small parties and hunted round for nooks and crannies underneath the rocks wherein to shelter. We spread our couches on a smooth slab-rock, over which a large granite boulder jutted out, forming shelter above us, and protecting us from the rain. Our men found other places in which to pass the night, and supped upon cold rice saved from their morning's meal, for there was neither water to cook with, nor wood to make a fire. The drizzle turned into heavy showers as the night advanced, but being on the sheltered side of the hill we kept dry until the rain commenced to percolate through the soil above and to trickle over the ledge on which we slept, gradually saturating our bedding, and making us wretchedly wet and cold, for the night was dark, and we dared not move for fear of falling into some crevasse. The morning's view was somewhat of a disappointment, as there was a haze over the distant country, although it was sufficiently clear to enable us to see where the hills fell away and rose again to the northward between us and Gunong Bintang, which is over 6000 feet in height. The descent of the mountain into the valley of the Perak river was at first, if anything, steeper than the side by which we had ascended, and we were fain to help ourselves along now and again by catching hold of some sapling that grew by the side of the track. On coming to the lower spurs we walked right through the abandoned camp of a party of Sakais, showing that the path along which we were travelling was but seldom used; and during the journey I saw alongside of the narrow track a large snake, with head erect and poised in the air ready to strike, within a few inches of the legs of my companion, who was walking on in front. I gave a warning cry, which not only startled him, but the snake as well, for it turned to go away, and we both watched it gradually uncoiling itself and leisurely gliding off. It proved to be an enormous python, and as we had nothing in our hands with which to attack it, it escaped unscathed; and it was fortunate it did not seize my comrade by the leg, for its bite is nasty and takes some time to heal.

In a couple of days we reached Janing, the most northerly station in Perak, and after some delay succeeded in engaging men to take us for some distance down the Perak river. We made an early start in the morning, having previously sent our carriers round by the path to meet us at the house of the headman of the village of Bruar, as the small dug-out in which we were to travel was but capable of holding two passengers besides the Malay boatmen, both of whom paddled, one sitting in the bow, the other in the stern, whilst we sat in the middle, our legs crossed in front of us, unable to move for fear of upsetting our crank little craft. As the height of the river made it more than dangerous for us to shoot the first rapids reached, we were obliged to get out, scramble over the rocks by it, helping our men to pass the empty boat through with the aid of poles and ropes.

A series of rapids, a little lower down, had still to be negotiated, and could only be passed by getting into the boat once more. This time we sat with a hand holding on to each gunwale in order to keep as steady as possible, and the men shoving off we were soon dashing along at a fine pace; every now and then the man in the bows would shout some directions to his comrade in the stern, and the paddles would be simultaneously plunged into the seething waters and the canoe almost lifted out of the way of a hidden rock in front, which we were suddenly almost on top of. The slightest carelessness or misunderstanding between the boatmen (who have a series of cries intimating what kind of stroke of the paddle is needed) would have caused a catastrophe. After we had safely passed the worst places and were gaining more open water I thought for a moment that after all we should not get through without being swamped, for a large rock was right in our course, against which the current dashed, and recoiling made the water so rough and broken that the waves splashed over; but the way on the boat and a few vigorous strokes of the paddles caused her to rush through this danger into smoother waters beyond. We soon afterwards came to the place where we intended to land, and parted with our boatmen, or "children of the rapids," as those accustomed to shoot the rapids are euphoniously called.

It was pouring with rain when we reached the village of Bruar, and our carriers not having arrived, the headman rigged us out in Malay garments, much to the amusement of his household. Next morning, our elephants having rejoined us, we still continued travelling to the southward (making some explorations on the way with a view to learning the topography of the adjacent country and finding out the height of some passes in the hills lying at right angles to the main range), until we crossed the Perak river and camped on a grassy headland on the southern bank of the Plus, and close by where it flows into the main river.

To all appearance we had chosen an ideal spot on which to pitch our tent; a beautiful sward of closely-cropped grass covered the dry ground on which we sat admiring the lovely view of the water, woods, and mountains, whilst below us on two sides there were different rivers; the larger one—the whiteness of whose waters has given the name of "Perak" (silver) to the state — flows sedately and swiftly by, and slight eddies alone break the smooth evenness of its surface, whilst the other one ripples over rocks and stones, a sparkling expanse of gently splashing wavelets; and close beside us was a grove of palms and fruit trees, from whence came sounds of laughter as our men recounted some amusing incident or tale to the inmates of a house occupied by the sole dwellers on this lovely knoll.

In the middle of the night a sudden squall of wind and rain arose, awakening us out of sleep just in time to save the tent from being blown over, and instead of pleasant slumber we spent what to us appeared a considerable time outside in the midst of thunder and lightning, holding on to the tent-pole and to the guy-ropes until the wind sufficiently abated to allow of our changing our dripping clothes, and once more to seek our couches; by which time we had agreed in future to pitch our tent only in sheltered spots, and not

## IPOH—A COFFEE PLANTATION.

to be tempted again by panoramic considerations. Travelling by easy stages to Ipoh, we passed on our way to Chumor some of the best soil I had come across in the peninsula.

Our journey was highly successful, for it confirmed the State Engineer in his opinion that the Kinta valley could be reached by this northern route without ascending the range of mountains that separated the two watersheds further south. The correctness of this supposition was subsequently fully proved by further explorations, during which I discovered a low and easy gap in the hills through which the road now runs. At the same time the line of country was selected over which the road from Thaiping to Salamah has since been made, as well as the road which skirts along the hills of the Perak valley, joining the Thaiping road some miles west of Kwala Kangsar.

During the construction of this section of the cart road between Ipoh and the Perak river, the opening up of a coffee estate was commenced on the very locality where I had been so struck with the excellence of the soil, and connected with this enterprise an event happened, so typical of many others, that I do not hesitate to relate it. The European upon whom devolved the active management of the estate was an old Ceylon planter, who had been in the Straits for a couple of years, and was a person of marvellous endurance, had never suffered even so much as a day's illness, and was far and away the best walker of anyone who had ever come to the native states. Notwithstanding the climate, he could seemingly without the slightest fatigue walk forty-two miles along a bridle-path, crossing a hill of close on 3000 feet in height, and arrive quite fresh and ready for dinner, returning the same distance the next day. I always considered thirty to thirty-five miles a very good day's walking over similar country, and although there were several of us who could do that distance, or walk for twelve consecutive hours over bad roads without stopping, none of us could equal the journeys he appeared to accomplish so easily. He felled the jungle, planted the estate, of which he had a share, and all promised well; but nature, indignant at being interfered with, had her revenge even on this man, the sturdiest of us all, for on one occasion while passing through Kwala Kangsar I found him suffering from an attack of fever which he could not shake off, and tried hard to persuade him to accompany me to Singapore, whither I intended going in a few days. He refused, having some accounts to make up, and coolies to pay on the estate, and declining all offers of help returned there against our advice, but agreed to meet me in Penang directly he had completed his work. As he did not arrive as arranged, before leaving Penang I sent a telegram to be forwarded to him, saying that another steamer was leaving in a day or so, and telling him to come on by that. But on reaching Singapore I received this short message in reply: "Poor Tommy is dead"; and that was all. He had returned to the estate, finished his accounts, paid his men, but had sacrificed himself to what he considered to be his duty, for by the time he once more reached Kwala Kangsar it was only to die before he could proceed further on his way.

Many similar cases occur, and will continue to do so in these hot climes as long as a self-sacrificing devotion to duty remains so strongly rooted a principle as it is at present amongst Britishers. I have often heard a beardless youth, still in the enjoyment of every boyish pastime, and with all his life before him, say to a friend (quartered in some more salubrious district, with whom he was on a visit to recruit his health), " I *must* go back; I have my work to do." An unanswerable argument; and the lad has returned perhaps only to succumb to his illness, with no witnesses to mark or appreciate his heroic disregard of all else but his sense of duty.

# CHAPTER XIII.

Pigeon shooting—Krian—Snipe shooting—A Tamil ruse—Buffaloes—Nipa Palms and making Attaps—Province Wellesley—Sugar Planting and Indian Immigrants—Penang—Its Botanical Gardens and Hills—The dwellers in the Island on the Esplanade—Drying and salting fish—Fishing stakes.

NEAR Thaiping during several weeks in the year, excellent pigeon shooting is obtainable every evening some little while before dusk, when flights of small green pigeons returned to roost amongst the branches of the mangrove trees along the shore, after having spent the day searching for ripe berries in the forest. These birds, which were of a dull green colour with a bright orange patch on the breast, generally followed the same line of flight for some days in succession, and once the sportsman had discovered it, all that it was necessary to do was to find some open space behind a belt of jungle, so as to be able to stand screened from the view of the approaching birds. The number that flew past at one time varied very much, sometimes a flock of twenty or thirty, at others only two or three, and after the birds had been fired at once, they remembered it, and directly they perceived they were being waited for they twisted in the air, and swooped, and dashed past as speedily as possible. The shooting only lasted at most an hour, but during that time very pretty sport was often obtainable and a good bag the result.

Northward of Thaiping is the district of Krian, a large agricultural settlement, which the industry of its inhabitants has in the course of a few years changed from a vast morass into extensive rice-growing fields, only needing an assured supply of water to render the cultivation stable and successful. At present the growing of rice in this district is largely dependent upon a precarious supply of surface water, and should the rain come at the wrong time the crops suffer accordingly, and in years of drought fail almost entirely, so that the cultivators who are dependent upon their crops are often obliged to sell their holdings owing to continuous bad harvests. A system of irrigation by gravitation is in course of construction, and when completed will materially benefit the paddy planters; and it is to be hoped that this method of irrigating will be further extended, for there is plenty of water and many large tracts of most suitable land for rice growing throughout the Malay States, only requiring settlement and an assured water supply to enable them to become yearly productive, and make the inhabitants not so dependent upon imported rice as they are at present.

At certain seasons these expanses of paddy fields abound in snipe, which of an evening may be heard whistling overhead, and flying in all directions, high in the air, circling round and round before settling on some attractive feeding ground. It is only for a couple of months that good sport can be obtained, as the snipe are migratory, and soon move elsewhere, but during the time they are plentiful thirty couple a day is a moderate and usual bag. Walking the birds up is hard work on a hot day, for at the season of the year when they arrive the cultivation of the paddy fields has already commenced, the ground is being ploughed and planted and the water turned on, so that the sportsman wades the whole day through slush and mud, and if the snipe are wild, wisp after wisp get up out of range and fly away; at other times they lie pretty well, apparently preferring the neighbourhood of the houses of the cultivators, around which the best shooting is generally to be had. The dwellers in these rice-growing flats are so constantly working in the fields that the snipe get accustomed to their presence and pay little heed to them; but the shooter has always to be careful in what direction he fires for fear of hitting someone who has remained unperceived. On one occasion, after shooting a snipe near a house, cries and shouts arose from within, and gradually the whole Tamil family came out, so I determined to see what was the matter. The surface of the ground all around was so covered with water that it was impossible to see where I was walking, and on approaching the house I inquired what had happened, but the only answer was a renewal of wails and shouts, and in the midst of the group stood a man with his head bandaged. Unable to get a reply I went nearer, only to fall into a large open well that supplied the house with water during the dry season. I scrambled out, not in the best of tempers after my ducking, and asked what it all meant. It was explained in a broken jargon of Malay that a shot from my gun had hit the man's eye and ruined his sight, but my request to have the bandage removed was met with the reply that his face was bleeding, and they endeavoured to prevent my going too near, pretending not to understand thoroughly what I said to them. Beginning to suspect that they were trying on a dodge I addressed them, much to their dismay, in their own language— Tamil—and proceeded to take off the dirty bandage round the man's head myself, and asked which eye was the damaged one; an unfortunate question for which my subject was unprepared, as he had become so nervous at his ruse being discovered that he first said one eye then the other. I examined them both and found absolutely nothing the matter with either, and left them all much chagrined that their plot for extorting a few dollars had miscarried and been so unsuccessful.

Upon the small ridges that separate the paddy fields numerous traps and snares are set to capture any snipe that happen to alight upon these divisions, which serve the double purpose of confining the water to its proper locality, and providing a path along which the cultivators are able to walk without wading in the slush or damaging the growing crops. Malays are not singular amongst eastern races in their indifference to the sufferings of all wild creatures, and most of them, until taught to the contrary, will pick up a wounded snipe and place it on the stick to die by degrees rather than take the trouble to kill it immediately.

Numbers of buffaloes wallow in the fields as yet untilled, and it is advisable not to approach too closely, for, although a native causes them no alarm and easily drives them away, directly a white man appears the herd collect together and advance with heads well thrown back and noses in the air, sniffing at the intruder; then one of them stamps his foot, and the herd draw a little nearer and shake their heads, apparently debating what the next move shall be, undismayed and unalarmed by your endeavour to drive them away; until a native appears with a stick, when they at once scamper off, and you trend your steps to some other field at a safe distance. It is always advisable not to shoot too near these herds of buffaloes, as they are of uncertain temper, and apt to charge a stranger.

In this district there is a Tamil settlement under the direction of a Roman Catholic Mission; and it is instructive to watch the quiet, earnest way in which the priests endeavour to keep their little colony together and to improve the welfare of their converts.

The manufacture of attaps for roofing purposes is another industry largely followed in this district, for on the banks of the streams and channels that wind with tortuous course through the mangrove swamps stretching along the western coast, where the salt and fresh water mingle, the nipa-attap flourishes.

This palm is indigenous, grows readily, and

requires but scant attention, it being only necessary to keep other growths in check, so that they shall not spring up and choke the plant. The full-grown leaves are cut off and used for roofing, whilst the young and immature ones are cut into short lengths and tied in bundles, being utilized instead of paper for cigarettes; they give to the tobacco a peculiar flavour not altogether disagreeable, but to which it is necessary to become accustomed.

The cultivation and gathering of the nipa-attap exactly suits the Malay, who drifts up with the flowing tide in his little dug-out boat, and making it fast to some root projecting from the bank, he lands, and wading through the mud amidst his grove of palms, cuts off the largest branches and denudes them of their leaves until sufficient have been collected and loaded, when he unties the rope, gets into his boat, and drifts home with the ebbing tide, smoking the while and paddling leisurely along. The next process is relegated to the women and children, and occupies their spare time, as sitting and chatting they deftly double the leaves over a small lath cut from the trunk of the nebong palm, sewing them together with rattan to keep them firm and in position. When finished they make excellent roofing, being laid in lengths overlapping each other, and last for about three years before requiring renewal, although thatch made with the larger and tougher leaves of the sago palm continues good for double that period. The houses of the dwellers in the coast districts adjoining the Straits of Malacca are for the most part roofed with these attaps, which are also exported in great numbers to Sumatra. There is a considerable trade in exporting the nipa-attaps along the coast carried on in large tongkongs with brown lateen sails, owned and navigated by Chinese, who only put to sea when the weather is fine, because the decks of their crafts are piled up to such a height with the light leaves, exposing so large a surface to the winds as to make their smacks unseaworthy in stormy weather.

To the north of Krian there is a wedge of British territory called Province Wellesley, which together with the adjacent island of Penang was ceded to an enterprising Britisher more than a hundred years ago by the then Sultan of Kedah, whose successors have since come under the sovereignty of Siam, and whose country now forms one of the group of semi-independent Malay States recognized as within the sphere of Siamese jurisdiction. Province Wellesley, like Krian, is an agricultural district, and its planters have suffered severely from the low price of sugar; consequently this industry has not spread throughout the Malay Peninsula, as it otherwise would have done, for there are considerable tracts of land further south suitable for the cultivation of the sugar-cane, and only awaiting remunerative prices to be opened up.

The greater proportion of the labourers employed on these estates are Indian immigrants, imported under agreements to work for a short term of years, on the expiration of which period they are free to go where they like. This constant importation of labour by planters has materially advanced the prosperity of the colony, as well as the native states, for numbers of these labourers, on becoming free and their own masters, have settled permanently in the country.

Only a narrow stretch of water separates the island of Penang from the mainland, and it is in this sheltered and natural harbour that ocean-going steamers anchor, as well as the smaller ones and

sailing crafts, which merely trade to the adjoining coasts.

The business houses of the merchants of Penang and the quarters of the native traders are all clustered together, and stretch along the shore close to this roadstead, which is alive with boats carrying various cargoes to and fro.

The town itself is situated on flat ground at the base of a group of hills, and is the chief centre of the trade of the northern parts of Sumatra and the Malay Peninsula. Its trade with the former place has for many years been hampered and adversely affected by the failure of the Dutch either to establish peaceful relations with the Achinese or to subjugate them. However, the general expansion of trade in other directions has now more than counter-balanced what has thus been lost.

A short drive along a well-made road, through thick groves of cocoanut palms, leads to the attractive-looking residences of the European merchants, which stretch along the sea-shore for several miles. Beyond are the botanical gardens, charmingly situated on the lower spurs of the hills. Rising abruptly behind, they form a varied background to the beautiful flowering plants and shrubs, amongst which wind well-laid-out paths that lead to the stream whose waters rush down through the garden from the hills above in a series of falls. The beautiful native, and tropical flora is well represented, the choicer plants being sheltered by small light sheds of split bamboo, and amongst the flowers flit swarms of gorgeous butterflies, which congregate together in large clusters on the ground, forming a mosaic of lovely colours.

The ascent of the hills is made along a small footpath, which winds up the mountain-side until it reaches a group of houses built on the very top, and occupied by Penang residents, who, desiring a change from the oft stifling heat below, come up and spend a few weeks on these hills, from which the views are glorious, and where the air is always cool and fresh. A comfortable hotel makes it also a favourite health resort for others of smaller means.

The dwellers in the island are of different races, and here, as in Singapore, the prosperous and successful Chinese merchants and traders are to be seen driving about in well-turned-out equipages drawn by a pair of horses, which are driven by Japanese or Boyanese coachmen in bright-coloured and fantastic liveries; and passing Chinese coolies toiling in the shafts of jinrickshas occupied by fares sitting inside, and quite unconcerned at the efforts of these human horses, who are often sickly, and always striving to reach the end of their journey as quickly as possible, mopping their faces as they run along, and audibly panting from their exertions.

During the heat of the day, and away from the busy quarters of the town, all seems quiet and almost deserted by the European community; for it is not till the afternoon is well advanced that the men are able to leave their offices and betake themselves to the golf-links or the cricket-field, for wherever sufficient English people reside both these games, as well as race-meetings, soon become firmly established and inevitable.

The European ladies and children remain within doors during the day out of the glare and the heat of the sun, but the pale faces of the latter only too clearly show that the fresher and cooler breezes of the closing day are insufficient to counteract the effects of the (to them) baneful climate. On the esplanade late of an afternoon the scene is varied and animated, for here representatives of most of the nationalities residing in Penang may be met with, and their different characteristics noted. Smartly-dressed, light-hearted Malays loll about, laughing and talking, gossiping and telling one another stories; tidily-clad Javanese, more serious and quiet of demeanour, walk in twos or threes watching the cricket, or a game of football, that is being played by Chinese youngsters to the accompaniment of much shouting and gesticulation. Slim, lithesome Achinese saunter around, carelessly dressed, and seemingly unmindful of the valour of their race that for over twenty years has stubbornly resisted Dutch encroachments, although they would be only too ready to give in their allegiance to British rule.

A tall and stalwart Sikh, wearing an enormous turban on his head, clothed in bright-coloured raiment, having a massive gold chain round his neck, and carrying a large stick in his hand, walks by, and the military regularity of his movements clearly shows that he has served in the Indian Army. He is on his way to take up his duties for the night of watching the residence of some Chinese merchant, or his business quarters in the town, and is seen to exchange nods and greetings as he passes two of his fellow-countrymen, whose dark blue uniforms proclaim them to be members of the police force, and who are bending over a perambulator trying to amuse the pallid-looking child of their superior officer, which is out for its daily airing accompanied by its Chinese amah (or nurse), who stretches out her hand, and waves it up and down, endeavouring to arouse and show off her charge. The Chinese woman's face is hard and wrinkled, for she is getting on in years, and has had many vicissitudes of fortune before taking to her present occupation. She is methodical and slow of movement, apparently overcome by the stiff and highly-starched coat and trousers that hang loosely on her person, whilst her feet are encased in awkward-looking, thick-soled shoes. A pleasant-faced, good-humoured, stout little Siamese ayah stands unconcerned and nonchalantly by the side of another perambulator, with an air which plainly indicates that her present duties are only undertaken for the sake of gain, and not from choice or pleasure; for she is seen to much greater advantage in her native country, of which with her bright, quick, and industrious habits she is the life and soul.

Should she be residing in her beloved Bangkok, the Venice of the East, she either sits alone in her own little boat, bargaining with some compatriot of whom she wishes to buy something, or whom she is endeavouring to persuade into purchasing some of her own wares, which are displayed and spread out in front of her, for her heart delights in trading as well as in amusements. Having completed her bargains, or disposed of her goods, she paddles to the river's bank and joins her friends, who, with their hair cut short to the neck, their yellow shawls thrown gracefully over their shoulders, and wearing bright-coloured cloths looped up at the back, and tied in such a way as to resemble short pantaloons, make a picturesque group standing together in some open space, or sitting beneath a shady tree, and as a fitting background rises one of the many "watts" or temples with which the chief town of Siam abounds, whose plaster coverings are encrusted with many-coloured bits of glass and china that glitter and shine in the sun. Or, perhaps, returning home, our little Siamese busies herself with household duties, or takes her place at the cumbrous loom, and deftly throwing wooden shuttles across the threads, she weaves the bright-coloured raiments peculiar to her country.

But after this digression, let us return to our description of Penang. At one corner of the green a group of dark-skinned Tamil ayahs talk and chatter in high-pitched tones, whilst the stolid Chinamen stand by the railings watching a game of cricket played by the Europeans, and as the cricket ball whizzes past their heads they turn to one another in an amused, laughing way and congratulate each other on the escape they have had, gazing after the ball that has rebounded from the wall of the public reading-room, although it never occurs to them to pick it up and return it to the players; that is left for the more quick-witted Tamil boy, who is also looking on with interest at the game, betokening that he is also a cricketer, and accustomed to play with other boys on some flat piece of grass near his home.

Carriages drive about or stand close by the sea-wall, so that their occupants may enjoy the sea breeze or watch what is going on around; a closed gharry drawn by a small pony and driven by a Tamil passes slowly along, and between the closed jalousies of its windows the eyes of the occupants peep out, these are Malay women, carefully screened from view, although they are able to observe all that is going on around. Quite different is the gharry that follows; the windows are all open, and sitting inside it is a Chinese family, well dressed and bedecked in jewels, fully enjoying the scene around, the children drawing one another's attention to anything that takes their fancy with animated gesture and shrill chatter. The scene is one of recreation and enjoyment, and even the fever-stricken white man, but recently arrived from some malarious district, shakes off his languor, and his haggard and drawn face relaxes into smiles at the kindly greetings he receives from his many friends.

The band plays selections of music, and in the intervals the ripple of the waves adds to the delight and harmony of the evening as they lap against the sea wall, urged on by the cool breeze the setting sun has left behind as a recompense for the fierce heat of the day. But avarice and the struggle for existence are represented even here, for stalking along appears a chetty, the usurer of the East, the blood-sucker of the poor; his head is closely shaven, his coal-black body is nude to the waist, which is encircled by a silver belt supporting a thin white cloth that hangs down in folds almost reaching to his sandalled feet; and by his side walks a Tamil coolie, who fawns upon him, and in wheedling tones entreats him not to sell up his home or to take from him his cart and bullocks with which he earns his livelihood; but he might as well talk to the granite blocks of which the sea-wall is composed, they would be equally unresponsive, and not less hard than the stony-hearted money-lender, once his victim is well within his toils.

Conjurers and snake-charmers from India are frequently to be seen exercising their art by the side of the road. The conjurer stands or squats in some open space and performs a series of sleight-of-hand; he has two principal tricks, one of which is without extraneous aid to plant the seed of a mango in the ground and make it grow into a healthy seedling; and the other is the well-known basket trick, when the conjurer places one of the troupe, generally a woman, into a basket and makes her disappear. In order to prove the genuineness of the trick, and that she is no longer inside the now closed basket, he pierces it with a sword in several directions.

The snake-charmer carries his venomous playthings about in small round baskets made from rushes, and taking the lid off one he deftly seizes its writhing occupant below the neck, and throwing it a little distance away commences to blow his pipe, which emits a dull monotonous music, to which the snake is attracted and stands with its head poised in the air, and when it glides too near the performer he again pushes it to a distance. One amongst a group of Europeans who happened to be spectators on an occasion when a snake-charmer was giving an exhibition on the steps of an hotel, under the impression that the cobra's fangs had been extracted, essayed to catch one of these snakes during the performance and pick it up. He was only prevented from doing so, and thereby running the risk of being bitten, by the snake-

## DRYING AND SALTING FISH.

charmer's urgent entreaties and warnings that the snakes were really venomous and the fangs intact. To prove his assertion a fowl was procured and the snake permitted to bite it, with the result that within a short while the fowl was dead.

Around Penang, as well as along the coasts of the native states, a large industry in drying and salting fish is carried on by the Chinese and Malays, who capture the fish both by netting them and with hook and line, and it is no unusual occur-

rence when travelling on board a steamer to see a light suddenly displayed ahead by some fisherman alone by himself, who never troubles about showing any signs of his whereabouts until the steamer is close upon him and he is afraid of being run down. The numbers of fish captured by the above methods are small when compared with those taken in the fishing-stakes, which are erected wherever a locality is suitable and fish plentiful. These stakes almost disappear from view when the tide is high, but as it goes out they can be seen stretching across the flat expanses of shallow foreshore and along the hidden sandbanks which are so common in the Straits of Malacca.

They consist of a line of long thin sticks stuck into the sand, and upon the lower portion of this fence a light removable paling, composed of split rattans tied together, is fastened so as to prevent the fish from passing through. At the end of these stakes there is a round circular fence into which the fish are able to pass as they swim along either side of the fence towards the deeper water in their endeavours to get round this obstacle to their progress; but when once they have entered the trap they cannot return, and remain until lifted out in a net that has been sunk to the bottom of the trap some hours before by the fishermen, who visit these stakes at regular intervals when the tide is low, to take out the fish that have entered, and returning to their houses close to the shore occupy themselves between whiles with salting and drying their captures. The take of fish is often a very mixed one; large and small are indiscriminately brought to shore, even including sharks, for the latter is considered quite a delicacy amongst the Chinese.

These stakes when once completed are a continuous source of revenue to their owners, only occasionally needing repairs, for they are always erected in positions somewhat sheltered from the prevailing winds to prevent their destruction by storms, and as much out of the beaten track of steamers and sailing crafts as possible to preserve the fence from being damaged on dark nights, when they cannot be discerned by those on watch until the steamer is close upon them or the noise of the sticks as they grate against her sides is heard, for in order to enter the rivers along the coast these trading boats are obliged to pass close to the shallow waters and the sandbanks and fore-shores near where the stakes are placed.

## CHAPTER XIV.

Island of Pangkor— Dutch Fort—Pirates—District Officer murdered —Station moved to Lumut—S'tiawan—Pandah Karim—Start upon a Survey—Tamil Boy murdered—Three Weeks in a Swamp— Thorns and Mosquitoes—A Tiger—Kota Stia—Rowing up the Perak river to Teluk Anson—The Bridle-path to Tapah—Poling up the Kinta and Tapah rivers and descending them.

To the southward of Penang there is another small piece of British territory called the Dindings, which was ceded in 1826 by the Sultan of Perak. It is a somewhat desolate if picturesque spot, consisting of the rocky Sembilan Islets as well as the island of Pangkor, which is clothed with forest trees, and separated from the mainland by a channel, the north entrance of which is beset with sunken rocks and dangerous on stormy nights or when the lights are not distinctly visible. Steaming up this channel, we pass a group of houses nearly hidden from view by the cocoanut trees amongst which they are situated, and in them dwell the fishermen who form a portion of the scanty population that reside in this small island; and a little distance further the steamer anchors in a bay, on the shore of which are the shops of the few traders who live here, also the police station, whilst close to this anchorage there are still the ruins of the old Dutch fort which was abandoned as long ago as 1670.

High and dry, along the beach, are several boats and tongkongs undergoing repair, and lying at anchor in this sheltered bay are various other crafts filled with wood cut from the mangrove trees that line the many creeks extending into the adjacent mainland. The wood of the mangrove tree, after being sawn in lengths and split, is used as fuel by the steamers trading between Penang and Teluk Anson, whilst the bark of the tree is exported for tanning and dyeing purposes.

The Sembilans, as the nine small islets to the south of Pangkor are called, are renowned for the quantities of turtles' eggs that are collected round their shores at the season of the year when the turtle lays her eggs.

The Dindings and its neighbourhood had formerly an unenviable notoriety as being a rendezvous of pirates, and I well remember on my first visit there seeing the blood marks on the floor of the house in which the district officer in charge was attacked and murdered, his wife and a lady friend being at the same time assaulted and wounded by a band of Chinese robbers, who afterwards ransacked the dwelling. Curiously enough, the next official who succeeded to the appointment very nearly met the same fate at the hands of a Malay Haji, who had given evidence in an amuck case in which a relative of his whilst running amuck had been killed. The affair seems to have upset the Haji's mental equilibrium to such an extent that he decided to run amuck himself, and in furtherance of this idea somewhat later crept up behind the chair of the district officer who happened to be lunching in company with the European inspector of police at the time, and would certainly have killed him on the spot had he not been noticed by the inspector, who jumped up just in time to somewhat divert the direction of the blow and save the life of his superior, who was nevertheless so badly stabbed that eventually he was compelled to resign his appointment.

Formerly the administration of this small piece of British territory was supervised by the Resident of Perak, but in 1886 it came under the direct control and management of the colony, and the station and residences of the Government servants have since been moved, owing to the continued unhealthiness of the island itself, to Lumut, a place on the adjacent mainland, which was ceded by the Sultan of Perak in 1874, some little distance up an inlet of the sea, and close to the Perak boundary. Further along the same creek is the village of S'tiawan, which is in Perak territory. In the neighbourhood there is a settlement of Kelantan Malays, who have opened a considerable tract of land, upon which they planted the shrub from which patchouli scent is distilled. Unfortunately such a large increase in the supply could not be disposed of; the price fell so much that the cultivation was no longer remunerative. Some of these Malays made a good living by capturing rhinoceros, which were somewhat plentiful in this part of the country. The method of their capture was very simple: a large hole was cut in a path they frequented and covered with brushwood, into which the animal fell if it happened to pass along the track across which the trap was dug. They were often injured by the fall, and died shortly after their release, which did not take place for several days, nor until the animal had become so weak from starvation that it had but little strength left, when a sloping way was cut leading to the pit, up which it was either driven straight into a cage just large enough to hold it, or led away to one; and in order to prevent its escape on the journey long ropes were fastened to its legs, so that directly it showed symptoms of restlessness they could be twisted round some tree and so render its struggles futile. In this confined space it was kept until purchased and loaded on some small boat, to be ferried across to the port at the Dindings for transhipment to Penang, where it usually died in a few days after arrival, and proved but a poor bargain for its purchaser.

My visit to S'tiawan was for the purpose of surveying for a road between that place and the Perak river, and I was fortunately accompanied by a number of Malays who were accustomed to work for me. They came from a village called Talum, close to Kwala Kangsar, the residence of the Sultan, who reserved the snipe-shooting in the vicinity of their village for himself and friends; and they were certainly the best Malays I ever had to deal with, always bright and cheerful, no day's work too long for them; and if I was anxious to complete any special work they were equally interested in it and continued labouring till dark, and upon its final completion they would return to their village with their headman, Pandah

Karim, who was a really upright and trustworthy man, and in whom I was able to place the most complete reliance. He was a good Mahomedan, acting up not only to the letter of his religion, but to the spirit of its teaching; he had great influence with his fellow-villagers who accompanied him, and at a few days' notice I could depend upon his having a gang of men ready and willing to meet and accompany me wherever required. He was a small man, well past middle age, and was obliged to use spectacles in order to read. After some practice he became quite expert in judging of the most practical line to take across a difficult country, and took as keen an interest in the work and the gradients of the road as I did myself, and his character was of a type that any race might be proud of. Only one other Malay of a somewhat similar disposition did I discover during the time of my residence in these regions, and he in the same way, without showing any signs of authority, seemed to have unbounded influence with the men who worked with him.

As the jungle to be traversed was remote and entangled, I supplemented the force of men I had brought with me by an equal number of strangers, about whom I knew nothing, and being anxious to commence working, took them on with as little delay as possible. Before I had gone far I recognized that I had to deal with a rough and queer lot, so gradually sent them all away and replaced them with others, as it was not pleasant dealing with men who refused to work, and who upon the slightest reprimand scowled and seized the handles of their parangs, intimating that if they only dared they would cut you down.

After some days, while I was working near camp, I heard a shout and answered it, but was unable to locate its exact direction, so concluded, after I had replied once more, that it was only someone collecting rattan calling to his companion, and continued what I was engaged upon until evening, when we all returned to camp together, and were met by a gruesome sight, for on the ground my Tamil servant, Pombayan, was lying quite dead with his throat cut, and the camp had been looted of everything that was of any value. There were indications where the struggle had taken place, and my camp bed was bespattered with my poor servant's blood, for he had fallen on to it; and a cut in front, as well as three cuts on the back of his head, showed how he had been felled and hacked whilst on the ground, and then dragged and thrown outside, where his throat was gashed from ear to ear to prevent any chance of his survival.

My camp was built at some distance away in the jungle, so it was exceedingly improbable that anybody should have chanced upon it; and as one of my workmen was absent during the whole day, although he had promised to return, my suspicions were aroused, and lighting torches I started for S'tiawan, and amongst the throng that crowded round my men when they were recounting what had happened was the man I was in pursuit of, so I had him arrested, and his house was searched, but he had made good use of his ten hours' grace, and his clothes were found hanging up wringing wet, but he had forgotten to clean his parang sheath, upon which were splashes of blood. Unfortunately, at this time Perak had been to some extent denuded of her police force and police officers, for service in Pahang, to which place they had been dispatched to quell some disturbances that had broken out amongst a portion of its inhabitants who were dissatisfied and discontented with the imposition of the Residential system; so that it was some while before any real steps were taken to work up the case, and in the meanwhile the man's friends had not been idle, and nothing could be found in his possession or in that of others to connect him with the murder, although he had been seen going and returning from the direction in which my camp was situated. His clothing, upon a portion of which were blood stains, and other things he wore on the day of the murder were sent from Perak to the Government analyst at Singapore, but on the journey thither the mail-bag which contained them fell into the water as it was being transhipped at Penang, and the contents were so soaked that nothing could be done with them. All this untoward chain of events prevented the assassin's being brought to justice, and the murder ranks amongst the number of those crimes of which the culprits have never been discovered. Amongst the Malays, life, and especially that of an unbeliever, is held of such slight value that none of that race would willingly give evidence against his compatriot, unless he had some private spite to satisfy, or revenge to gratify.

Pombayan was a Tamil, a native of Puducottah in Southern India, and at the time of his death he had been with me for sixteen years, having entered my service when quite a lad, and had accompanied me on a great many of my travels, although I used to leave him at home when possible, because he never quite recovered from the frequent attacks of malarial fever contracted during the early years of pioneering upon the hills and the hardships he then endured; but during the whole time he was a thoroughly faithful and attached companion, and I felt his loss keenly.

Another of my servants was a Chinaman, who was with me for ten years, and when I returned to civilization once more and related to him what had occurred in the meanwhile, his first exclamation was that he must accompany me, and he did so on the next expedition I made; but as he was elderly I usually delegated to him the looking after my house during my absence. He had a wife and family in China, whom he used to go and see at intervals of several years, always coming back at the agreed-upon date. He was loyal and trustworthy, and on being told on his return from China that I was not returning to the East, he sat down on the steps of the verandah and gave vent to his feelings by weeping, and refused for some time to be comforted.

The Hailam Chinese make excellent servants, and they are perfectly honest with anyone who treats them well and understands them. They are born cooks, all knowing something of the culinary art, so that there is never any difficulty in finding a person to cook at a pinch; and as long as you have a reliable head *boy*, as these servants are called, he can always obtain under ones at the shortest notice. Constant travelling about necessitated my keeping three servants, as the journeys knocked them up, and it was necessary for them to rest, and to take it in turns to accompany me. I usually arranged to take the youngest on my roughest excursions, and after six months he generally used to try and obtain some easier situation.

On many future occasions, when accompanied by some of the men who were with me at that time, I often heard the story of Pombayan's murder repeated to new-comers sitting round the camp-fire of an evening, who always inquired what I did when I arrived in camp and found my servant murdered, and upon being told that I was much distressed invariably replied, " How strange, I did not think that a white man would really care what happened to a black one."

But to return to the survey upon which I was engaged, and where, after moving camp several times, we erected one on a nice sandy ridge not far from the seashore and bordering upon a vast swamp, across which we were obliged to pass in order to reach the Perak river. Our camp consisted of a rough shelter open all round and quite unprotected. It was not pleasant each morning on waking up to see the footprints of a tigress and her cubs, who had been disporting and amusing themselves close to where we had been sleeping, but owing to the darkness of the nights we had been unable to perceive them, and never knew of their presence until daybreak. As this sandy ridge appeared to be the regular playground of these animals, we changed our camp into the swamp itself, building it upon the roots of trees and sticks above the level of the water. After proceeding a short distance the character of the swamp changed, and instead of wading waist-deep in mud we found that a little distance below the surface of the ground the earth was fairly hard and firm, and the water only occasionally more than knee-deep. Progress would have been less difficult had it not been for continuous clumps of thorns, the stems of which were covered with sharp needle-like spikes, necessitating the use of a pronged stick with which to cast them on one side when cut, as they were too prickly to take hold of. Even when a passage had been cleared it took the whole day for my men to change camp a mile and a half, so tedious was it for them to carry their burdens over the track strewn with long spiked thorns and bristling with prickly roots, and to cut sticks at the end of their journey with which to build a new camp.

Most of the men wore canvas shoes, which in great measure protected their feet, as the thorns could not penetrate the leather soles, but they readily pierced the canvas tops; and every evening after work a considerable time was spent by the coolies cutting out and extracting thorns from their hands and limbs.

Nearly as numerous as the thorns were the black clouds of mosquitoes that settled upon your clothes and face and hands, and which it was vain to try and escape from, and useless to brush off, for others immediately took their place. At first they were most vexatious, but after a day or so they ceased to give the same annoyance, for the irritation caused by their proboscis piercing your flesh was so continuous that you became accustomed to it, and no bad results followed; for although their bite is often poisonous, creating painful swellings and sometimes sores on newcomers, it ceases to have any effect upon those who have resided some while in the tropics and become acclimatized, and is only troublesome at the time and for a few hours afterwards. Their constant buzzing and trumpeting could be heard all the day long, and at night they persistently tried to find some small opening in the mosquito nets through which they could enter. Over three weeks were spent in this morass of roots and thorns, of mud and water, always wet and damp, where the sun never penetrated, and where the vision was circumscribed, being limited by a thick and thorny tangle that not only prevented anything from being seen at a distance of a few yards, but also obstructed progress, as it was impossible to penetrate it without a considerable amount of cutting. It was only along this narrow cleared track fenced by the thorns thrown to each side that it was practicable to walk at all; and if twenty men chopping steadily for eight hours succeeded in making half a mile of progress it was a satisfactory day's work, and had there been much rain as well life would have been almost unendurable.

The only river we came to was so blocked with

rank, coarse grasses, that we were able to cross —although it was of considerable depth—by simply walking on the top of the matted growth, which was sufficiently strong to easily support our weight and allow us to walk across with scarcely wetting more than the soles of our feet. Two days more after crossing this river brought us to the bank of the Perak river, and into the glare of the sun once more, and it was a delightful change to see signs of life and human habitations.

The day before getting out into the open, after work was finished, I lingered somewhat behind my men, who returned to camp, and on my arrival there one of them inquired of me in a quizzing manner whether I had seen anything by the way, and on my replying in the negative I was informed that as they were walking along a tiger had growled at them quite close by, and since their arrival they had been wondering whether I should encounter it on my way back alone.

Before ascending the Perak river I stopped a day at the police station at Kota Stia, which was in charge of a Sikh corporal who had been all through the Afghan war, and about which he related many interesting reminiscences. The village is situated on the banks of the river, and the centre of the attap trade of Lower Perak.

I have already described in a previous chapter the same industry on a smaller scale in the district of Krian, but a much larger one is carried on here. The fortunate dwellers along the banks of the river, as far as the tide extends, possess groves of these attap palms, so that all the year round a lucrative occupation is close at hand, and they can at any moment sally forth and cut and make the attap thatch, for which a ready market exists; and not only that, but the Chinese traders are always only too ready to advance money or goods to be repaid in kind at a small reduction on the prevailing market price.

Several Chinese tongkongs were anchored in the river off the village loading these attap-leaves for shipment to Sumatra, where they are much used to thatch the large sheds in which tobacco plants, after being cut, are hung up to dry and wither before the leaves are detached and fermented; while yet more tongkongs were waiting for a favourable breeze before putting to sea. The crew of these craft live in a little cabin in the poop, which has a window looking out astern; but should one of the sailors fall overboard at any time he need look for no assistance from his comrades, who consider it unlucky to rescue a drowning person, and imagine that some calamity would certainly overtake them if they did so. Steamers used to load firewood off this place, but the mangrove trees have been so much destroyed and cut in the neighbourhood that the trade in fuel has been abandoned.

Near to Kota Stia were the remains of an old Siamese fort, and not far off a stretch of land now covered by forest trees, and known by the name of "Bendong Siam," or the paddy fields of the Siamese. There is a tradition amongst the present inhabitants that a large settlement of these people existed, and certainly there were signs that a considerable extent of country in this district had been under cultivation at some former time. No doubt this neighbourhood was a peculiarly well-suited one for the residence of conquering and marauding settlers, as they were remote enough from the districts populated by the Malays to be safe from any sudden raids, whilst the river was broad and sufficiently deep to allow of their ships lying safely at anchor, and guarding the only route by which any numbers could come to attack them. They were able to collect their toll on the trade of the country without difficulty, as a considerable proportion of the imports and exports had of necessity to pass up or down the Perak river. At the same time they had an ample expanse of suitable land on which to grow sufficient rice for their own wants, and were close to the sea, whence they could not only obtain the fish they themselves needed, but were able to monopolize the industry of drying and salting them; the sandbanks off the coast in this neighbourhood being still noted for the quantities of fish daily taken in the fishing-stakes by those pursuing this trade.

As the tide commenced to flow in the morning we embarked in a small boat, having an easily removable roof at the stern made from the leaves of the nipa palm, which sewn together make an excellent covering, keeping out the sun and rain, and lasting for a considerable while. My bedding was spread under this shelter upon a flat deck, made by covering sticks placed crosswise with a flooring of cut rattan, upon which a mat is placed.

The roof came down so close as only to permit of the occupant's adopting a sitting position, and if he wishes to stand upright, he is obliged to crawl out of this shelter before he can do so. Lazily reclining on my couch I read a book, whilst my boy was busy preparing food in the bows of the boat, which, propelled by the rowers, and assisted by the incoming tide, travelled along at a fair pace, passing on the way Kota Blanda, the site of a fort built during Dutch supremacy, as well as several huge roots of the attap palm, which, growing close to the water's edge, had become detached and fallen into the stream, and were carried up or down by the flowing or ebbing tide until caught by some overhanging branches, or taken out to sea.

On one occasion, floating in a boat up this river by night, my boatmen lost their way in the darkness, and I awoke to find the boat amongst some trees growing in a backwater which impeded our further progress, and none of us knew in the slightest degree where we were. Daylight enabled us to extricate ourselves by cutting our way through the bushes, following the direction of the ebbing water until it brought us back into the river again; but it was early the next morning before we reached Teluk Anson, so the mishap delayed us some twelve hours on the journey. This time my rowers endeavoured to save the tide, which had already changed, but had not gained sufficient strength to entirely stop us as we turned round the last bend in the river and the town came into view, the first name of which, Teluk, means promontory in Malay, and the last word, Anson, was the name of a former Lieutenant-Governor of Penang. The old port of this part of Perak was called Durian Sebatang, but owing to the silting of the river and some difficult turns it was abandoned, and the present place being selected as suitable, the jungle was cleared and the site of the town located; but at high tides the water rises in the ditches, and the ground itself becomes moist and sodden, so that it is anything but an agreeable place of residence.

The town consists of a number of wooden houses, with plank walls and tiled roofs. The railway now transports goods into the interior, to the tin-mining districts of Tapah and Kinta, but at the time of my first visit Teluk Anson was an isolated village with absolutely no roads, and the interior could only be reached by taking boat. As far as foot passengers were concerned this was not to last long, for a small bridle path was made to Tapah, through a district where not a single house was met with on the line.

The first time I made the journey—walking over the narrow track, cleared with the aid of a compass, and from which the smaller saplings had been cut a short distance from the ground, so that their stumps required to be carefully avoided in walking along—I outpaced my carrying coolies, who could only proceed slowly and with difficulty, so sat down to await their coming, as I did not wish to leave them altogether for fear they should lose their way. Whilst waiting I was interested to hear a bear and her cubs snorting and grunting not far off, which were entirely unaware of my presence. Bears are but seldom encountered in these parts, and are mostly small and not vicious like those of Ceylon, which will follow and attack the wayfarer, even when unprovoked and unmolested; nor can they compare with the fine bears to be met with in the Rocky Mountains and other parts of America and Canada.

The cutting of the road was very unhealthy work and difficult of accomplishment, for the real Perak Malay has an aversion to manual labour when it can possibly be avoided, and the work had to be carried out by Chinese but lately arrived in the country, unacclimatized and unused to the felling and uprooting of trees, besides knowing nothing as to the manner in which the earthwork of the road should be commenced, necessitating constant teaching and continuous supervision. The village of Tapah even now is noted for a peculiar fever that attacks those living in it; especially is it so with Europeans, who seldom escape if their residence is of any duration.

After the path was finished it was constantly being damaged by elephants, who during the wet weather made many holes in the portions over which they walked, but fortunately did not venture to test the strength of the bridges that crossed the many streams. Even when the railway was constructed these animals trampled about its banks, and one large tusker went so far in his dislike to the innovations of civilization as to dispute the passage of a train. In this encounter, however, he came off badly, for he was instantly knocked down and killed.

The twenty-four miles of bridle path connecting Tapah with Teluk Anson were extremely fatiguing to walk along during wet weather owing to the greasy and slippery nature of the soil for a considerable proportion of the journey. At each step forward the foot would slip back nearly as much as the distance gained; half way, a house where travellers could pass the night was erected, and on one occasion, while walking along this road, I met a friend who had lately been employed in erecting a cairn of stones for trigonometrical observations on the summit of Gunong Inas, where we had spent such an unpleasant night. He seemed to have had an equally uncomfortable stay, though for a longer period, and was now *en route* to some mountain beyond Tapah. During our conversation I discovered he had passed the night at the half-way house, only having heard on his arrival that two men had died there of cholera a few days before, but as it was raining at the time, and too late to continue his journey until the following day, he was forced to remain there. The path happened to be more slippery than usual and travelling was very difficult, and as we rose to part he said that this walk always appeared to him the longest journey he knew of anywhere. But he was shortly on a longer and more distant one, however, for before many more days' sun had set the cholera had claimed him as a victim.

Close to the bank of the river adjoining the town of Teluk Anson numerous boats were tied, and these so increased in numbers as the interior of the state became opened up and developed as to be quite a wonderful sight shortly before the railway was completed. The boats stretched out into the river two or three feet deep, and were either waiting to be loaded, or for the tide to turn to help them on the first portion of the journey up the different streams which joined the main river above this port. The steamers discharged their cargoes in many instances direct into these broad, shallow boats until there were but a very few inches of freeboard left before their rowers were satisfied that they were sufficiently loaded. The crews in some instances consisted of Chinese, in other cases of Malays, the former always possessing larger boats and fitted with a plank outside upon which the polers walked, whereas the latter had smaller boats and the polers walked up and down inside the gunwale of the boat itself, and thus were able to navigate smaller and swifter rivers than the former. Once these boats were loaded the crew were anxious to get away on to the higher reaches of the river, where the wind was powerless to disturb the surface of the water, for they dreaded the slightest ripple for fear it should swamp their craft; but when they got into the narrower streams that flowed from the Kinta and Tapah hills their perils were not over, for snags and roots and sunken trees were a constant source of danger, and many were the boats upset in ascending and descending these rivers. The sharp corners, when the currents were strong, were difficult to turn, and it was no uncommon thing for the polers to have to exert all their efforts to keep the boat stationary and to prevent her being swept down by the current,

THE TAPAH RIVER.

which nevertheless sometimes happened. The men were often hurt trying to fend her off the trees and bushes that line the banks, and were obliged to tie up for several days until the freshet ceased and the volume of the descending waters had decreased.

On the Tapah river, where it usually took a week or more to pole up a laden boat against the stream, the descent could be made within the twenty-four hours; and very exhilarating it was to be swept rapidly down, especially if the river happened to be in flood. The steerer sat in the stern of the boat, two rowers occupied the thwarts, ready to row when necessary, whilst another man stood in the bows, pole in hand, every now and again calling on the helmsman who manipulated a large circular paddle fixed to the stern of the boat, which made a powerful rudder, and could not only be turned to both sides, but also used as an oar, either to straighten the course of the boat or to keep her off the bank.

The voyagers were sure to be once or twice carried against the river sides and to get mixed up amongst the branches and thorns, of which a species known as "wait a bit," having long trails covered with fish-hook thorns that catch and tear your clothes, and were sometimes even so numerous as to stop the boat itself. All had knives handy to cut these long, overhanging, whip-like detainers should they catch hold of anyone, and all loose articles had to be stowed carefully out of the way. Once I took off my coat and left it by my side, but it was not long before it was snatched out of the boat and I saw it disappearing in the water as we rounded the next corner, for we could not stop for some distance, and then all chance of recovering my lost property, which contained my watch and note-book, was gone. Cargoes were frequently lost, and the merchant up country never knew whether his goods would come to hand or not; but these accidents did not so often happen to the boats carrying tin down stream as to the ascending ones laden with miscellaneous merchandise, for the downward freight was so much more valuable that the traders insisted upon the boats being lightly loaded, which was practicable, as the weight and bulk of the goods imported largely exceeded that of those exported from these districts.

# CHAPTER XV.

Mr. Noel Denison—An arduous Exploration through Floods—Destruction of Gutta Trees—Method of collecting Gutta by Dyaks—Through the Floods of the Bernam River—Fever-stricken Followers—Rembau, its Stockades, Politics, and Inhabitants—Tampin—Johol—Jempol—Ulu-Moar—S'trimenanti—Exploring—A Message from the Datoh—Small-pox—A Cock Fight—Coffee trees—Fruit trees—Irrigation—Graves—Eam Tuan of S'trimenanti—Bukit Putus, its Defence and Capture—Meeting between Sir Frederick A. Weld and Chiefs.

THE district of Lower Perak, of which Teluk Anson was the chief town — and where the Government offices of the superintendent's staff are situated—was fortunate in having Mr. Noel Denison as principal officer, an indefatigable and zealous official, and very popular amongst Malays, and the phenomenal success of the agricultural district of Krian was due to his hard work and exertions; for at his advent, there was no population, but before he left settlers had come from many parts, and had brought quite a large area under cultivation. So much was he respected and liked by the inhabitants, that upon his death they wished to erect some memorial to the officer who had done so much for them and benefited the district generally; but the Government used its influence, perhaps wisely, to prevent the scheme being carried out by the public, and itself perpetuated his memory by a tablet let into a water-tower then in course of erection.

Some distance below Teluk Anson a canal is cut, joining the Perak with the Bernam river further to the south, and which was made to enable the small river boats to proceed from one river to the other without going out to sea, along a coast so liable to sudden squalls.

The most trying journey, although it was only of short duration, I ever made was from Teluk Anson, during the rainy season, to explore a line of country between the Bernam river on the one side and the valley of the Sungkai river on the other. It rained every day; all the rivers were in flood, and it was with the object of discovering the extent of country inundated, and the feasibility of constructing a road, that the exploration was undertaken. I commenced by spending over a week partially immersed in mud and water, where the Sungkai river had overflowed its banks, and where our camp each evening had to be constructed above the flood water, a tedious proceeding causing much delay; and besides, there was the uncertainty of how high the water all around us would rise during the night from the continuous rain, or a freshet, coming down from the higher lands, might at any moment have made further progress impossible. The thorny growth was not so dense as seriously to impede our progress, which was fairly good, although it rained constantly, but of that we took little notice, and beyond causing all our clothes to become saturated and sodden it did not retard our movements. At last we reached a

## DESTRUCTION OF GUTTA TREES.

village by the banks of the river, and here we took a well-earned rest, mending and drying our wearing apparel and laying in a stock of fresh provisions for the continuance of our journey.

Leaving this village we skirted and traversed some hills, where numbers of gutta-producing trees were lying in the jungle in every direction; and this portion of the country probably had remained untouched

until a party of Dyaks from Borneo came over to collect gutta in these parts, and they are so accustomed to this employment that they scarcely leave a gutta-producing tree undiscovered. Their method of obtaining the juice is wasteful in the extreme, for not content with tapping the trees and obtaining a small quantity at frequent intervals, they devastate the woods of gutta trees by cutting them down, so that they may make as much profit as possible as the result of their expedition. Having felled the tree, they cut rings through the bark round its stem and branches about a foot apart, into which channels the juice flows, coagulates, and is collected. Large and small trees are indiscriminately cut down, and the whole country is denuded of its gutta trees in a very short while. From indications remaining, the collectors must have had a very successful expedition in these regions, as numbers of trees were met with which had been entirely destroyed and were lying rotting on the ground. The moist climate and frequent showers of the Malay States appear to be especially favourable to these trees, which are indigenous, grow luxuriantly, and yield copiously. In fact, taking example from the few trees that have escaped destruction, or have been grown near some Malay house, whose owner has been content to tap the tree frequently and has not cut it down, there is no reason to doubt that the quantity of gutta that could be exported, once the inhabitants took to systematic planting of the trees (which there are signs of their doing), would be very large, and have a considerable effect on the market, for the supply in the future will be continuous instead of, as formerly, evanescent.

Besides gutta trees there are several kinds of creepers that produce gutta-percha; and a case has been known of a thirsty explorer, who, mistaking a gutta-creeper for one of the many varieties which exude water, placed his mouth beneath one that he had cut in two, and drank its juice, with the result that the liquid he swallowed coagulated and solidified in his bowels, thereby causing his death.

Traversing several small ridges we passed through this district so prolific of gutta trees, and came to the watershed of the Bernam river, where we found the country through which we had to go inundated, and our progress was more difficult than it had previously been, for, instead of a large flat covered with water of fairly equal depth, the surface was broken up into hillocks and depressions, the flood water just reaching to the tops of the former, but quite deep and impassable wherever the latter happened to be.

On arriving at places which were too deep for us to wade through, the men hung up their loads on the branches of any small adjacent trees, and commenced to erect light and frail bridges, or to cut down some large tree to span a spot where the water would not admit of their fixing the light posts of the temporary structures made. The expert swimmers of the party undertook the making of these light bridges, which were just sufficiently strong to allow of one man crossing at a time, whilst the rest cut long, slender, whippy saplings and sticks. The construction was simple in the extreme; each span was supported by two sticks stuck into the ground leaning inwards, being tied just above the level of the water, and into the fork thus formed two sticks were placed to make the footway, level with which the end of one of the supports was cut off, whilst that of the other was allowed to project up some distance; and a light lath being fastened to it formed a slight rail, enabling those crossing to keep their balance by lightly touching it. Upon completion of the bridge loads were once more taken up and the journey recommenced until another similar place was reached. So arduous and hard did my men find their labours that they lightened their burdens as much as possible by discarding everything that was not absolutely necessary, and preferred to go on short commons rather than carry more rice than just sufficient for their expected requirements. It rained at frequent intervals both night and day; the men fell ill from being continually wet through and from having to be constantly in the water erecting bridges. So much was this the case that on the last day's march a portion of the number were delayed two days in conveying their sick comrades along.

On reaching Slim—where I could obtain a fresh supply of men—I paid off and dismissed any who wished to leave; and, with the exception of two Malays and my Chinese carriers who elected to remain, every one of the twenty-five were more or less fever-stricken, although they had been with me barely a month, and appeared very delighted at returning to their homes, notwithstanding that they were receiving nearly double wages, for it was only that inducement which enabled me to collect a fair-sized gang to accompany me; for, knowing the hardships of the journey I was undertaking, I did not employ the men that I usually obtained from Talum, so as not to incapacitate them if wanted at some future time. Another fortnight enabled me to finish the work I was engaged upon, and returning to Tapah I was just able to complete my plans before being laid low myself with a virulent attack of fever, necessitating a journey to and sojourn in Penang to recover from it. The two men who accompanied me throughout did not escape either, for I met them later on looking thin and wan, just recovering from a bad attack of malarial fever. My Chinese servant left my employment very shortly afterwards, although he to all appearances came through unscathed, and my Chinese carriers I never met again.

Adjoining the territory of Malacca is the native state of Rembau, which I traversed, walking from Sungie Ujong to Malacca in the days when it was free and independent, and had not yet accepted British protection.

The houses in which the principal families of each village dwelt were protected by forts and stockades, which had been erected to prevent their being rushed and looted during the inter-tribal and internal fights which were so constantly occurring. The defences in every case were similar, and consisted of a dry moat, the earth from which had been thrown up so as to form a bank, and into this a palisade of split logs was firmly planted, and the tops were strongly bound together, and being constructed of the hardest wood procurable lasted many years, and formed an excellent protection, behind which those inside could shoot at an approaching enemy. The weapons used were old flint muskets and small cannon—made in the last century, and not much larger than an ordinary blunderbuss—also spears and krises. The chief was a Penghulu, an office somewhat corresponding to that of ruler and chief magistrate combined, the occupant being elected for life, and chosen from amongst certain families, whose privilege it was to supply in rotation the chief of the state.

There is little wonder under these circumstances that the death of each chief was made an occasion for disputes and dissensions, in which the inhabitants of the neighbouring states joined, for there were always free lances only too ready and willing to give their assistance to one side or the other, and to bring a following as lawless as themselves ready to join in any fighting to be had. Their method of warfare was desultory and undisciplined, and is aptly described in a Malay proverb, "To retreat when hard pressed, not ashamed to fly, and not satisfied when pursuing."

At the time of my visit there still existed a great deal of ill-feeling and enmity between the people of Rembau and those of the adjacent state of Tampin, whose chief was descended through the paternal side from a Syed (a lineal descendant of the Prophet Mahomet), and therefore had considerable influence amongst his co-religionists; and being ambitious to extend his authority over the neighbouring state of Rembau, a series of intrigues and disturbances took place, but without success, for the sturdy inhabitants of that state were too fond of their old-established form of government to quietly allow of a change, and objected to the prospect of contributing to the support of a prince who owed his rank to the prophet, and not to any family of royal Malay descent.

The Government of Malacca set its face against

these continuous intrigues and eruptions on its frontier, and in order to gain some ascendency and influence at the courts of the native rulers in the neighbouring native states which came within the sphere of its influence, commenced a policy of supplying the chiefs with money in order to enable them to improve their country and open up communications. Finding that the money was being wasted and ill-spent from ignorance, the Government decided that the roads constructed with their money should be properly laid out and supervised by some competent person. The contract for this work was placed with me on the understanding that I should, as far as possible, work in agreement with the chiefs and employ the labour of the country, so that the money set aside for the purposes of road-making should be distributed amongst and benefit the inhabitants of the districts through which it passed; and therefore prior to commencing work I had to pay a formal visit to the Datoh. I was received with every courtesy; guns were fired in my honour, but I recognized that, notwithstanding the apparent cordiality of my welcome, I was being regarded with a good deal of suspicion; but his mistrust was allayed when he discovered that I had undertaken the work to make money out of it, and not to dabble in the internal politics of his state, and upon finding out who I was, for he had heard of me by repute owing to a relation of his having been in my employment for some years in a very responsible position. This relative was more closely allied to the family of the old Datoh than that of the present one, who had banished him from the country for some intrigue, and although refusing him permission to return, felt no active animosity against him as long as he kept away, but had he come back there is no doubt his life would have been taken before many days had passed. The Datoh was a man of strong character and great influence, and thought more of the proposed road being a convenience to himself personally than to the public generally, therefore our ideas of where it should pass were at variance; but on hearing I had also been employed by the Government of Malacca to lay out roads for them, as well as to alter and deviate existing ones that joined his frontier with the town of Malacca, likewise also in other parts of the Malay States, he gave in, unconvinced and unsatisfied, but not caring to argue the point any further with a person differing so much from his usual advisers, who were only too ready to agree with all he said, and to acquiesce in every suggestion he made.

These Rembau Malays were settlers from the district of Menangkabau in Sumatra, and still kept up a certain intercourse with that country, speaking a much broader Malay dialect than those in other portions of the peninsula, and changing the *a* at the end of a word into *o*. They were by far the sturdiest and best workers of all, and plucky as well; but notwithstanding their good qualities they were somewhat looked down upon by their neighbours as being thievishly inclined and treacherous in the extreme.

On the Malacca side of Rembau is the small

state of Naning, which caused considerable trouble between 1831–1834 by refusing to acknowledge the jurisdiction of Malacca, and being helped by Rembau, successfully resisted the first expedition sent against it and obliged it to return to Malacca, where a fresh one was organized. The density of the jungle was such, and the means of transporting supplies so inadequate, that this second punitive expedition, although better equipped than the previous one, took some three weeks to advance for twelve miles, carrying on a guerilla warfare the whole way.

Beyond Tampin there was a cluster of small states, including Johol, Jempol, Ulu-Moar, and S'trimenanti, where the Government were pursuing a similar policy, and by whom I was engaged to mark out the main road through them.

I spent a week in the hills between Tampin and these states before being satisfied that the best gap had been discovered over which the road should pass, and then set out exploring in order to obtain a general idea of the main features of the country before proceeding farther with the survey. It was whilst thus engaged that one of the chiefs sent a message to inform me that he had decided no road should pass through his territory, and that rather than allow it he had made up his mind to kill the intruder. The only reply I could send back to him was that the taking of my life would not help him much, for someone else was sure to come in my place; and to lessen the sting of the above speech I added, of course he could do as he liked, and concluded with the Malay saying that "the plucking of a bud would not stop the growth of the tree," to show him that the policy the Government had initiated would continue whatever might happen to me.

As I walked through the village of this chief a day or so afterwards, the men were sitting at the doors of their houses watching me as I passed by. They were all fully armed, for in these independent states no one moved about without a weapon of some sort on his person, to be used on the slightest provocation. As I approached a house one of its inmates came down a ladder, threw up his hand to show me he had no weapon in it, and saluting me in a most friendly manner, asked if I had forgotten him, as he had formerly worked on the coffee estates of Gunong Brembong. On assuring him to the contrary, and after conversing with him for a short while, he informed all his friends who I was, and so amicable relations were established, and our former acquaintance stood me in good stead.

It was during this expedition that I came upon an awful example of the desolation following a bad epidemic of small-pox. Upon reaching a small and beautiful valley, where the rice fields although planted were neglected, and as we passed house after house standing empty and uninhabited, my guide recalled to mind its former inmates, of whom perhaps one or two were still alive; but in many instances whole families had succumbed and died, and all their little possessions that were of small value remained as they had been left, for none cared to remove them. The spread of vaccination has been amongst the greatest of the benefits that have followed British protection, but it was difficult to persuade the people of its efficacy, and in many instances the idea was so repugnant to the people of certain districts that it often took years of discussion to obtain their consent to submit to it, unless in the meanwhile small-pox broke out, and then there would be a general request for some vaccinator to be sent amongst them with as little delay as possible.

The inhabitants of these states were of lighter build than the Rembau men, more pleasure-loving, and throughout there was an air of easy-going contentment, and the appearance of having nothing to do beyond enjoyment.

Cock-fighting was a popular pastime, and one much in evidence. The possession of a champion cock was something to be proud of and to boast about, and a battle between different well-known favourites was quite a local event, and much money was wagered on the result. The cocks were prepared for the fight by having a long, sharp spur tied carefully to each leg; their owners would then carry them, stroking and talking to them the whole time, whilst the spectators crowded round the space reserved to view the fight. The following is an account of a fight I witnessed. The owners approached one another, and, crouching down, placed their birds on the ground, and smoothed down their feathers. The birds themselves seemed to fully share in the excitement of the scene, and to know what was expected of them, for, on being confronted by one another, they became eager and exultant, and their necks craned forwards and the surrounding feathers bristled up. Twice were they drawn back after touching each other's beaks to stir up their enthusiasm, but the third time their owners released them from their grasp, and the fight commenced. The birds faced each other with outstretched necks, then struck viciously at one another with their spurs which disappeared amongst their respective feathers, but failed to pierce the flesh; they pecked and jumped at each other the whole while, although neither gained any advantage at first, for both were well-trained birds. One round was finished, and they were caught up and smoothed down and refreshed by their owners, who placed the bird's beak between their lips, and thus moistened their throats. Time was up, and the fight recommenced. During this bout one of them jumped over the other's guard, and made a quick stab at him as he passed over his back, and another round was finished. The cocks were already showing signs of exhaustion, but faced one another as pluckily as ever, and the fight recommenced, during which one of them again managed to jump over his adversary, and struck again at his back as he passed, but it was done so quickly that the onlookers did not perceive that the spur had been driven home, for the cocks turned round face to face as unwaveringly as ever, and continued the fight. The victory seemed still in doubt, when all of a sudden one of them was seen to turn giddy and run round in a circle and fall over dead in his tracks, game to the last. The favourite had won. The delight of its backers was manifest, but to me it seemed but poor sport, and the sudden death of the wounded bird almost uncanny, and although I often saw cock-fights in progress as I passed along, I never stopped to witness another.

The many bright-plumaged birds of the jungle had been almost exterminated, having been ruthlessly shot whenever seen for the sake of their skins, which were collected for export, until a very sensible local law came into force forbidding the taking or killing of birds, and the sale of their plumage or feathers, thus putting a stop to this wanton and wholesale destruction.

A few Arabian coffee trees grew in some of the gardens of the villages, but curiously enough the natives did not drink a liquor obtained from the berries in the usual way, but made an infusion by boiling the leaves.

Fruit trees abounded, and grew extremely well, the soil being suitable, cocoanuts, rambutans, durians, rambei, mangosteens, langsats, and many other varieties flourished. Chinamen came all the way from Malacca to buy fruit at the season when it was ripe, conveying it away in baskets.

Herds of buffaloes were numerous, and previous to an attack of foot-and-mouth disease, which killed them off in large numbers, they formed the principal wealth of the inhabitants.

The country was much broken up into valleys, through which streams flowed, making the irrigation of the paddy fields easy, and there was every appearance of there having been a settled population in this part of the country for many generations. The graves were in many instances better cared for here than elsewhere, and wooden monuments supplemented the mound of turned sods, which is the usual way of marking the spot where Malays have been buried.

The first Sumatra Malay colonists who settled in this part of the country intermarried with the original inhabitants, and even to this day the right of their descendants, through the female line, to the ownership of the soil is still recognized, and from them the Penghulu, or chief of the state, is selected in rotation. Beneath the Penghulu was the "Lembaga," who ruled his tribe, and below him again the "heads of families."

All these minor chiefs were in direct subjection to the kings of Malacca until the conquest of that place by the Portuguese, early in the sixteenth century, caused the flight to Johore of the royal family, who, although still retaining their nominal sovereignty, were unable to maintain their authority over these "Negri Sembilan," or nine states, as their power was broken. As was only natural with such a complicated system of chieftainship, disputes and disturbances arose ; the chiefs of various tribes fought the chiefs of states, and the heads of families the chiefs of tribes, and the chaos became such that in the middle of the eighteenth century the then ruler of Johore, not caring any longer to be responsible for their behaviour and good conduct, released them from their allegiance. After a quarter of a century of misrule and fighting, these states petitioned the Rajah of Johore to appoint a prince to rule over them in order to keep up the Mohammedan religion and observances, which were becoming discarded and falling into disuse. After considerable negotiations it was decided that the king of Menang-Kabau should send some royal prince belonging to his family as viceroy, and that certain taxes should be imposed for his maintenance, but that he should in nowise have authority to interfere with the vested interests, of the different tribes, in the soil nor meddle in the internal politics of the several states, and beyond being titular princes they had but slight jurisdiction. Several viceroys succeeded one another, and the system continued for half a century; but by that time the very fact of the appointment of succeeding viceroys had introduced a new element of discord, for each viceroy married, and as their children and descendants increased, these in their turn commenced not only to assert their claims to the titular sovereignty but to the penghuluships as well; and the succeeding half-century was simply a series of internal disputes and disturbances between the different royal families and their adherents, until in 1876 the British Government recognized the claims of one of these, not merely to S'trimenanti and Ulu-Moar, but to Jempol and Jellye as well.

Between 1873 and 1876 not only were these states, through which I was travelling, torn by dissensions, but Rembau and Sungie Ujong, which were both included in the original nine states, joined in them, the latter place becoming especially embroiled, its ruler at this time being Syed Ahman, who although not the proper heir had got himself elected klana or chief, and whose authority was well-nigh gone; for the Banda, a chief equally powerful, had revolted, and was being assisted by some of the Selangor Rajahs and freebooters, whose piracies and murders had been put a stop to in that country. This opportunity was too favourable a one for the people of S'trimenanti and these states to forego, and they invaded Sungie Ujong to pay off many a long-standing score and to take their revenge. In his extremity Syed Ahman appealed to the British for protection, having previously asked for someone to be appointed to help him rule the state and to maintain his authority. His request was granted, and assistance and troops were sent, and after quelling the rising of the Banda's followers they proceeded in the direction of S'trimenanti, travelling up the valley of Ampangan to Paroe, which had been the scene of many a former fight between the peoples of both states, and drove the invaders before them into the hills that separate the two countries. On the S'trimenanti side of these hills were the districts of Terachi and Bandole, both well protected by stockades and forts, and the only path between the two countries was through a deep cleft in the range of mountains called Bukit Putus, or "the broken place in the hills," which locality has been notable for two events in recent Malay history.

The S'trimenanti men, hopeless of combating with British troops in the open, retired to their

## BUKIT PUTUS—DEFENCE AND CAPTURE.

strongholds in the Bukit Putus pass, where the defile was guarded by several stockades, which, being surrounded on all sides by jungle and steep approaches, would have been most difficult to capture had it not been for a very unexpected event. A few Goorkhas, under an English officer

(who received a V.C. for the exploit), and guided by an Arab called Sheikh Abdulrahman, were reconnoitring in the forest, when a Malay was perceived going in the direction of one of the stockades, and being silently followed, was seen to enter through a narrow aperture which, as it was screened by forest and could only have been found by those conversant with the stockade, had been left unguarded. The Malays inside felt secure from attack, as their stockade was situated some distance up the hill, and the approach was too steep for any sudden assault; it did not contain as many occupants as the forts in a more vulnerable position, and had only been erected to prevent the principal defence from being outflanked or fired into from above.

Seeing this Malay enter unchallenged, the reconnoitring party was collected, and stealthily approached unperceived to the small opening, through which they crept and took the Malays inside entirely by surprise, who, springing up, precipitately fled, offering but slight resistance, for they had been quite unaware of their enemies being in their vicinity, and had carelessly laid down their arms and left their defences unwatched whilst they all sat down to partake of the midday meal, which was so unpleasantly interrupted. By the loss of this fort the key of their position was in the hands of the British troops, who, training and firing the guns, that had been for the defence of the stockade which they had captured, upon one at a lower elevation into which the defeated Malays had fled, soon made it untenable, so that it had to be evacuated by its defenders and the passage of the pass was gained. Thus it was that the strongest position in the country was taken with hardly any loss, and the S'trimenanti people were unable to prolong the contest, and to take to flight to escape capture; for a force of soldiers under Captain Murray, R.N., having made a long detour, were already climbing over the hills with the object of outflanking them and cutting off their retreat.

When I visited this place for the first time the signs were still discernible of where the stockades had formerly been, and the steep hills on either side appeared to render the position so secure that the Malays seem not to have contemplated any possible danger of their being outflanked and attacked from the rear.

Even after this defeat some of the S'trimenanti Malays continued for some while to attack isolated bodies of police, and to plunder and murder wherever they could, until the principal bandits were killed; and to show that at last there was a chance of disturbances ceasing, the decapitated head of the chief of them was carried to Sungie Ujong in proof of his death. The method of this chief's assassination was related to me with gusto by the man who committed the deed, which was one of vile and barefaced treachery. The narrator, accompanied by a few friends, arrived one evening at the house of the man they had determined to take the first opportunity of killing, and with many vows of friendship stated that they had come to join his band of freebooters. They ate the meal he placed before them, chewed betel leaf with him, and helped themselves to his tobacco, and by bedtime had so gained his confidence that he invited his newly-made friend to sleep within his house, whilst his companions were allowed to lie down in the verandah outside. In the middle of the night the murderer crept to where his host lay asleep and plunged his krise into his heart, killing him instantly, and quickly cutting off his head as a trophy, he managed to escape with his companions before the bandit's followers had fully realized what had occurred.

The Malays had a great reverence for and fear of the Goorkha troops, for they were more than their match in guerilla fighting, and equal to them in their knowledge of jungle warfare, as well as possessing more dash and bravery.

The next event of historical interest at Bukit Putus was when Sir Frederick Weld met the chiefs of the neighbouring states at that place in 1880, at a time when disturbances were feared, owing to the continued refusal of some of these small states to recognize the authority of the Eam Tuan. It was during a rather hot discussion upon political subjects that one of the chiefs flung down his krise on the floor of the house in which the meeting was held, and required some pacifying, for the chiefs and people complained on the one hand of the newly-recognized Eam Tuan's indifference to their affairs, and on the other hand of the interference of the neighbouring state of Johore in their internal politics. There was no satisfying their manifold wants, nor any means of allaying their jealousies, for the penghuluship of several of these states, and other honourable appointments, instead of being occupied by the rightful heirs, had been seized upon and appropriated by the strongest faction, whereby was formed an antagonistic minority, who were only too ready to take advantage of the slightest opportunity to oust the present holders of authority, and to create disturbances on the smallest of pretexts. Matters were patched up so as to prevent any serious or open breach of the peace, but the relations between the Eam Tuan of S'trimenanti and the neighbouring states were never cordial, and all friction did not cease until the appointment of a British Resident in 1889, who had not only the difficult task of settling numberless disputes, for each state afforded several instances of power usurped by might, but also of allaying many long-standing jealousies and feuds.

# CHAPTER XVI.

Jelebu—Crossing the Mountains—Tigers—Kanaboi—Tin—Kwala Klawang—Eam Tuan—Terrified Elephants—Bukit Tanah—Exploring Hills—Road-making—Malays—Chinese—Tamils—The Malay Peninsula—Geology—Climate and Rainfall—Some of its Products, Flora, Fauna, and Minerals—Its Inhabitants, Education, and Administration—Comparisons of Revenue and Trade.

THE state of Jelebu was separated from S'trimenanti by a ridge, and over it there was a seldom-used and hilly track, which I had once occasion to traverse when engaged upon a journey of exploration connected with the extension of the Sungie Ujong railway. I had several times previously travelled through Jelebu, crossing the mountain ranges that separate it from the western state in no less than three places.

The first journey I made was from Kwala Lumpor, and as far as Ulu Langat the path was good, but as soon as we left that mining village behind the track became indistinct, for travellers along it were few and far between.

Our party consisted of myself, four Malays, and the Arab sheikh, who had made himself famous during the Sungie Ujong war, for in addition to his exploit at Bukit Putus, he had on another occasion distinguished himself when the troops were unable to scale the palisade of a Malay fort by having himself hoisted up and helped over the defences, to find, fortunately for him, the stronghold already evacuated.

During our ascent of this mountain range we passed several shelters all palisaded round so as to protect their occupants from becoming a prey to the many tigers which frequented the neighbourhood. Arriving at the summit there were signs of where the Malays had been mining the hill for tin, and the shed they had lived in afforded us a shelter for the night. It was here that some wayfarers met with a curious adventure. Being accompanied by several goats, which they were leading across the hill for sale in Selangor, they determined to pass the night in this structure, and were cooking their food when a passing tiger, attracted by the idea of having a goat for supper, entered. One of the Malays, nothing daunted, sprang up, seizing his parang at the same time, and placed himself in front of the goats whilst the tiger was deliberating what he should do next. The man's plucky action, instead of ending disastrously for him, caused the tiger to hesitate still further, and finally to withdraw without molesting any of the occupants of the house.

This Malay man was more fortunate than a couple of Chinese coolies who were working near each other on a path in the jungle. One of them being seized by a tiger cried out to attract the attention of his comrade, who gallantly came to his rescue with the implement with which he was working, and successfully caused the tiger to drop his prey; but it was only for the purpose of turning upon him, and it was next his turn to shout out and to cry as the animal sprang at him. In his case it was of no avail, as his companion, whom he had so bravely rescued, in the meantime had got up and run away, leaving his more plucky comrade to his fate, and to replace him in affording the tiger a meal.

During our occupation of the shed we were undisturbed, and commenced the descent of the range of mountains the next morning. The slopes of the hills were, if anything, steeper than on the western side of the range, and the streams, instead of dashing amongst granite boulders and rocks, flowed over a species of trap-rock that was greasy and slimy from the constant moisture. At the foot of the hills we reached the small village of Kanaboi, situated on the banks of a river of the same name; this, as well as all the other streams and rivers of Jelebu, flows into the large Pahang river, which empties itself into the Gulf of Siam on the eastern coast of the Malay Peninsula. I spent several days here endeavouring to ascertain whether there was any truth in the reports as to its richness in gold, but beyond discovering some prospects of the precious metal amongst the alluvial deposits of the river, I could in nowise further substantiate the rumours that reached me.

Travelling to the southward, and climbing over a curious steep ridge of hill composed of sharp quartz pebbles, and called by the natives the "Hill of Fire," because the edges of its stones were so sharp that they pricked and lacerated the feet of all who crossed it barefoot; to the westward as we journeyed along was a high granite cliff that rose abruptly from a fine valley, which had formerly been cultivated but was now devoid of inhabitants. The country round was rich in alluvial tin, which was found to lie but a little distance below the surface of the ground, and proved easily workable and remunerative whilst the supply lasted.

Reaching Kwala Klawang, a small village then consisting of two or three houses, built close to the Klawang stream at the highest point where it was navigable for even the smallest of boats, and which has since become the site where the District Officer's house, the Government offices, and the traders' shops have been built.

Further up the valley another small group of houses was reached, in one of which dwelt the Eam Tuan, or titular ruler of Jelebu, a descendant of a son of a former Rajah of S'trimenanti, who had succeeded, with the help of his kinsmen, in getting himself recognized and his position secured. Although he was accorded all homage as the supreme head of the state, the ownership of the land still remained vested in the families of the local headmen, and he had no power personally to dispose of it in any way. Such a peaceful state of affairs was not to endure for very long, and the state became split into factions, one of which led by the Penghulu, who felt that some of his authority had gone by the new appointment, was in favour of ousting the Eam Tuan; but eventually a compromise was arrived at, and he went to reside at Klawang, a valley which, although adjoining Jelebu, really by inheritance belonged to Sungie Ujong.

Here his successors also lived, still recognized by a portion of the inhabitants in the state, but disregarded by the others, or what was left of them, for during the disturbances the country had become depopulated and deserted.

The Eam Tuan, who was the holder of this almost empty title, was a man of mild and pleasant manners, and had accepted with resignation his present position, only desiring to be left in peace to follow unmolested agricultural pursuits, and to enjoy country sports.

In the vicinity of his house, as I arrived, a group of Malays were playing a kind of football or kickabout, using a light, hollow ball made of rattans entwined and laced together in a spherical shape. The object of this game is to keep the ball in the air as long as possible, kicking it with instep or ankle, and thus tossing it indiscriminately from one to the other. Some players become very expert, and will return the ball by kicking it over their backs with the soles of their feet, and when this trick is successful the assembled players shout a Ha! ha! of approval; others toss it in the air by butting it with their heads; in fact, there seem no special rules in this game other than to try and keep the ball alive without the aid of hands, and from touching the ground.

Pitch-and-toss is not unknown to Malay boys, and when in funds they are often to be seen tossing coppers into a small hole in the ground, and watching the result of each throw of the coin with as much eagerness and interest as any street arab. Grown-up lads also amuse themselves by a trial of skill with their comrades.

In the verandah of the Eam Tuan's house a dove was confined in a cage made of rattan, and was kept for fighting, for dove fights are watched with the same keen interest and excitement by Malays as cock fights, and a champion dove is a very valued treasure to its owner, and worth a considerable sum. In a smaller cage there was a captive quail, used as a decoy to attract others of its kind to where snares had been prepared.

Malays are very expert bird catchers, and quite happy when so engaged. There are several methods of capturing wild birds; by bird-lime obtained from the milky juice of many trees, and especially from those producing gutta-percha; another way is to place snares made of hair on the ground, and so arranged that directly the bird gets its leg within the noose which is attached to a peg stuck into the ground, it tightens at the pressure and holds the captive fast. Often as many as twenty or thirty of these snares are placed around the decoy, and some food is sprinkled on the ground as a further attraction. Still another plan adopted to catch pigeons is for the snarer to build himself a little conical shelter of palm leaves, in which he can hide and remain unseen by the birds, who come to the decoy and commence feeding on a smooth piece of ground that has been prepared for them. The snarer watches his opportunity, and stealthily pushes a stick, on the end of which is fastened a running noose, along the ground to where the bird is feeding, captures it, and draws it into his little shelter and places it in a cage he has brought with him for the purpose, and is soon again ready to try and catch another. Curiously enough, the birds, as long as the man remains unperceived by them, do not suspect his presence, and take but little notice of their snared companions, and continue feeding unconcerned. The pigeons thus caught are often kept and fed for some days before being carried to the nearest market, where they meet with a ready sale.

Both Malays and Sakais are clever at constructing and setting traps for wild animals, making the jungle unsafe where they are placed, and care has to be taken in passing through it. Pits are dug for rhinoceros and pigs; beams to which a sharp spear-head is fastened are set so that the point shall fall upon the passing beast, which brings about its own doom by touching a twig placed in its path, and so arranged that upon its being knocked on one side it lets loose the string that keeps the beam in place. Spring guns are sometimes set, but the most common trap of all is one made for the different kinds of smaller game and deer, and which is very effective. This trap is prepared by cutting and laying a few branches and twigs on the ground to make two low fences, over which the smaller creatures are afraid to pass, and which gradually approach each other until they meet and form a point where the trap, consisting of a log held suspended between two rows of sticks firmly fixed in the ground, is set. Anything entering this narrow passage touches the trigger and down comes the log of wood on the unsuspecting creature's back, often squeezing the life out of it. The larger kinds of birds are frequently caught in traps of this kind, as well as deer and porcupine, and other lesser animals. Birds and beasts are also captured by using calls, and in the case of the timid mouse-deer, two sticks are tapped together in a peculiar way, and the little creature thinks that it is a buck of its own species stamping on the ground and answers it, gradually drawing nearer to the challenge, thus enabling the Malay or Sakai to shoot it with a gun or poisoned dart.

Some years after my first visit, the state of Jelebu, so called after the name of a man who was drowned in the Triang river, came under the jurisdiction of the Resident of Sungie Ujong, whose locum tenens, finding the distance too far for him to walk, imported a couple of elephants from Perak and set out to visit the Eam Tuan, borne upon their backs. This magnate, wishing to accord his guest all the honour in his power, and being absolutely ignorant of the peculiarities of tame elephants, fired a salute from the small and rusty cannon that guarded the entrance to his house upon the arrival of the cavalcade. The noise and flash of the powder was too much for the elephants, who, becoming terrified, bolted, carrying their riders into the adjacent forest, where fortunately they were unseated without injury, and were able to enjoy the comicality of their position and escape from what might have been a serious accident. The example of introducing elephants as beasts of burden was not followed by others, and as these soon became a nuisance on account of the damage they did to the gardens of the villagers, who were afraid to drive them off at night when they strayed into their compounds, they were in a short while returned to Perak. After the death of the Eam Tuan the dignity lapsed, as no successor was installed in his place, the Government rightly refusing to recognize the claims of those who considered they had some right to the position so lately acquired and merely retained only on sufferance.

I was on very friendly terms with the Eam Tuan, and at his death became acquainted with a curious custom and piece of etiquette existing amongst the Malay rajahs of his rank, and which prevented any of their number from being buried, should he owe any money, until his creditors were paid in full. At the time of the Eam Tuan's death he happened to be indebted to me for quite a trifling sum, but so particular were his family that this small amount should be repaid before the funeral, that they delayed it for two whole days whilst they endeavoured to find me; but as I happened to be on some distant journey, a friend of mine, an Arab sheikh of good standing, assured them that this was a case where some relaxation might be reasonably made in existing custom, and took upon himself the responsibility of receiving the amount on my behalf, and in my name requested the family no longer to hesitate to accord to their chief a suitable and fitting funeral, which they did, and thus died and was buried the last of the rulers of Jelebu.

The paddy fields in this state are irrigated by an ingenious method. A frail and light undershot water-wheel is placed by the side of a small stream, and on its outer circumference, attached to each of its blades, is a section of bamboo tied at a certain angle, and having one end open, so that as the wheel revolves water is scooped up and carried overhead to be emptied in continuous rotation into a trough, from whence it flows to irrigate the fields.

Ascending the Klawang valley, I crossed a gap in the hills called Bukit Tangga, and it is through this pass that the road now passes which connects Jelebu with Sungie Ujong. It is a peculiarity of the Malay that he in nowise can calculate the height of a hill, and is but of small use in helping you to determine the lowest point where the mountains can be crossed. Hearing subsequently of a lower gap to the northward, I made a week's exploration, only to discover the ridges of the hills to be knife-edged and the approaches to them exceedingly steep and precipitous, whilst the lowest part was considerably higher than the one at Bukit Tangga.

It may be as well for me to give the reader some account of the work upon which I was engaged in constructing roads throughout most parts of the Malay Peninsula (upon the principal number of the journeys I have described), and which in their turn have, in many instances, been already superseded by railways.

First of all it was necessary to make the selection of the line of country to be followed and to ascertain the correct points of the compass, for that was the only reliable guide as to direction. Then the site of the road itself not only required surveying and staking out, but the gradients necessitated the greatest care being exercised so as to utilize the configuration of the country to the best advantage. The maximum steepness of any portion of a road was a gradient of one foot in twenty, or, to make my meaning clearer, only fifteen feet of gradual rise or fall could be ascended, or descended, in every hundred yards of length.

Ridges and hills were numerous, and the whole country was covered with a dense mass of jungle through which the eye could penetrate but a few feet in advance, rendering the task of laying down and staking out a good and proper line for the road to follow very difficult, also causing a constant repetition of the work when some unforeseen difficulty necessitated a change of direction or gradient. Added to this, food was often hard to procure, its transport difficult, and the life most arduous and unhealthy.

After the line of the road was staked out, with a numbered peg at every chain, the gradients and levels to be followed marked, and a detailed plan made of the direction and the physical features of the country passed through, all was ready for the jungle to be cleared along the line, which was necessary before the road itself could be constructed.

First of all the undergrowth was cut down and thrown to one side, then the smaller trees were uprooted and the larger ones dug round about, so as to expose their roots some little distance below the ground before being cut, so that no roots should remain in the roadway. The heavy tops of the larger trees saved much axe work, but even then it was often a week before two men were able to cut through sufficient of the roots to cause the tree to fall, and by itself drag up the remainder, leaving a large hole where it once stood. In places where charcoal-burners had cut down and burnt the

large hard-wood trees, leaving their roots in the ground, the work was more difficult, owing to the wood having become so tough and hard as to resist the axes, causing them to chip and splinter, and necessitating the making of large fires over the roots and the keeping of them alight until they had been consumed; all very well in dry weather, but most troublesome when it was wet. After the trees had fallen they were then cut into lengths and rolled to one side, when it was no unusual sight to see twenty men straining at one huge log, endeavouring to remove it with poles, to the accompaniment of yells and shouts. The width of the clearing of course depended on the breadth of the road to be constructed. Where long distances had to be traversed through sparsely-populated districts, bridle paths were made, so as to enable travellers on foot or horseback to get from one place to another, and where the necessity of a cart road had not as yet become apparent. Timber bridges of hard-wood beams and sawn planks were made across all streams and rivers. Obtaining and keeping a sufficient supply of labour together, besides arranging for their supplies of food, and sickness, constituted the principal difficulties in constructing these smaller paths, which were six feet in breadth.

Cart roads required much more labour, and were of three varieties, all of them sixteen to twenty feet in width.

The earth roads were most unsatisfactory, for directly bullock and buffalo carts travelled along them they got so damaged and cut up that in wet weather they became impassable; the carts stuck in the deep ruts and holes, churning up the mud and destroying the formation of the roadway.

The gravelled roads were somewhat more satisfactory, but it entirely depended upon the pits whence supplies could be obtained. In Malacca there were excellent gravelled roads, made with the small hard laterite and ironstone pebbles which abounded in the earth at the sides of the roads in many parts; and this formation also existed in some parts of Sungie Ujong, and occasionally in Selangor, but where inferior gravels were employed it was quickly changed into dirt and mire.

The metalled roads, besides being excellent, were a pleasure to construct, for the results were permanent and lasting. The roads in Perak were for the most part constructed on this principle, and were far superior to those made in the other Malay states. They were metalled to a width of twelve feet, slightly higher in the centre than at the sides, to allow of the rain-water draining off. First of all a layer of larger stones—broken so as to be approximately of the same size—was carefully placed in position and laid by hand, then there was a top layer of smaller stones, and the whole was nine inches in thickness after it had been well consolidated by a small steam road-roller, weighing about four tons, which was very suitable for this class of work, as heavier rollers could not be used with advantage on newly-made banks and excavations. A thin dressing of earth and sand, well watered and rolled, completed capital and durable roads. The stone used had often to be carted several miles from the quarries, and was either granite or limestone, according to the kind of rock which happened to be within most convenient distance. In long stretches of forest, grass for the bullocks had often to be fetched a considerable distance.

The labourers employed were Malays, Chinese, and Tamils, each nationality requiring different treatment, and their own special idiosyncrasies had to be studied and understood before it was possible to get them to put forth their best efforts and to keep them going. Everything had to be explained and shown at the commencement, and the labourers instructed as to what was expected of them.

On each work many of those employed collapsed from fever or dysentery, both constant sources of sickness, whilst many left owing to ill-health; especially was this the case when cutting through soil containing much decomposed granite, then whole gangs became fever-stricken, and were compelled to leave, and substitutes for them had to be found, who in their turn also became incapacitated in a very short while.

Malays were only of use for jungle-clearing and light earthwork, and even they, inured to the climate and not prone to exhaust themselves by too much labour, were often ill, and usually only worked for short periods at a time.

Chinese were the most useful all-round workmen, for they were also able to clear the jungle, though less expert in doing so than the Malays. They were excellent for all earthwork, and when well trained, graded and levelled the surface satisfactorily. They required very firm treatment and to be made to understand that it was better policy to do their work properly than to scamp it. They were excellent on contract, and as long as money was owed to them most easy to deal with; but if the case was reversed by faulty supervision, or the dishonesty of their headman at the commencement of the work upon which they were engaged, then there were endless difficulties and troubles to get them to finish what they had begun, or to work at all, for once all prospect of a profit had disappeared it became their endeavour to obtain advances of money and goods, doing as little as possible the while, until it was convenient for them to go off somewhere else. They were good blasters and metal breakers once they became used to drilling, and expert in the use of the hammer.

Tamils were not nearly so physically or constitutionally strong as the Chinese, and suffered much more from the climate, becoming thin and fever-stricken. They are especially sensitive to any alteration of diet; even a difference in the rice supplied or a change of drinking water is sufficient to cause them to lose their health, and often the reason given for leaving a place or changing their abode is that "the water there did not agree with them." They are useless as wood-cutters, and work best on daily wages and when set a task. They are amenable and easily managed by anyone speaking their language who treats them justly and fairly. Although inferior to the Chinese in any kind of heavy earthwork, they are equal to them in drilling and in breaking stones, and superior to them in laying and spreading metal; also working for less wages, they are more suitable for all classes of light work and agricultural employment.

The geology of the country is a most interesting study. The main range of hills are granite—a crystallized compound of quartz, feldspar, and mica; the spurs and smaller hills are for the most part composed of slates, sandstones, and clays. All the paleozoic rocks—the ancient formation above the granite—have been much distorted and altered by the upheaval of the granite, which has been more violent and greater between 3° and 6° than between 1° and 3°. Laterite of a rich red colour, due to peroxide of iron, is most common in the southern portion of the peninsula, and in the northern half, crystalline limestone hills are frequently met with standing out by themselves with precipitous cliffs. Much of the tin ore is found in the bed of ancient streams beneath a covering of fine silt, above which there is a layer of china clay or kaolin, as well as in clays and sandy loams at varying depths from a few inches to many feet. There is an entire absence of marine fossils; an old cannon has been found in a tin mine in Larut thirty feet below the present surface of the ground, as well as an old paddy mortar similar to those now in use, and trees are constantly discovered in the old river drifts. The surface of a portion of the country in the neighbourhood of Thaiping has been proved by borings taken, to have recently sunk over a hundred feet. Stone implements—mostly axes and adzes—have been frequently discovered; and one type of stone axe, which is fairly common, has also been found in several parts of Europe, Indiana, and Java, being similar in shape to some old axes made of copper and bronze, but no fossil remains, or other relics of human life or mammalia have been brought to light. A hoard of Portuguese coins of the fifteenth century was dug up in Kinta.

The climate is a moist, depressing heat, unaffected by the monsoons. There is no true rainy season; the six wettest months are March, April,

May, October, November, and December. The rainfall varies from ninety to two hundred inches in Thaiping, which is the wettest district in the Straits. The nights are cool, and to some extent counteract the unvarying damp heat which slowly but steadily undermines the European constitution; and those of a fair complexion usually appear to be the most susceptible to its banefulness. Malarial diseases have become less virulent since the country has been more opened up and inhabited; but whenever new settlements are made and soil disturbed fevers are sure to be prevalent in the neighbourhood for the first few years.

The products of the Malay Peninsula are varied, for the very heat and moisture that makes humanity decay forces plant-life to grow and bear abundantly. Areca-nuts increase quickly in size, and bear profusely. Cocoanuts yield abundant crops as long as properly cared for. Coffee arabica flourishes on the hills, but in the plains it soon over-bears itself if in the open and dies. Liberian coffee grows in the plains, yielding heavy crops, but the trees, if not kept up with liberal manuring, deteriorate, and leaf-disease, which is ever present, obtains a firmer hold and lessens their productiveness. Fruit trees flourish except those of the orange species, which not only suffer from blight, but the constant wet rots the fruit before it ripens. Nutmegs were once a flourishing and paying cultivation, but a blight in 1856 killed most of the trees, since which but few new plantations have been opened. Gutta-percha-producing trees and creepers are indigenous, and grow wild in the forests. Tapioca grows readily, and on the lighter soils the tubers arrive at a goodly size. Tobacco plants are cultivated by the natives to a small extent, producing leaves suitable for the commoner kinds of tobacco, but unadapted for the outside covering of cigars. Up to the present, all efforts to grow a tobacco similar to that produced in Sumatra have failed. A trial plantation opened on the light alluvial flats near Thaiping, as well as one on the stiffer black deposits of Krian, resulted in pecuniary loss, for in the first instance the leaves lacked the colour and substance of those grown for cigar-coverings in Deli, and in the second the leaves were coarse and lacked the proper texture to fetch the high price requisite to repay the extensive outlay necessary in this kind of tobacco cultivation, which is at all times risky, a good year being relied upon to recoup the losses of several bad ones. Pineapples grow readily everywhere, and it is only necessary to stick the crown of one into the ground in order to obtain a new plant producing several pines. Rubber and caoutchouc trees grow rapidly, and yield well, as the moist climate is in every way favourable to all kinds of trees producing milky juices. Wood oil is obtained from two varieties of trees.

Plant life is tropical and luxuriant; tree-ferns and various kinds of calladium flourish in damp localities, there are ground and aerial orchids, pitcher and other trailing plants grow in dense masses, and a free-flowering crimson creeper causes the trees which it covers to be a blaze of colour. Rhododendrons flower on the hill-tops, and on their slopes all kinds of European vegetables can be cultivated. The virgin forest is singularly deficient in flowering plants, and beyond a solitary specimen now and again, they are seldom to be met with, excepting during the few days when the fruit trees blossom. What gives to the jungle its peculiar charm are the different shades and sombre hues of colour, not only of the leaves and shoots of the different trees, but their bark as well.

The fauna is disappointing from a sportsman's point of view, for the luxuriance of the vegetation so clothes the ground with forest as to leave no large area of grass. The elephant, bison or seladang, tiger, panther, pig, bear, and different kinds of deer are the most frequently met with, but the last named are not gregarious varieties, and do not congregate in herds. Many kinds of wild cat abound, all of which are not only wicked and vicious, but most destructive to the smaller kinds of game.

The inhabitants are Aborigines, Malays, Chinese, Tamils, a few Arab and Indian traders, Jawi Pakans—a mixed Tamil-Malay class, and Babas —a mixed Chinese-Malay class, besides the descendants of former Portuguese and Dutch settlers. The population of the western states under British protection in 1880 was about 200,000, and in 1891 it had reached over 361,000, and the following is an approximate return of the numbers of the different nationalities: Aborigines, 11,000; Malays, 166,500; Chinese, 164,000; Tamils, 17,500; mixed and other nationalities, 2,000. It was estimated that in 1896 the population had increased to 540,000.

There are English, Malay, and Tamil schools for both boys and girls, although for the latter the number is as yet very small. The Chinese mostly patronize the English schools, and all Malay boys attend their village vernacular school, where they are given a very fair elementary education, which does not in the least unfit them for agricultural pursuits, as on the completion of their studies they become paddy-planters, boatmen, and labourers; so that the spread of education in the Straits is in every respect an advantage to the population, and has no tendency to demoralize the masses by making them above their stations in life, or their ordinary every-day occupations.

Each state is administered by an organized staff of British officials under the control of a Resident, who advises the rulers upon all matters, and is responsible to his chief, who up to June, 1895, was the Governor of the Colony of the Straits Settlements; but since that date a Resident-General has been interposed, and the Sultans of the federated states have agreed to provide him with a suitable salary and staff, as well as to follow his advice in all matters of administration other than those touching on the Mohammedan religion, and they have also agreed to help in money, men, and other respects, states in the federation needing it—as well as to provide a force of soldiers for the defence of the colony should the necessity arise.

The accompanying statistics of the progressive

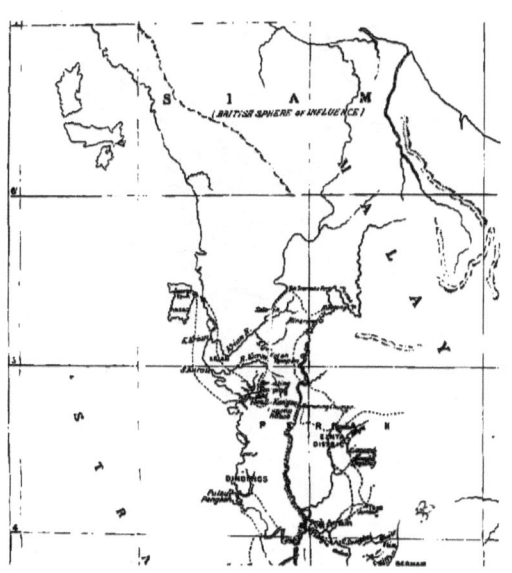

# COMPARISONS OF REVENUE AND TRADE.

increase of total revenue, exports, imports, duty on tin, land, postal and telegraph and railway revenues, exemplify the continuous prosperity and advancement of the Western Protected Malay States more eloquently than any words, and show how they are almost entirely due to the alluvial tin-mining industry. The values are expressed in dollars.

### TOTAL REVENUE.

| | |
|---|---|
| 1880 | 881,910. |
| 1890 | 4,777,988. |
| 1895 | 8,374,264. |

| | Value of Imports. | Value of Exports. | Duty on Tin. | Land Revenue. | Postal and Telegraph. | Railway Receipts. |
|---|---|---|---|---|---|---|
| 1880 | *3,250,000 | *3,100,000 | 399,391 | 38,844 | 233 | Nil. |
| 1890 | 15,443,809 | 17,602,093 | 1,604,778 | 146,487 | 36,524 | 406,032 |
| 1895 | 21,865,412 | 30,847,492 | 3,355,346 | 444,397 | 107,943 | 1,294,390 |

\* Approximate.

PLYMOUTH:
WILLIAM BRENDON AND SON,
PRINTERS.

www.ingramcontent.com/pod-product-compliance
Lightning Source LLC
Chambersburg PA
CBHW030303240426
43673CB00040B/1047